Flexibility and Real Estate Valuation under Uncertainty:
A Practical Guide for Developers

Flexibility and Real Estate Valuation under Uncertainty: A Practical Guide for Developers

David Geltner
Massachusetts Institute of Technology
Cambridge, MA, USA

Richard de Neufville
Massachusetts Institute of Technology
Cambridge, MA, USA

WILEY Blackwell

Registered Offices
John Wiley & Sons, Inc., 111 River Street, Hoboken, NJ 07030, USA
John Wiley & Sons Ltd, The Atrium, Southern Gate, Chichester, West Sussex, PO19 8SQ, UK

Editorial Office
9600 Garsington Road, Oxford, OX4 2DQ, UK

For details of our global editorial offices, customer services, and more information about Wiley products visit us at www.wiley.com.

Wiley also publishes its books in a variety of electronic formats and by print-on-demand. Some content that appears in standard print versions of this book may not be available in other formats.

Library of Congress Cataloging-in-Publication Data

Names: Geltner, David, 1951– author. | De Neufville, Richard, 1939– author.
Title: Flexibility and real estate valuation under uncertainty : a practical guide for developers /
    by David Geltner, Massachusetts Institute of Technology, Richard de Neufville,
    Massachusetts Institute of Technology.
Description: Hoboken, NJ : John Wiley & Sons, [2018] | Includes bibliographical references and index. |
Identifiers: LCCN 2017051519 (print) | LCCN 2017054517 (ebook) | ISBN 9781119106456 (pdf) |
    ISBN 9781119106487 (epub) | ISBN 9781119106494 (pbk.)
Subjects: LCSH: Real property–Valuation. | Real estate development. | Real estate investment.
Classification: LCC HD1387 (ebook) | LCC HD1387 .G45 2018 (print) | DDC 333.33/2–dc23
LC record available at https://lccn.loc.gov/2017051519

Cover Design: Wiley
Cover Image: © Lava 4 images/Shutterstock

Set in 10/12pt Warnock by SPi Global, Pondicherry, India

10 9 8 7 6 5 4 3 2 1

to Debby and Ginger

Contents

Foreword

Major leaps forward in real estate thought leadership are few and far between, such as the application of discounted cash flow to real estate valuation in the 1970s, and of portfolio theory to property investment in the 1980s and 1990s. This seminal book by Professors Geltner and de Neufville provides the vanguard for the next major leap in thought leadership, being *optionality* in real estate.

While optionality, as distinct from option pricing theory, has been conceptually discussed by the world's leading real estate academics for the last few years, including at the landmark RICS Foundation Global Symposium on "Optionality" in early 2012, little has been written until now.

Similarly, while the use of spreadsheets for development cash flows and the application of probability analysis and scenario analysis are not new ideas, their combination within a framework of flexibility or optionality is a new concept. This changes the way we think about real estate valuation, with their guided application through the use of spreadsheets rendering them accessible to all practitioners. Such techniques as probability analysis and scenario analysis are no longer possible add-ons to development cash flows, but now have a central role.

Henry Ford is often misquoted as saying:

> If I had asked people what they wanted, they would have said "faster horses."

This was academia's previous response to the real estate industry and profession through such developments as *financial management rate of return* and the *modified internal rate of return* for discounted cash flow. This book does not provide a faster spreadsheet or a simpler probability application, but instead provides a new way to conceptualize real estate as a bundle of opportunities with positive or negative contributions to value that can be combined to optimize value to an individual party or to a market. Significantly, rather than the traditional view of land value theory, this book views land as a call option on development. As the authors note in the Preface:

> You can think of our approach as providing a way for decision-makers—with more, or less, experience—to transform their intuitive sense of managing risks and exploiting opportunities into more solid, defensible quantitative economic valuations of real estate options.

Optionality in real estate valuation essentially addresses the three realms made famous by former US defense secretary Donald Rumsfeld—known knowns, known unknowns, and unknown unknowns—providing a framework within which each may be quantified and modelled. It is optionality manifest in flexibility arising from uncertainty in the investment and development process, which is the focus of this book.

This book logically and sequentially moves through three phases—acquainting the reader with the quantitative foundations, then introducing the concept and framework of optionality, before combining these through application to an increasingly detailed example of a real estate project.

Chapter 1 sets out the rationale for and structure of the cash flow model, with a focus on retrospective and prospective assessment, while Chapter 2 extends the discussion to net present value (NPV) and internal rate of return (IRR), with a focus on the opportunity cost of capital and the discount rate. Chapters 3–8 introduce the recognition of uncertainty through probabilities and scenarios, simulation, pricing factors, and random walks, importantly recognizing the differences between inputs and outputs. Chapters 9 and 10 apply these quantitative foundations to a simple example of optionality in real estate, being the sale timing decision. Chapter 11 moves to the development process and the opportunity cost of capital for construction, while Chapter 12 focuses on the decision of whether and/or when to develop.

The concept and framework of optionality in the context of real estate are introduced in Chapter 13, with Chapter 14 focusing on product options and Chapter 15 on timing options. The quantitative foundations and concept and framework of optionality are then combined through application to the large-scale Garden City residential development project. Chapter 16 presents the traditional cash flow, with uncertainty (but without flexibility) discussed in Chapter 17. Both uncertainty and flexibility are examined in Chapters 18 and 19 through the start date, in Chapter 20 through modular production timing flexibility, in Chapter 21 through product mix flexibility, and in Chapters 22 and 23 through sequential phasing delay. The use of the same example evolving through a series of chapters allows the reader to easily understand the respective applications and their differing impacts on the outputs of the analysis.

Chapter 24 then summarizes the book. Text boxes throughout provide illuminating commentary, and the Appendix provides key information on the real estate system, uncertainty, and the eight components of real estate price dynamics. The accompanying website provides very helpful sample spreadsheets and supporting material. Usefully, each chapter is bite-sized, being generally 15 pages or less and written in a conversational style that makes reading both quick and enjoyable, satisfying the author's intention to present:

> … common-sense methods rooted in the spirit of engineering, rather than highly complex models typical of academic literature in the field of economics. (Chapter 24)

Significantly, the book bridges concepts of value with development analysis. Rather than the traditional focus on concepts of *market value*, the book views development through the lens of *investment value* (or its economic equivalent, *private value*) from the perspective of the developer, which is contingent on the ability and willingness of the developer to exercise the flexibility being modelled. A key output of this book for valuation theory is the bridging of *investment value* and *market value* in a development context:

> Furthermore, at a deeper level, private valuations underlie, and determine, market values. Buyers will not pay more than their private valuations for an asset, and sellers will not take less than their private valuations for assets they own. The equilibrium prices that we define as market values evidenced by consummated transaction prices can therefore reflect private valuations. (Chapter 19)

The overall contribution of this book to an understanding of flexibility and optionality in real estate is aptly summarized by the authors:

> We can distill the results of our analysis into a general rule: *Make as much of the project as flexible as possible, as early as possible, but think about the implications of the market cycle.*

Professors Geltner and de Neufville are to be commended for their contribution to the next major leap in real estate thought leadership, being optionality in real estate.

April 2017

Professor David Parker
Professor of Property
University of South Australia

Authors' Preface

What this book is about, and how to use it.

This book is a groundbreaking text for real estate developers and investors. It is about uncertainty: "unknown unknowns." It shows how the flexibility that exists in real estate investments and development projects unlocks hidden value, and it provides easy-to-use tools to quantify that hidden value. If you are a developer or investor, you *know* that *uncertainty* pervades your decision-making, and you *intuitively* realize the importance of *flexibility* for dealing with unexpected future outcomes. Flexibility includes such capabilities as the ability to sell a property whenever you choose, to delay a second phase of construction, or to change from building a hotel to building apartments. This book describes an approach to realistically quantifying the nature and effect of future uncertainty, and to putting a monetary value on these types of flexibilities.

Our approach is easy to use because it is based on the industry-standard spreadsheets of discounted cash flow analysis. It efficiently calculates the values of flexibilities and options, and quantifies the nature of risks and opportunities. In contrast to the complex, highly mathematical procedures that academics and some Wall Street or City "rocket scientists" often use to calculate option value, the approach we present is intuitive, transparent, easy to implement, and, we think, more informative for real estate decision-makers. The procedures described in this book are direct analogs of management decision-making, not academic economic models of market equilibrium. In the real world of real estate investment decision-making, this approach adds fundamental and crucial aspects of reality that are currently too much ignored or treated only with seat-of-the-pants intuition. Namely, we include the explicit and quantitative consideration of uncertainty and flexibility.

The text presents and describes in detail this innovative and simple approach to valuing the types of real estate flexibility that commonly exist in real-world investment and development. Building naturally and easily on the familiar current practice of project valuation and financial analysis, the procedure we present completes the analysis and makes it much more powerful and useful. It enhances one's capability to evaluate the multiple, interacting options and contingencies that arise from market changes. Importantly, it does more than calculate the expected, or average, value of real estate options. It describes the range of possible outcomes, and so informs users about the possible risks and rewards, quantifying the "downside" and the "upside." We believe it does so with sufficient depth and realism to usefully inform project planning and design decisions.

Essentially, we exploit the power of modern personal computers, combined with knowledge derived from newly available empirical data about real estate markets. Instead of using complex mathematical computations based on limited assumptions about the nature of uncertainty (for example, the random walk assumption), we use laptops to explore in detail what may actually occur. The procedure simulates the effects of the many different kinds of uncertainties that may exist, and considers the implications of a range of possible decisions that managers might take. This enables users to explore strategies of management and development in the light of a sophisticated valuation of the flexibility that exists. You can think of our approach as providing a way for decision-makers—with more, or less, experience—to transform their intuitive sense of managing risks and exploiting opportunities into more solid, defensible, quantitative economic valuations of real estate options. Our approach is:

- *Valuable*: It unlocks added value by exploring options that might provide a significant increase in expected value; this may be done by exploiting upside opportunities, avoiding downside risks, and, in some cases, decreasing initial costs;
- *Practical*: It simply extends the standard spreadsheet-based discounted cash flow analyses for valuing real estate projects that practitioners are already at ease with, requiring no additional special software; and
- *Realistic*: It builds on over 30 years of collaboration between the commercial real estate industry and the Center for Real Estate at the Massachusetts Institute of Technology (MIT), and over 90 years of combined professional investment, engineering, and teaching experience of the authors.

The Value Proposition

The book enables real-world practitioners—managers, investors, and developers of real estate properties and projects—to evaluate their real estate options quantitatively. Practitioners can use this book to identify opportunities to increase their expected value using various types of flexibilities that can exist in real estate investment, and particularly in development projects. These opportunities arise from the possibilities to:

- Time the start, stop, or sale of developments or investments to their advantage;
- Change the mix of uses, or even the scale and density, in a development in accordance with changing market priorities; and
- In general, manage and develop properties' flexibilities to exploit opportunities as they arise, while also avoiding risks that may crop up.

Taken together, these options allow developers to deal proactively with the many uncertainties that inevitably confront the development of real estate projects.

The use of options in real estate can significantly increase the expected value of real estate development in three ways. It can enable decision-makers to:

- Exploit new opportunities arising from favorable upticks in market conditions;
- Reduce or avoid the downward consequences associated with unfavorable circumstances; and
- Increase the rate of return while reducing the risk in the return on investments, or reduce their initial capital requirements—for example, by delaying the implementation of project stages until the market becomes more favorable, or by resizing the initial investment to consider future expansion possibilities.

Users taking advantage of the flexibility of real options can put themselves ahead of the competition. The ability to identify greater value in investment and development projects will enable practitioners to win more opportunities. The capability to deploy innovative designs that enhance the value of new developments by incorporating valuable options should improve investment performance.

Using this approach to quantitatively document the value of options can strengthen the case for certain projects. In other cases, scenario exploration can reveal cautionary considerations that are important for investors and principals to take into account before launching the project. The methods in this book can help test the intuitive sense of opportunities and, where appropriate, demonstrate the value of options that developers are considering for a project. Reducing uncertainty by shining a more quantitative "light" on the nature of the risks faced by the developer, scenario and simulation analysis can better facilitate financing of potential projects (or weed out more risky projects). Overall, the solid analysis and the use of real estate options give practitioners an advantage over any competitors who ignore this new capability.

This innovative book is inherently future-oriented. It describes how real estate valuation can evolve, learning from, but not repeating, the past. It's for the new generation used to living in a world of "big data."

Accessibility

Our approach is eminently accessible. It builds on the standard spreadsheet analyses that industry practitioners already use to evaluate projects. It extends this method to the valuation of options through commonsense and logic. It simply exploits the power of modern computers to search through a range of possibilities, to calculate the results of alternative actions, and to display those results in intuitively understandable ways. The process thus avoids the use of complicated mathematics.

We have designed the presentation for easy learning and adoption. We provide a suite of practical, realistic tools to value real estate options in different circumstances. We present this material in easy-to-read, bite-sized steps. These steps build up from simple demonstrations to examples that have a degree of realism useful for actual business decision-making. Illustrative cases and simple worked-out examples guide users through the process. Beyond the book, an accompanying website provides spreadsheet templates that practitioners can download and adapt to their own needs.

The approach presented here results from the collaboration of two leading teachers at MIT, David Geltner and Richard de Neufville. Professor Geltner is the principal author of a leading industry text, *Commercial Real Estate Analysis and Investments* (3rd edition, OnCourse Learning). Professor de Neufville is the lead author of *Flexibility in Engineering Design* (MIT Press) and six other textbooks on systems analysis, planning, and design.

How to Use this Book

Before diving in, please take a moment to look at how we have structured the text. We have designed this book to smoothly and easily introduce real estate managers, investors, and developers to new ways to evaluate and improve their projects. The book presents the new approach one concept at a time. It builds up your understanding, step by step, in short chapters that you can cover in about an hour each. We illustrate topics with practical examples. And we have written the text in straightforward language. The goal is to help you quickly understand the concepts and the principles of how you can use flexibility and options to create and increase value in real estate.

The basic idea is to imagine what could happen and then examine the consequences. It's a "what if?" analysis. We show how to do this simply and quickly using laptops. A computer simulates the possibilities and the consequences rapidly—thousands of times in just seconds. The process then compares the results to identify the benefits of possible flexible strategies and options.

The process mechanics should be accessible to practicing real estate analysts. The calculations build on the standard financial spreadsheets (such as Microsoft Excel®) that are almost everywhere in real estate valuations. The approach does not involve fancy mathematics—we just calculate possible values many, many times. Nor does it require special software beyond standard spreadsheets such as Microsoft Excel®. We use a disciplined approach structured to provide the results numerically and graphically.

In addition, the analyses are transparent. The spreadsheets clearly display inputs and assumptions and allow users to change them easily. Users are not required to assume that uncertainties and trends are stationary (that is, do not alter over time), a commonly required assumption in academic economic options models.

We describe (and provide freely via the web) a series of spreadsheet templates to simulate a plausible range of possible uncertain outcomes based on our knowledge of real estate markets, and to calculate the resulting distribution of the investment performance outcome for a typical illustrative project. The electronic templates effectively supplement the examples in the text for readers who want to replicate the examples or build on them to create their own applications. Thus, the web material, which is well annotated at the "nuts-and-bolts" level in Microsoft Excel®, can be used by readers who want to value flexible real estate strategies themselves. The web material is also suitable for students, either in class or for self-study.

In a nutshell, the way to access the material is to:

- Read the text for overall comprehension of our approach;
- Dip into the web material for detailed explanations as desired; and
- Draw on the web material for detailed examples and templates you can use as starting points for your own projects.

Acknowledgments

The authors gratefully acknowledge the professional support and advice of Professor David Parker of the University of South Australia and Dr. Paul McNamara of Linden Parkside Ltd in the UK; the technical support of our graduate assistants Nick Foran, Saurabh Jalori, Eric Mo, and Qing Ye; the helpful feedback of the hundreds of MIT and Harvard students who have followed our class at MIT over the years; our home copy editor Susan Matheson; our Wiley-Blackwell editor Paul Sayer; and of course the Wiley-Blackwell production team in the UK and India, including Blessy Regulas, Adalfin Jayasingh, Shalisha Sukanya Sam and Aravind Kannankara.

About the Companion Website

This book is accompanied by a companion website:

www.wiley.com/go/geltner-deneufville/
flexibility-and-real-estate-valuation

The website includes:
- Excel files

1

Discounted Cash Flow Valuation

The Basic Procedures and Concepts Underlying Spreadsheet Valuation
Constitute the Springboard to our Approach of Analyzing Flexibility
Under Uncertainty

LEARNING OBJECTIVES

- Share the reasons why we focus on the discounted cash flow (DCF) model;
- Establish the basic terminology and setup that we use throughout the text;
- Review the mechanics of the DCF valuation model;
- Understand the use of the DCF model for prospective (ex-ante) and retrospective (ex-post) valuations.

OUTLINE OF THE CHAPTER

1.1 Why the Focus on the Discounted Cash Flow Model?
1.2 Structure of a Discounted Cash Flow Spreadsheet
1.3 The Cash Flow Projection
1.4 Discount Rate
1.5 Market Value and Forward-Looking (Ex-Ante) Analysis
1.6 Backward-Looking (Ex-Post) Analysis
1.7 Conclusion

The focus of this book is on the valuation of properties and development projects in the face of uncertainty. We concentrate particularly on management and design flexibility, which is the ability to respond to circumstances in order to reduce downside risks and take advantage of upside opportunities.

To this end, everything in this book builds on and uses the basic discounted cash flow (DCF) model. So, to ensure we're all on the same page, and using the same terminology and basic understanding about this tool, this first chapter introduces and reviews the DCF model, and thereby sets the stage for all that follows.

First, we discuss why it makes sense for us to focus on the DCF model. What makes the DCF model so appropriate for our purpose? (See Section 1.1.)

Second, we describe the essential elements of the DCF model. We define both the terminology and structure of the model that we use throughout the book. We do this to establish a common vocabulary and to avoid confusion that might arise from different professional practices. This quick review also introduces DCF modeling for those who might not be familiar with the procedure (see Sections 1.2–1.4).

Flexibility and Real Estate Valuation under Uncertainty: A Practical Guide for Developers, First Edition.
David Geltner and Richard de Neufville.
© 2018 John Wiley & Sons Ltd. Published 2018 by John Wiley & Sons Ltd.
Companion website: www.wiley.com/go/geltner-deneufville/flexibility-and-real-estate-valuation

Third, we illustrate the two basic ways to use the DCF model to value projects. We can use it to value projects *prospectively*—in advance of making investments, as an aid to decision-making. We can also use it *retrospectively*—to assess the actual past performance of a real estate asset and investment, to help diagnose the causes of success and failure (see Sections 1.5 and 1.6).

1.1   Why the Focus on the Discounted Cash Flow Model?

Three factors make the DCF model the most appropriate basis for valuation of real estate properties and developments in the face of uncertainty:

- DCF is based on fundamental financial economic theory, explicitly recognizing and valuing, based on opportunity cost, the three seminal considerations in investment: *cash flow*, *time*, and *risk*.
- The DCF model is already the analytic workhorse for valuation of real estate investments. Many of you are probably already familiar with it.
- Implemented in modern computer spreadsheet software, the DCF model is very efficient and widely applicable. The relevant calculations usually take seconds or less. And the model can realistically represent a wide range of complex situations useful for valuing flexibility under uncertainty.

Allow us to elaborate briefly on these three points.

The focus of DCF on cash contrasts with a focus on accounting metrics such as net income. Of course, such accounting metrics are very important, and DCF models often include and use accounting metrics. Nevertheless, cash is what you can actually use—in investments, in business, in life. The accounting metrics are indirect representatives, reflections, or predictors of the existing or future cash flow that ultimately matters.

The "D" part of "DCF" is how we account for time and risk in the valuation. Future money is worth less than present money for two reasons:

1) You could be using the money in the meantime (maybe to spend on consumption, maybe to earn returns in investment); and
2) The future money might not materialize in full or at all, since the future is uncertain (no one has a crystal ball).

The discount rate by which the DCF procedure reduces future expected cash flow to present value (PV) accounts for both of these considerations. It does this accounting based on the fundamental economic principle of opportunity cost, using a discount rate that reflects what the investor could expect to earn by investing in a similar investment of similar risk. In short, the DCF model is solid, elegant, and intuitive.

The DCF model is not just sound from an economic theory perspective—its use too is widespread. DCF models operate using computer spreadsheets, which are a common way to organize data for valuation analysis. Spreadsheets are everywhere in financial analysis. Business analysts and decision-makers worldwide use common spreadsheet programs such as Microsoft Excel®. Such spreadsheet software is, in effect, a common language in the business and financial world. This can greatly facilitate communication, transparency, understanding, and use.

Finally, DCF models based on computer spreadsheets have tremendous range and flexibility in what they can do for us analytically, especially in our quest to bring uncertainty and flexibility explicitly into valuation. Spreadsheets take in numerical data and calculate outputs, allowing us to easily change one or more entries and recalculate to see the results instantaneously. Spreadsheets have two special capabilities that enable us to represent uncertainty and flexibility. These capabilities are easy to implement and use, and are essential to the approach we present in this book.

- First, we can easily use spreadsheets to calculate thousands of variations of the same problem automatically, in seconds. This feature allows us to deal with the range of possible economic and other variations that could affect the performance of an investment and hence the valuation of the real estate. This frees us from the need to confine our analysis to just a few estimates of the possible future. It enables us to look at probabilistic distributions of possibilities in detail, such as the effects of business cycles and market movements—a step that is necessary for the proper valuation of flexibility. This capability is available through the random number generation capability and the "data table" function in Microsoft Excel®.
- Second, we can set up the spreadsheet to represent the actions of a decision-maker choosing to take appropriate actions under the conditions we specify. In effect, we can create an analog model of the investment and decision-making process. Thus, we can program potential decisions to take advantage of the flexibility to sell a property under favorable circumstances, or to delay development in a down economic cycle, for example. This capability enables us to represent and quantify the advantages of certain options and certain types of decision flexibility. This approach also enables us to value several options simultaneously, a capability largely beyond the ability of many of the formal academic models of option valuation. In essence, we employ "IF statements" in Microsoft Excel® formulas.

1.2 Structure of a Discounted Cash Flow Spreadsheet

Let's now review the widely accepted and somewhat standardized structure and procedure for the DCF analysis we use for valuation, arguably a canonical framework in real estate. As we have said, this structure is tailor-made for spreadsheets (and vice versa). It is usual to call this setup and framework a "pro forma analysis," or, simply, a DCF "pro forma."

Table 1.1 presents a simple numerical example of such a DCF valuation for a stylized commercial rental property. As Table 1.1 illustrates, the DCF pro forma is a table (or matrix) showing the state of an investment over time in two dimensions (rows and columns). The overall structure is that:

- The columns specify different periods, for example, years. For generality, a usual practice is to number the columns starting with "0," which refers to the present—that is, the time when the analysis and evaluation are applicable. "Column 1" is the first year (or period) in the future, "Column 2" the second, and so on.
- The rows represent revenue and expenditure items relevant for analysis and valuation. We speak of these as the "cash flow over time" of the line item represented in the row. The normal convention is to assume that cash flows occur "in arrears"—that is,

Table 1.1 Illustrative "pro forma" spreadsheet for the DCF valuation of a rental property.

ASSUMPTIONS

Discount Rate:	7.0%	=r	Vacancy*:	5.0%	=v	Capital Expenditures*:	10.0%	=CI
Growth Rate:	2.0%	=g	Expenses*:	35.0%	=Expense Ratio	Exit Cap-Rate:	5.0%	=y

PRO FORMA	YEAR 0	YEAR 1	YEAR 2	YEAR 3	YEAR 4	YEAR 5	YEAR 6	YEAR 7	YEAR 8	YEAR 9	YEAR 10	YEAR 11
4 Potential Gross Income		$100.00	$102.00	$104.04	$106.12	$108.24	$110.41	$112.62	$114.87	$117.17	$119.51	$121.90
5 Vacancy Allowance		5.00	5.10	5.20	5.31	5.41	5.52	5.63	5.74	5.86	5.98	6.09
6 Effective Gross Income		95.00	96.90	98.84	100.81	102.83	104.89	106.99	109.13	111.31	113.53	115.80
7 Operating Expenses		35.00	35.70	36.41	37.14	37.89	38.64	39.42	40.20	41.01	41.83	42.66
8 Net Operating Income		60.00	61.20	62.42	63.67	64.95	66.24	67.57	68.92	70.30	71.71	73.14
9 Capital Expenditures		10.00	10.20	10.40	10.61	10.82	11.04	11.26	11.49	11.72	11.95	12.19
10 Net Annual Cash Flows		50.00	51.00	52.02	53.06	54.12	55.20	56.31	57.43	58.58	59.75	60.95
11 Reversion Cash Flows											1218.99	1278.75
12 Net Cash Flows with		50.00	51.00	52.02	53.06	54.12	55.20	56.31	57.43	58.58	1218.99	1278.75
13 PV @7.0% Discount Rate	$1,000											

* Percentage (%) of Potential Gross Income (PGI)

as of the end of the indicated period. Some rows are sometimes used to display the underlying physical source amounts, such as the quantity of units sold or the square meters of space occupied.

1.3   The Cash Flow Projection

In this and the next sections, we review the essential mechanics of the DCF valuation procedure. We first focus on the future stream of cash flow we expect from the property—that is, the estimates of its future revenues and expenditures, period by period. It's important to note that we specify these estimates by period. It isn't enough to estimate the overall revenues and expenses; one must assess how they evolve over time. This is because the discounting process noted previously (and as elaborated in the following section) will give different present values to future cash flows, depending on how far in the future they occur.

We base cash flow projections on a variety of sources. These include:

- Knowledge of fixed contractual obligations (such as mortgage payments and lease terms);
- Informed best estimates of specific income and expenses; and
- Assumptions about the relevant real estate market and overall economic conditions, such as future prices.

Table 1.1 presents a simple numerical example of a commercial rental property, in which the cash flows are all speculative estimates. You might think of the property as an apartment property.

Later in this book, we focus primarily on development projects—that is, investments that require considerable construction up front as well as possibly in later stages. Development projects can have major net negative cash flows for extended periods or at different times during the project's life. But, to begin, we focus on a simpler and more fundamental type of capital asset, as represented by the fully operational rental property depicted in Table 1.1. (A fully operational property occupied to a normal level is also referred to as a "stabilized" property.)

The property owner takes in rental revenue and pays out cash to cover operating and capital expenses. The difference between the money in and the money out is the "net cash flow." This can be either positive or negative in any given period. *Positive cash flow* means that the property owner receives money, net, from the asset. *Negative cash flow* means that expenditures exceed revenues, and that the property owner must somehow provide cash to the property.

While we have not labeled the cash flows in any particular currency, we refer to them in "dollars" for illustrative purposes. Note also that Table 1.1 uses real estate terms typical for the United States.

Table 1.1 projects all the estimated cash flow components in our property to grow at a steady rate. This practice does occur in the real world as a simplification, but here this simplification is for ease of illustration, to allow us to make some essential points more clearly. For the property in our example, we use a projected growth rate of income and expenses of 2% each year, as indicated at the top of the spreadsheet. While this might be a typical rate of growth for rental property in a mature economy, it is just an example of growth projection.

It is usual to structure the rows so that annual revenues are generally at the top of each column, followed by costs, leading to net cash flow for the year at the bottom. Table 1.1 is reasonably standard in this respect. To see how this works, consider the entries in the column for Year 3. Taking each row in turn, we have:

- *Potential gross income* (PGI): This refers to the revenue that the property would generate if it were fully occupied. (This is also sometimes referred to as *Gross Revenue*, or *Rent Roll*.) We project this as $104.04 in Year 3, which is the $100 of Year 1 grown by 2% over 2 years.
- *Vacancy allowance*: This implies that some fraction (which we assume to be 5%, or $5.20) of the potential revenue will *not* be generated, owing to vacancy in the property during the year.
- *Effective gross income* (EGI): $98.84 equals PGI minus vacancy allowance.
- *Operating expenses*: This refers to the estimated regularly recurring costs for operating the property, such as utilities, insurance, property taxes, maintenance, and management costs.
- *Net operating income* (NOI): $62.42 equals EGI minus operating expenses.
- *Capital improvement expenditures* ("Capex"): This refers to the longer-term, less regularly recurring expenditures incurred to improve the property and keep it running—for example, a new roof, new heating or air conditioning system, repaving the parking lot or re-landscaping the grounds, refurbishing and refitting apartments with new appliances, etc.
- *Net cash flow*: $52.02 equals NOI minus Capex; this is the overall difference between the money in and the money out, at the property level. (In this book, we focus on the asset level, not considering specifically investor-level cash flows such as debt payments or income taxes—although, of course, the DCF model may also be applied at that level.) Net cash flow is our "bottom-line" projection for operations in Year 3. As noted, the net cash flow can be either positive or negative in any given year.

A complete DCF valuation, in addition to its ongoing annual cash flows, has to account properly for the projected value of the asset at the time it might be sold. We do this by projecting what real estate analysts call the "reversion" cash flow. This amount corresponds to what in other fields of capital budgeting might be termed "terminal value" or "salvage value." In real estate, this is the expected resale price for the property.

In practice, real estate analysts usually consider that the resale of the property will occur at some finite horizon, often using the nice round number of 10 years. (Many leases and mortgages have terms equal to or less than 10 years, and many owners in fact resell investment properties after about that length of holding.) We can use other horizons, but Table 1.1 conventionally calculates the reversion cash flow with the standard 10-year horizon.

The reversion is logically the capitalized value of the future stream of net cash flow that the property will provide beyond the resale horizon date (the present value for the next buyer). The common way to estimate this is to divide the projected net cash flow for the year beyond the resale horizon (in our case, Year 11) by a projected cash yield rate for that time. Thus:

$$\text{Reversion cash flow Year } 10 = \frac{(\text{Year 11 Net Cash Flow})}{\text{Cash yield rate}} \tag{1.1}$$

This "ratio valuation" formula is a practical, acceptable procedure for reversion valuation. It skips the full, multi-year DCF valuation, which might require difficult or excessively speculative projections beyond the 10-year horizon.

Our example assumes a "going-out" (or "terminal") yield rate of 5% for a valuation as of the end of Year 10 (which is therefore applied to the projected cash flow of Year 11). Thus, the estimated Year 10 reversion cash flow equals the Year 11 projected net cash flow of $60.95 divided by 0.05, which is (rounding out) $1218.99, shown as reversion in the Year 10 column.

The overall bottom line for our DCF valuation model in Table 1.1 consists of the operating net cash flow amounts during the first 9 years plus, for the terminal tenth year, the sum of its operating cash flow and the projected reversion. Thus, the Year 10 net cash flow projection is $1278.75 (operating net cash flow of $59.75 plus the projected reversion of $1218.99).

We now have all the cash flow data needed to perform the DCF valuation analysis. To value the asset, in addition to cash flow, we need another crucial parameter: the discount rate. Let's think about what this should be.

1.4 Discount Rate

The role of the discount rate—that is, how the DCF valuation accounts for time and risk—was noted in Section 1.1. The discount rate has its name because it discounts—that is, reduces the value of—future amounts in terms of the present value (PV). The formula for this reduction is:

$$PV = \frac{(\text{Future amount})}{(1 + \text{discount rate})^{(\text{number of periods})}} \tag{1.2}$$

These reductions can be huge. Figure 1.1 illustrates the phenomenon, showing how several discount rates reduce the value of $100 received in future years.

What should the discount rate be in our DCF valuation? This is a most important issue, since the rate strongly affects the perceived economic value of the project. As noted in Section 1.1, for market valuation purposes, the discount rate should equal the opportunity cost of capital (OCC). We discuss this important concept in some depth in Chapter 2. For the moment, we assume in Table 1.1 that the appropriate discount rate is 7% per year.

1.5 Market Value and Forward-Looking (Ex-Ante) Analysis

We can now value the asset. In terms of mechanics, once we have set up the spreadsheet, filled in our estimates of cash flows, and selected the discount rate, all we have to do is place the proper formula in the desired cell and initiate calculation. In our example, the result is the $1000 value that appears in the bottom left-hand corner. This is the present value (PV) of the property. It is the value of all the net future cash flows placed on the common basis of the present, controlling for time and risk.

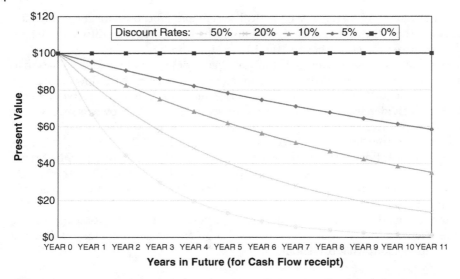

Figure 1.1 Present value of a single $100 future cash flow promised at various future times and discounted at various rates.

In detail, the calculation works as follows. (These steps are not visible on the pro forma.) The computer spreadsheet reduces the net cash flow in each year to its present value and sums up the result across all the years; this equals the value of the asset. The reduction for any year depends on a compounding of the discount rate by the number of years between it and the present, as Equation 1.2 indicates. Thus, Year 1 net cash flow of 50.00 reduces to the PV:

$$46.73 = \frac{50.00}{1.07}$$

Year 2 net cash flow of 51.00 reduces to the PV:

$$44.55 = \frac{51.00}{(1.07)^2}$$

And so on. Finally, the PV of the Year 10 net cash flow is:

$$\frac{1278.75}{(1.07)^{10}} = 650.05$$

The sum of all these present values of the future cash flow expectations is:

$$(46.73 + 44.55 + 42.46 + \ldots + 650.05) = 1000$$

This DCF valuation is forward-looking; that is, its data come from projections of future years' cash flows (including the resale). It is a typical pro forma application of the model that is appropriate for evaluating a property asset at the present time (Time 0).

This is because the present value of the asset depends on the net cash flow that we anticipate it to produce in the future. We refer to this as an "ex-ante" analysis. This way of using DCF valuation is typical for estimating the "market value" of a property asset, presuming the cash flows are unbiased estimates and the discount rate is a realistic estimate of the market OCC. The market value is an estimate of what the property would sell for. Ex-ante DCF analysis is also useful to estimate "investment value," which is a private valuation for a particular investor. Investment value may differ from market value if the investor differs from the typical marginal buyer in the market, or if the investor knows something that the market does not know.

1.6 Backward-Looking (Ex-Post) Analysis

We can also apply the DCF model to a past investment. In this case, our cash flows are historical—they have already happened—so we use actual amounts rather than estimated future amounts. We might do this as part of a retrospective, "post mortem" analysis of an investment. We refer to this as an "ex-post" analysis.

The spreadsheet for the ex-post analysis of a project has the same structure as Table 1.1. However, the year headings at the tops of the columns would refer to specific past years, and the cash flow amounts in the table would equal the actual recorded historical cash flows in those years.

The focus of the ex-post analysis differs from that of the ex-ante analysis. The ex-ante analysis often aims to estimate the value of an investment, for example, so that we can have an idea of how much to pay for it, given the current opportunity cost of capital. In the ex-post analysis, we know what we paid for the investment, and can apply the DCF to learn what rate of return we actually achieved. This can be helpful in conducting diagnostics, to learn the causes of investment successes and failures.

In later chapters, we introduce another way to use the DCF model in an ex-post manner. We will create scenarios of future cash flow streams that could conceivably happen; in effect, we will calculate possible "future histories." We can use the present values of these scenarios as a metric of interest in our simulation modeling. In effect, we will be conducting ex-post DCF analyses of the possible future scenarios. The distribution of possible future ex-post results then effectively presents us with an ex-ante probability distribution.

1.7 Conclusion

This chapter introduced (or briefly reviewed for you) the discounted cash flow valuation model, perhaps the most basic construct in property valuation, and in the tools we present in this book. We discussed the basic rationale, terminology, and mechanics of the model, and pointed out how it may be used in either a forward-looking or backward-looking manner. The next chapter deepens this discussion by going further into the economics of the model.

2

Economics of the Discounted Cash Flow Valuation Model

Understanding the Discount Rate is Critical

LEARNING OBJECTIVES

- Understand the opportunity cost of capital (OCC) and its basis for the discount rate;
- Understand the differences between discount rate, OCC, and internal rate of return (IRR);
- Learn the concept of net present value (NPV) and how it differs in concept and use from the IRR;
- Understand the relationship between discount rate, growth rate, and yield;
- Understand the relationship between discount rate and risk.

OUTLINE OF THE CHAPTER

2.1 Choice of Discount Rate
2.2 Differences between Discount Rate, Opportunity Cost of Capital, and Internal Rate of Return
2.3 Net Present Value
2.4 Relationship between Discount Rate, Growth Rate, and Income Yield
2.5 Relationship between Discount Rate and Risk
2.6 Conclusion

This chapter explains the concepts needed for a good economic valuation of a real estate property or development, and distinguishes between the various terms used in this process. You may think of this chapter as the conceptual counterpart to the discussion of the mechanics of discounted cash flow (DCF) in the preceding chapter. It is our opportunity to make sure that we are all on the same page regarding the basic concepts and meanings associated with the valuation of real estate and use of the DCF model.

2.1   Choice of Discount Rate

Mechanically, the discount rate we use in the DCF valuation model simply converts future cash flow amounts to present values (PVs). But the economic meaning of this mechanical process can differ depending on what the future cash flows represent and on what type of value is used for the discount rate.

If, as is usually the case, we are interested in estimating the "market value" (see Box 2.1) of the asset, then the future cash flows should represent unbiased expectations, and the discount rate should equal the "opportunity cost of capital" (OCC) faced by

Flexibility and Real Estate Valuation under Uncertainty: A Practical Guide for Developers, First Edition.
David Geltner and Richard de Neufville.
© 2018 John Wiley & Sons Ltd. Published 2018 by John Wiley & Sons Ltd.
Companion website: www.wiley.com/go/geltner-deneufville/flexibility-and-real-estate-valuation

---

Box 2.1 Different Conceptions of Value and Price

At first, it may seem like the "value" of an investment asset is a very straightforward and unambiguous concept. Think again! Investors, economists, and lawyers may be interested in different conceptions of the value of a real estate asset.

The most common concept is that of "market value," which we sometimes refer to as "exchange value." It's the price you could expect the asset to sell for in the market today, assuming an arms-length transaction (not some sort of "special deal") between reasonably informed buyers and sellers. Of course, no one knows exactly what this value is for any given property at any given time.

Whenever a property actually does sell, we can observe an exact transaction "price." That price might be above or below the (unknowable) market value, since one party to the deal might have gotten the better of the other. But we usually consider an arms-length transaction price to be an unbiased indication of what the market value was at the time of the transaction. In this way, "price" and "value" are not the same thing in real estate, although they are related. Prices are statistically distributed and centered around market values.

Now consider other conceptions of value that might be of interest. For example, a tax assessing authority might have a special definition of value upon which they want to base assessments for property tax. A bank or potential lender might require a special valuation that purposely errs on the conservative side.

A particularly important and fundamental conception of value that specifically contrasts with market value is what economists often call "private value." A closely related concept is "inherent value" or "intrinsic value" or "usage value" (or "value in use"). These concepts refer to the value of the asset for particular owners or users apart from its exchange value—that is, ignoring how much the asset might sell for if it could be traded. The investment community often refers to this type of valuation as "investment value." We might view it as the maximum price a particular investor would be willing to pay for the asset *if he or she had to pay that much*. Or, for existing property owners, it might the price they would be willing to sell the property for *if they had to sell that low*. Investment value depends on the net incremental after-tax cash flow that a particular investor can obtain as a result of owning the asset indefinitely without selling it, including consideration not just of the subject asset itself but also of possible synergies to other assets owned by the investor. Buyers are motivated for transactions in which the price is lower than their investment value, while sellers are motivated for transactions in which the price is greater than their investment values.

---

investors dealing in the market where the asset is traded. Anyone who invests in our project or property asset is foregoing investing in other similar investments, and therefore is foregoing the opportunity to earn the returns that such alternative investments could provide. This is the sense in which the potential buyer of our property faces an "opportunity cost." Therefore, to be competitively attractive, the expected return on our project should equal this opportunity cost, namely, the expected return on other assets of similar investment risk.

In practice, we can never know the exact OCC for any property precisely and definitively. It is not something you can just look up on the Internet! We can estimate the OCC based on surveys, experience, guidance from expert reports, relevant historical and market data, and our own understanding of the market and its investment opportunities, as well as our understanding of the risk of the project. Importantly, we are looking to represent what the *market* requires as an expected return, and not necessarily what we ourselves personally might think it should be.

In this regard, assets (investments) that seem more "risky" (in some sense) command higher expected returns; that is, they have higher OCC, relatively speaking. This is a widely documented market phenomenon. It is worth reiterating that this means that the OCC for a project that we are analyzing should equal the return on investment of properties with similar risk.

While this is the classical framework and is certainly true and good practice, we would be naïve not to raise another consideration. In many asset markets, the OCC depends on the competition for investment projects. This is related to the classical risk/return concept. But it does add an important additional perspective. The fact is that the OCC can reflect capital flows, which reflect the overall demand for real estate investment. Are there many good opportunities available? Is there a flood of investors with a lot of money looking to make investments? Is the central bank keeping interest rates very low? An abundance of good investment opportunities with a scarcity of investors will result in relatively low asset prices (as the projects compete with one another for scarce investment capital), and this will increase OCCs generally (picture a rapidly growing, emerging market country). In contrast, a flood of money will drive up asset prices and reduce OCCs as the ability of the assets to generate future operating profits remains largely unaffected by the capital inflow (picture the US commercial property market in 2007 or 2017). This money flow consideration can explain a lot of the variation over time, and between countries, in the typical magnitude of OCC rates applicable to real estate project valuation.

2.2 Differences between Discount Rate, Opportunity Cost of Capital, and Internal Rate of Return

Having introduced the construct of the discount rate and the concept of the OCC, we need to define and distinguish a third related metric, the internal rate of return (IRR). Students and practitioners often confuse these three terms (discount rate, OCC, IRR). Indeed, they are related. It can therefore be helpful for sharp, analytical thinking to try to grasp the subtle distinctions between these three constructs.

The discount rate is just a *mechanical device*. It is the rate we use to reduce future values to present values. There is not necessarily any normative implication in the term "discount rate." In other words, someone might posit or use some rate as the discount rate, whether or not that rate has any particular economic meaning. For example, a corporation might dictate a "hurdle rate" as a management tool (but defined somewhat arbitrarily from an economic perspective), to be used as the discount rate in benefit–cost analyses for capital budgeting.

In contrast, the OCC is a *normative economic construct*. It is the rate that, when we employ it as the discount rate, gives a present value equal to the estimated market value of the asset (assuming the future cash flows are correctly estimated). This is because, as discussed in the previous section, the OCC represents the return that the investor could expect to get from investing in a typical asset with similar risk and return as the subject asset, in the asset marketplace, simply by paying market value for the asset.

The third construct, the IRR, is like the discount rate, in that it is *not a normative construct but merely a mechanical or mathematical device*. It is simply a way of measuring investment returns when the investment involves multiple cash flows occurring in several future periods. By definition, the IRR is the rate that discounts a stream of cash flows to an NPV of zero. Equivalently, if the investor has an upfront negative cash flow (having paid for the asset at the beginning of the investment), then the IRR is the discount rate that causes the resulting present value of the subsequent complete project cash flow stream to equal the magnitude of that initial investment amount or asset price. Thus, IRR is the discount rate such that:

$$\left(Present\ Value\ of\ project\right) = \left(Up\ front\ investment\right) \tag{2.1}$$

To illustrate the concept of the IRR, let's refer to the DCF analysis in Chapter 1. In that case:

- We made the discount rate 7%;
- We then derived a present value (PV) for the project, $1000;
- If 7% is the OCC, then $1000 is the estimated market value (MV);
- An investor who bought the project for $1000 would obtain a net present value (NPV) of: $MV - Price = \$1000 - \$1000 = 0$;
- So, the investor's implied expected return equals 7%, expressed as the IRR of the investment at the given price of $1000.

The preceding scenario is an example of an *ex-ante* IRR, an expected future return computed *going into* the investment (also referred to as a "going-in IRR"). On the other hand, computing the realized IRR in an ex-post DCF analysis is a way to measure how well the investment performed. For example, one can compare the achieved IRRs across different investments. (However, in making any such comparisons, we shouldn't forget our previous point that more risky investments should provide higher returns, on average and over the long run.)

Thus, to summarize: if you discount at the OCC, the present value you obtain will be the estimated market value (assuming unbiased projected cash flows). If you then pay a price equal to that market value, your going-in IRR in the investment will be the OCC, the fair return given the amount of risk.

2.3 Net Present Value

The net present value (NPV) is the value of what you're getting minus the value of what you give up to get it, evaluating the benefits and costs in "apples-to-apples" money terms—that is, controlling for time and risk (reflecting opportunity costs). Formally, the NPV of a project is the excess of its present value (PV) over its investment cost, which is often simply the price paid (P) for the asset. Thus:

$$Net\ present\ value = \left(present\ value\ of\ project\right) - \left(investment\ cost\right) \tag{2.2}$$

To illustrate the concept, we build upon the DCF example from the preceding chapter. We assume that the cash flow projections remain as in Table 1.1 (including the reversion). However, we now suppose that the correct OCC is 6%, not the 7% discount rate employed in Table 1.1. In other words, we suppose that the investment marketplace has "decided" that it only needs a 6% return for assets like our subject property (perhaps interest rates have fallen, or the property is now viewed by the market as being less risky). In that case, the market value of the property, the sum of the present values of all the future cash flows discounted at 6%, would be $1080. At the lower discount rate, future expected cash flows are more valuable in the present, and the PV is higher than the $1000 calculated for a discount rate of 7%. But if we could still buy the property for $1000 (somehow, even though its market value is $1080, perhaps owing to the seller being misinformed or distressed), then our NPV would be: $1080 − $1000 = +$80.

The existence of a positive, non-zero NPV based on market value indicates that the investment is a bargain for the investor. It provides above market-expected returns. Another way of arriving at the same conclusion is to observe that the ex-ante IRR of the project at the $1000 price is still 7% (that is, the going-in expected total return on the investment), and this is greater than the OCC of the investment, which is 6%. In general, in the market, you could not expect to buy other assets of similar risk at prices that would present you with more than a 6% going-in IRR.

In most well-functioning asset markets, it is hard to find such "bargains." The definition of "market value" is that the property owner can expect to sell at that price. If the market value were $1080, why would the owner sell for $1000? In fact, paying a price equal to the (estimate of) market value provides $NPV = 0$. From such a market value perspective, this is not a "bad deal" for the investor (for the one buying *or* the one selling). From the market value perspective, the buyer receives $MV − P$, while the seller receives $P − MV$, where P is the price, and MV is the market value. Buying the asset for a price equal to its market value provides the investor with an expected return equal to the OCC, a "fair return" (ex-ante). Nevertheless, in real estate and some other circumstances, non-zero NPV deals can occur, even when evaluated from a market value perspective. In part, this is because it is usually difficult to know exactly and precisely what the OCC is or what the market value is of any given asset.

Non-zero NPV opportunities are probably more common when the investment involves construction of new assets, as such entrepreneurial actions often create value. Of course, such development projects can be quite risky.

Perhaps a more common way for non-zero NPV to occur, and, in particular, for positive NPV to occur, is to measure the NPV not from the perspective of market value but from that of some relevant type of "private value" (as defined in Box 2.1). Viewed from the private value perspectives of both parties, it is possible for NPV > 0 for *both* sides of the transaction, since the two parties' private values may differ (and they transact at a price above the seller's valuation and below the buyer's). If we let "IV(B)" be the buyer's "investment value" (as defined Box 2.1) and "IV(S)" be the seller's investment value, then a typical real estate transaction might look like this:

$$IV(S) < MV = P < IV(B) \tag{2.3}$$

And, the NPV from the buyer's investment value perspective is: NPV(B) = IV(B) − P = IV(B) − MV > 0; while, from the seller's perspective, it is: NPV(S) = P − IV(S) = MV − IV(S) > 0.

2.4 Relationship between Discount Rate, Growth Rate, and Income Yield

Now, let us stand back from the details of the DCF spreadsheet to consider some general relationships that will help you understand the terminology and basic economics of the DCF valuation model. In particular, let's focus on the three rates involved in the basic DCF analysis: the discount rate, r; the growth rate, g; and the going-in net cash yield rate, y. In a stylized model that simplifies but retains the important essence, the discount rate is the sum of the growth rate and the going-in cash yield. In equation form, we have:

$$r = g + y \qquad (2.4)$$

In the case of the illustrative DCF that we discussed in Chapter 1 (with the 7% discount rate), we have: $r = 7\%$, $g = 2\%$, and $y = 5\%$.

At this point, a few words about the net cash yield are in order. It is the ratio of current income to price:

$$\text{Net cash yield} = \frac{\left(\text{Current Income}\right)}{\text{Price}} \qquad (2.5)$$

In our example from Table 2.1 (from Chapter 1), the net cash yield is the "going-in" yield at the start of the project:

$$\frac{\left(\$50 \text{ net cash flow in Year 1}\right)}{\left(\$1000 \text{ project value}\right)} = 5\%$$

It is also the "going-out" yield at end of the projected investment:

$$\frac{\left(\$60.95 \text{ net cash flow in Year 11}\right)}{\left(\$1218.99 \text{ reversion value}\right)} = 5\%$$

That both yields are 5% reflects (and helps to cause) the fact that our asset value is a constant multiple of its current income.

Note that the cash yield rate is simply the inverse of the asset's current price/income multiple (which is another way of quoting asset prices):

$$\text{Current price/income multiple} = \frac{\left(\text{Price}\right)}{\left(\text{Current income}\right)} = \frac{1}{\left(\text{Net cash yield}\right)} \qquad (2.6)$$

Box 2.2 contains more detail on the various conceptions of yield in the United States and United Kingdom. It is a useful reference, which you can easily skip if you want.

Table 2.1 Repeating Table 1.1 pro forma spreadsheet (r=7.0%).

ASSUMPTIONS											
Discount Rate:	7.0% =r		Vacancy*:	5.0% =v			Capital Expenditures*:		10.0% =CI		
Growth Rate:	2.0% =g		Expenses*:	35.0% =Expense Ratio			Exit Cap-Rate:		5.0% =y		

PRO FORMA	YEAR 0	YEAR 1	YEAR 2	YEAR 3	YEAR 4	YEAR 5	YEAR 6	YEAR 7	YEAR 8	YEAR 9	YEAR 10	YEAR 11
Potential Gross Income		$100.00	$102.00	$104.04	$106.12	$108.24	$110.41	$112.62	$114.87	$117.17	$119.51	$121.90
Vacancy Allowance		5.00	5.10	5.20	5.31	5.41	5.52	5.63	5.74	5.86	5.98	6.09
Effective Gross Income		95.00	96.90	98.84	100.81	102.83	104.89	106.99	109.13	111.31	113.53	115.80
Operating Expenses		35.00	35.70	36.41	37.14	37.89	38.64	39.42	40.20	41.01	41.83	42.66
Net Operating Income		60.00	61.20	62.42	63.67	64.95	66.24	67.57	68.92	70.30	71.71	73.14
Capital Expenditures		10.00	10.20	10.40	10.61	10.82	11.04	11.26	11.49	11.72	11.95	12.19
Net Annual Cash Flows		50.00	51.00	52.02	53.06	54.12	55.20	56.31	57.43	58.58	59.75	60.95
Reversion Cash Flows											1218.99	
Net Cash Flows with		50.00	51.00	52.02	53.06	54.12	55.20	56.31	57.43	58.58	1278.75	
PV @7.0% Discount Rate	$1,000											

* Percentage (%) of Potential Gross Income (PGI)

Box 2.2 What is this thing called "yield"?

While people commonly use the term "yield" as the ratio of current income to price as in Equation 2.5, be careful. In other contexts, the term "yield" refers to the total return, the "r" in our nomenclature. For example, the "yields" of government bonds are generally total returns, generally defined as the IRRs on investments in bonds. That is, the bond "yield" is the discount rate that determines the price of the bond based on its contractual cash flows.

To clarify, it is sometimes helpful to specify the "cash yield," "initial yield," or "current yield" when referring to the "net cash yield" in Equation 2.5.

Terminology can also confuse matters when dealing just with the cash yield. A closely related construct is what US practitioners refer to as the "capitalization rate," or "cap rate" for short. You would think that this term would refer to the discount rate in the DCF valuation, and in some contexts indeed it does. However, in the US real estate industry, the term "cap rate" has come to refer to something akin to the cash yield, but not quite. In the United States, "cap rate" usually refers to an accounting-based income or earnings yield rather than a cash yield: cap rate = net operating income / property value. The net operating income (NOI) exceeds the actual net cash flow (CF) by the amount of the annual capital improvement expenditures: CF = NOI − Capex. for typical income-generating properties in the United States, capital expenditures average 1–2% of property value per year.

In the United Kingdom and in the appraisal profession, practitioners use further elaborations of the yield concept, with labels such as "equivalent yield" and "equated yield" (among others). These generally have to do with the definition of the numerator in the yield equation—for example, how much to consider only current in-place leases and Capex versus space market considerations and stabilizations. For our purposes, we need not delve into such depth.

2.5 Relationship between Discount Rate and Risk

Continuing with our elaboration of the basic DCF constructs, let's expand on our previous point that expected returns are related to risk. We can express the discount rate as the sum of two factors, a risk-free interest rate (rf) and a risk premium (RP):

$$r = rf + RP \tag{2.7}$$

The risk-free interest rate is what investors can get by investing without any risk, such as perhaps in government bonds. If r is the OCC for the investment, then the RP in Equation 2.7 represents what the asset market "offers" to investors as the amount of extra expected return (ex-ante) that compensates investors for taking on the risk associated with the given investment. (Of course, the market's ex-ante RP may not materialize ex-post; that is what we mean when we say the asset is a "risky" investment!)

Putting Equations 2.4 and 2.7 together, we see that the investment cash yield is:

$$y = rf + RP - g \tag{2.8}$$

In other words, the yield is the sum of the rf prevailing in the economy, plus the RP reflecting the amount of risk in the subject asset as perceived (and priced) by the investment marketplace, minus the growth expected in the asset cash flows and future values.

These relationships make sense:

- The higher the interest rates are, the greater in general is the opportunity cost of investing in any one asset (thereby foregoing investing in any other asset); and hence, the lower the price/income multiple will be (higher yield).
- The riskier the asset, the more investors will demand a higher expected return; and hence, again, the lower the price/income multiple must be (other things remaining equal).
- Finally, the greater the expected growth in the asset's future cash flow and value, the more the investor will pay per dollar of current net income; that is, the higher the price/income multiple will be, given that future income is expected to grow more.

These relationships are fundamental and important in the real world. While we present them as coming from Equations 2.4 and 2.7, we should point out that Equation 2.4 holds *exactly* only if the asset's cash flows grow in perpetuity at a constant rate (the rate g), and the asset value will always be a constant multiple of its current cash flow level. Nevertheless, the above general points still hold in the real world even if Equation 2.4 is not true exactly.

2.6 Conclusion

This chapter elaborated some of the basic constructs and mechanics of the DCF model introduced in Chapter 1 to reveal some important economic considerations. We hope you can see that the DCF valuation model is essentially intuitive, as well as rigorously based in solid economic theory, at least, as far as it goes. The model provides a good basis and tool for us to use in the remainder of this book.

3

Future Scenarios Matter

We Need to Recognize that Future Projections are Uncertain

LEARNING OBJECTIVES

- Learn the concept of "scenarios";
- Recognize the relationship between the DCF model and uncertainty about the future;
- Understand future projections as "expectations";
- See the difference between "flexibility" and economic "options."

OUTLINE OF THE CHAPTER

3.1 The Standard Discounted Cash Flow Model Appears to be Deterministic
3.2 We Live in a World of Uncertainty
3.3 Discounted Cash Flow Pro Forma Cash Flows Are Expectations
3.4 Flexibility and Options
3.5 Conclusion

Everybody loves the DCF model as a tool for valuing investment assets. And valuation is very important in real estate. But this book is about how flexibility can add value. So now we need to take a step beyond the traditional DCF model presented in the previous chapters. In this chapter, we explicitly introduce uncertainty into the cash flow projections in the DCF pro forma.

We suggest the concept of scenarios to describe uncertainties in real estate. Scenarios refer to the fact that the future may turn out differently than the prior projection. A scenario is one specific sequence of events, of circumstances that we may face. A scenario would describe the sequence of combinations of possibilities (price, vacancy, costs, etc.) in Year 1, Year 2, and so on. Any particular real estate project faces many possible scenarios. The price could go up in the first and second years, or it could go up and then down, or down and then up, and so on.

3.1 The Standard Discounted Cash Flow Model Appears to be Deterministic

Looking at our example DCF pro forma, shown again in Table 3.1, it's obvious that its future cash flow projection is a single stream of numbers. Each cash flow line item, each row in the spreadsheet, has a single amount in each future period. The top-line potential

Flexibility and Real Estate Valuation under Uncertainty: A Practical Guide for Developers, First Edition.
David Geltner and Richard de Neufville.
© 2018 John Wiley & Sons Ltd. Published 2018 by John Wiley & Sons Ltd.
Companion website: www.wiley.com/go/geltner-deneufville/flexibility-and-real-estate-valuation

Table 3.1 Pro forma spreadsheet for the DCF valuation of a rental property.

ASSUMPTIONS

1	Discount Rate:	7.0%	=r	Vacancy*:	5.0%	=v	Capital Expenditures*:	10.0%	=CI
2	Growth Rate:	2.0%	=g	Expenses*:	35.0%	=Expense Ratio	Exit Cap-Rate:	5.0%	=y

PRO FORMA	YEAR 0	YEAR 1	YEAR 2	YEAR 3	YEAR 4	YEAR 5	YEAR 6	YEAR 7	YEAR 8	YEAR 9	YEAR 10	YEAR 11
4 Potential Gross Income		$100.00	$102.00	$104.04	$106.12	$108.24	$110.41	$112.62	$114.87	$117.17	$119.51	$121.90
5 Vacancy Allowance		5.00	5.10	5.20	5.31	5.41	5.52	5.63	5.74	5.86	5.98	6.09
6 Effective Gross Income		95.00	96.90	98.84	100.81	102.83	104.89	106.99	109.13	111.31	113.53	115.80
7 Operating Expenses		35.00	35.70	36.41	37.14	37.89	38.64	39.42	40.20	41.01	41.83	42.66
8 Net Operating Income		60.00	61.20	62.42	63.67	64.95	66.24	67.57	68.92	70.30	71.71	73.14
9 Capital Expenditures		10.00	10.20	10.40	10.61	10.82	11.04	11.26	11.49	11.72	11.95	12.19
10 Net Annual Cash Flows		50.00	51.00	52.02	53.06	54.12	55.20	56.31	57.43	58.58	59.75	60.95
11 Reversion Cash Flows											1218.99	
12 Net Cash Flows with		50.00	51.00	52.02	53.06	54.12	55.20	56.31	57.43	58.58	1278.75	
13 PV @ 7.0% Discount Rate	$1,000											

* Percentage (%) of Potential Gross Income (PGI)

revenue stream starts with 100.00 in Year 1 (1 year from the present Time 0), increases to 102.00 in Year 2, and so on, all the way through to 121.90 in Year 11. After we account for vacancy and various expenses and expenditures, the bottom-line net cash flow stream (which more directly determines the estimate of the present value of the property) starts at 50.00 in Year 1 and grows to 60.95 in Year 11 with, again, a single projected value in each of the intermediate years. The point is, the standard DCF pro forma reflects, and utilizes, a *single stream of future cash flows*.

This makes it appear as though the DCF is treating the world as if the future were deterministic, a single possibility. Everybody knows this isn't really true, but the basic, traditional DCF model makes it easy to think, analyze, and make decisions as if the world were deterministic.

If we apply the DCF analysis retrospectively, then the single stream of cash flow amounts in each year might be all the information we need to know. There is only one realized history, and we can know it deterministically. The cash flow stream represented in the analysis would be the actual, recorded amounts in each year.

But DCF analyses usually need to be forward-looking. The value of the property today depends on how much cash it can deliver in the future. The objective is thus to peer into the future, to try to estimate the future cash flows to help us make the best decisions we can today. This perspective has significant implications.

At first, you might think it is fine to represent the future by a single stream of cash flow. In the real world, as the future happens, becoming the present fleetingly, and then the past permanently, there will be only one actual history. And if we make the single stream of cash flows in the pro forma be an unbiased expectation of what the future cash flows will be, then surely those cash flows are the best numbers to base our analyses and decisions upon, aren't they? Well, they are, in fact, often importantly insufficient, as we demonstrate in detail in Chapter 5. It is critical to recognize that, before the future happens, as far as we know in the present, there are many possible futures, many scenarios that could happen. We need to recognize this explicitly.

3.2 We Live in a World of Uncertainty

The future is uncertain. This is a fundamental fact about valuation and management and, come to think of it, life itself. No one has a crystal ball, as the cliché goes. How can we dare to represent the future in our DCF pro forma by a single stream of future cash flows? If the property in the example pro forma were a rental apartment building, for example, how likely do you think it would be that the gross rent in Year 11 would be exactly 121.90? Indeed, how likely is it even that the net cash flow in the first year would be exactly 50.00? And how accurately can we estimate the vacancy rate?

If we are to use the DCF model for more than just the estimation of market value, that is, if we are to use it to help make management decisions and value flexibility, then the model explicitly needs to recognize the uncertainties that realistically exist in the future.

The DCF model can help to provide the basis for important management, design, and programming decisions. For example:

- As the property owner, should you lease a vacant space in the building to Tenant A, who will pay $10 per square foot per year but only for 3 years, or to Tenant B, who will only pay $8 but will commit to a 10-year lease?

- As a designer or developer of a new residential complex, should you plan for all the units to be rental, or all to be condominiums, or half and half? How much should you let an upsurge in property prices tempt you to sell the property sooner than you had been planning to (or, on the contrary, to hold it longer than you had planned)?

Properly elaborated, the DCF model can help you understand the value of alternatives such as these and help you make ongoing management decisions.

In addition, such analysis can actually suggest possible changes in the cash flow projections themselves. The analysis can even change the value estimation of the property today, at least from your own private perspective.

3.3   Discounted Cash Flow Pro Forma Cash Flows Are Expectations

If the single stream of cash flows in the traditional DCF pro forma is not a set of deterministic guarantees, then what does (or should) this stream represent, realistically, in a world of uncertainty? The answer is that the single stream of cash flows in the traditional pro forma is, in principle, a stream of *expected values* of the future cash flows. Traditionally, this is interpreted as implying that each period's cash flow projection in the pro forma is the mean (the probability-weighted average) of the ex-ante probability distribution (as of Time 0) that governs the future cash flow that will actually be realized in that future time period. (For further explanation of "expected value," see Box 3.1.)

The traditional DCF valuation model does not totally ignore the fact that we live in a world of uncertainty. If we apply it correctly, the traditional model reflects uncertainty in two ways.

- First, the cash flow projections should represent expectations of probability distributions, as mentioned in the preceding text.
- Second, the valuation model should reflect risk through the discount rate. As we noted in Chapter 2, the discount rate should properly reflect the risky nature of the future operating cash flows and asset resale value, and so represent the opportunity cost of capital (OCC). Riskier investments will command a higher OCC with a higher risk premium.

But this recognition and reflection of risk and uncertainty in the traditional DCF valuation model is not sufficient to help with management decision-making and with the valuation of flexibility in the context of the private valuations that are of great importance in real estate. The single-stream pro forma tempts users to ignore or overlook important contingencies and opportunities. It makes it too easy to pretend that the world is deterministic, that you can pin everything on that simple, single, projected stream. This undercuts the potential of the DCF model as a management tool.

The reality is that the future is unknown, and that the exact cash flow amounts in the pro forma will almost certainly *not* happen. If the pro forma is very good, then the cash flow projections in it do represent the statistical means (expected values) of the probability distributions that govern what each future year's cash flows will actually

---

Box 3.1 What is the expected value?

An expected value of some variable X, written as $E(X)$, is a concept from probability theory. Mechanically, $E(X)$ is a weighted average of the variable over all of its possible outcome values. It is an extension of the basic notion of an average, which is:

$$\textit{Average} = \textit{[Sum of all values] / [number of values]} \tag{3.1}$$

For example, the average of the three numbers 10, 9, and 5 is $\frac{24}{3} = 8$.

The formula for $E(X)$ expands on the concept of average for the case when we have many possible values. It uses the frequency or probability that any one value occurs as the weighting factor for that value in computing the average. Thus:

$$\text{Expected value} = (\text{probability of value})(\text{value}) + (\text{probability of value})$$
$$(\text{value}) + (\text{probability of value})(\text{value}) + \ldots = \Sigma\left[P(X_i)X_i\right] = E(X) \tag{3.2}$$

Thus, the expectation of X is the average of the possible values of X weighted by the probability of occurrence of each value. We also refer to it as the "mean" of the probability distribution of X.

For example, suppose there are two possible results, either an outcome of 0 or an outcome of 1. If the two outcomes are equally likely, then the expectation is 0.5. But if the zero outcome is twice as likely, then the expectation is: $\left(\frac{2}{3}\right) \times 0 + \left(\frac{1}{3}\right) \times 1 = 0.33$. Note that the actual result, the outcome, will either be 0 or 1, neither of which was the expected value of 0.5 or 0.33.

In principle, the single-stream cash flows in the traditional DCF pro forma should be in the nature of expectations like these. For example, if, during a certain future period, a lease in the building will produce \$100 revenue if the tenant renews, and \$0 during that period if the tenant does not renew, and if the probability of renewal is 75%, then the traditional pro forma will project a cash flow (for that space for that period) of \$75.

Box 3.2 Average Is Not Necessarily Most Likely

Note that, in general, the "most likely" result can differ from the mean or expected value. For example, it is most likely that your house will not burn down; but your expected loss from fire is certainly not zero, considering the small possibility that you could lose the house to fire. This is why people buy fire insurance. Technically, we say that the *mode* (the number that appears most often) does not necessarily equal the *mean* of the probability distribution.

That said, the mode often does equal the mean. Some of the most common probability distributions are symmetrical (such as the famous "normal" probability distribution, which we discuss in Chapter 5), and their most likely value is indeed their "expected" value.

---

turn out to be, as best we can estimate as of Year 0 (the present). The fact that the cash flows are expected values implies that the cash flows actually realized ex-post are as likely to be above as below their projected values in the pro forma. Furthermore, the expected value (the pro forma projection) is not always even the single most likely outcome (see Box 3.2).

3.4   Flexibility and Options

Finally, a word on terminology. We've been focusing on "flexibility." But how does this differ from "options," as economists use this term? In fact, there is a lot of overlap. An option provides a "right without obligation." And this provides flexibility. Thus, options are a form of flexibility.

But the term "flexibility" is broader and more general than options. There are types of flexibilities that most economists would not describe using the word "option." In economics, "option" usually has a somewhat specialized meaning. It connotes a specific claim that we could in principle carve out and evaluate as if we could trade it separately. An example would be the option to tear down an existing building and redevelop the site, which is normally an inherent part of the value of fee simple land ownership.

On the other hand, we do not normally view the flexibility that a property owner has in choosing when to sell the property as an "option," as such, in economics terminology. Thus, while there is certainly considerable overlap, the term "flexibility" is broader than "option" in the context of this book. We will sometimes use the terms interchangeably when the distinction does not matter. But we have tried to use the terms carefully when it might matter.

3.5   Conclusion

"Uncertainty" means that it is possible to have a range of different future scenarios in most investments and development projects. The single-stream, traditional DCF valuation model tends to hide this important fact, even though it recognizes the presence of investment risk by defining the cash flow stream as the probabilistic expectation of possible cash flows in future periods, and includes a risk premium in the OCC employed as the discount rate. We need to recognize cash flow uncertainties explicitly, so that we can unlock and quantify the value of flexibility.

4

Scenario Analysis

Future Scenarios can Significantly and Surprisingly Affect the Present Value

---

LEARNING OBJECTIVES

- Learn to analyze the impact of uncertainty on valuation by creating and using future "scenarios";
- Understand that scenarios affect values;
- See how flexibility can have great value.

OUTLINE OF THE CHAPTER

4.1 Discounted Cash Flow Scenario Analysis
4.2 Scenarios Affect Value
4.3 Flexibility Has Value
4.4 Conclusion

This chapter presents an initial example of how we can identify hidden value using the DCF model to analyze scenarios. It provides a first demonstration of the value of flexibility. We quantify the added value we can obtain by modeling our management of properties to respond to downside and upside contingencies. The example we use is a simplified consideration of when to resell the property that we're evaluating.

4.1 Discounted Cash Flow Scenario Analysis

Let's now look at more than just the mean of the future cash flow, more than just the single-stream pro forma. We can learn a lot by looking at what might actually occur in the future. A good first step for doing this is to think about future cash flow "scenarios" rather than just a single expectation. A scenario analysis can reveal important management possibilities or dangers. This enlightenment can lead the analyst to revise the original pro forma or asset valuation, especially (perhaps) from a private valuation perspective.

Flexibility and Real Estate Valuation under Uncertainty: A Practical Guide for Developers, First Edition.
David Geltner and Richard de Neufville.
© 2018 John Wiley & Sons Ltd. Published 2018 by John Wiley & Sons Ltd.
Companion website: www.wiley.com/go/geltner-deneufville/flexibility-and-real-estate-valuation

Let's take a simple example that builds on the DCF for our example rental property. Table 4.1 shows three DCF pro formas.

- In the top panel, Panel A, the numbers are the same as in the original DCF (Table 1.1). As indicated in Section 3.3, its cash flow projections should be the expectations, the average of future cash flow possibilities in each period.
- Panel B represents a future, optimistic scenario, with a 50% chance of happening. In this example, we suppose that there are only two possible future scenarios, equally probable as of Time 0. For example, suppose the rental property could be near the site of a prospective attractive development (for example, a new metro station), with a 50:50 chance of going forward. Panel B assumes that the new development goes forward and that rents in the property we're considering will be high. Compared to the DCF in Panel A, the optimistic scenario cash flows start out $10 higher in Year 1 and subsequently grow faster.
- Panel C represents the pessimistic scenario where the new development doesn't occur. Compared to Panel A, rents in the property start out $10 lower than the expected value and decline over time.

Note that the two scenarios average out exactly to the entries in Panel A. Thus, Panel A is the true expectations, the unbiased projection of the future possibilities, like what a

Table 4.1 Three DCF scenarios

A) EXPECTED CASH FLOWS

PRO FORMA CASH FLOWS	YEAR 1	YEAR 2	YEAR 3	YEAR 4	YEAR 5	YEAR 6	YEAR 7	YEAR 8	YEAR 9	YEAR 10	YEAR 11
Potential Gross Income	$100.00	$102.00	$104.04	$106.12	$108.24	$110.41	$112.62	$114.87	$117.17	$119.51	$121.90
Vacancy Allowance	5.00	5.10	5.20	5.31	5.41	5.52	5.63	5.74	5.86	5.98	6.09
Effective Gross Income	95.00	96.90	98.84	100.81	102.83	104.89	106.99	109.13	111.31	113.53	115.80
Operating Expenses	35.00	35.70	36.41	37.14	37.89	38.64	39.42	40.20	41.01	41.83	42.66
Net Operating Income	60.00	61.20	62.42	63.67	64.95	66.24	67.57	68.92	70.30	71.71	73.14
Capital Expenditures	10.00	10.20	10.40	10.61	10.82	11.04	11.26	11.49	11.72	11.95	12.19
Net Cash Flow from Operations	50.00	51.00	52.02	53.06	54.12	55.20	56.31	57.43	58.58	59.75	60.95
Reversion Only If/When Sold	1020.00	1040.40	1061.21	1082.43	1104.08	1126.16	1148.69	1171.66	1195.09	1218.99	
Sale Horizon Year Cash Flow (including Reversion	1070.00	1091.40	1113.23	1135.49	1158.20	1181.37	1204.99	1229.09	1253.68	1278.75	
Time 0 PV @ 7% OCC By Year of Sale Horizon	$1,000	$1,000	$1,000	$1,000	$1,000	$1,000	$1,000	$1,000	$1,000	$1,000	

B) OPTIMISTIC CASH FLOWS (50% CHANCE)

PRO FORMA CASH FLOWS	YEAR 1	YEAR 2	YEAR 3	YEAR 4	YEAR 5	YEAR 6	YEAR 7	YEAR 8	YEAR 9	YEAR 10	YEAR 11
Potential Gross Income	$110.00	$115.20	$120.44	$125.73	$131.07	$136.45	$141.88	$147.36	$152.88	$158.46	$164.09
Vacancy Allowance	5.50	5.76	6.02	6.29	6.55	6.82	7.09	7.37	7.64	7.92	8.20
Effective Gross Income	104.50	109.44	114.42	119.45	124.51	129.63	134.78	139.99	145.24	150.54	155.88
Operating Expenses	38.50	40.32	42.16	44.01	45.87	47.76	49.66	51.57	53.51	55.46	57.43
Net Operating Income	66.00	69.12	72.27	75.44	78.64	81.87	85.13	88.41	91.73	95.08	98.45
Capital Expenditures	11.00	11.52	12.04	12.57	13.11	13.64	14.19	14.74	15.29	15.85	16.41
Net Cash Flow from Operations	55.00	57.60	60.22	62.87	65.53	68.22	70.94	73.68	76.44	79.23	82.04
Reversion Only If/When Sold	1152.00	1204.44	1257.33	1310.68	1364.49	1418.78	1473.55	1528.83	1584.60	1640.89	
Sale Horizon Year Cash Flow (including Reversion	1207.00	1262.04	1317.55	1373.54	1430.02	1487.00	1544.49	1602.50	1661.04	1720.12	
Time 0 PV @ 7% OCC By Year of Sale Horizon	$1,128	$1,154	$1,177	$1,199	$1,218	$1,236	$1,253	$1,268	$1,282	$1,294	

C) PESSIMISTIC CASH FLOWS (50% CHANCE)

PRO FORMA CASH FLOWS	YEAR 1	YEAR 2	YEAR 3	YEAR 4	YEAR 5	YEAR 6	YEAR 7	YEAR 8	YEAR 9	YEAR 10	YEAR 11
Potential Gross Income	$90.00	$88.80	$87.64	$86.51	$85.42	$84.37	$83.35	$82.38	$81.45	$80.56	$79.71
Vacancy Allowance	4.50	4.44	4.38	4.33	4.27	4.22	4.17	4.12	4.07	4.03	3.99
Effective Gross Income	85.50	84.36	83.25	82.18	81.15	80.15	79.19	78.26	77.38	76.53	75.72
Operating Expenses	31.50	31.08	30.67	30.28	29.90	29.53	29.17	28.83	28.51	28.20	27.90
Net Operating Income	54.00	53.28	52.58	51.91	51.25	50.62	50.01	49.43	48.87	48.33	47.83
Capital Expenditures	9.00	8.88	8.76	8.65	8.54	8.44	8.34	8.24	8.14	8.06	7.97
Net Cash Flow from Operations	45.00	44.40	43.82	43.25	42.71	42.18	41.68	41.19	40.72	40.28	39.85
Reversion Only If/When Sold	888.00	876.36	865.09	854.19	843.67	833.55	823.82	814.49	805.58	797.09	
Sale Horizon Year Cash Flow (including Reversion	933.00	920.76	908.91	897.44	886.38	875.73	865.49	855.68	846.31	837.37	
Time 0 PV @ 7% OCC By Year of Sale Horizon	$872	$846	$823	$801	$782	$764	$747	$732	$718	$706	

AS A FUNCTION OF SALE HORIZON YEAR	YEAR 1	YEAR 2	YEAR 3	YEAR 4	YEAR 5	YEAR 6	YEAR 7	YEAR 8	YEAR 9	YEAR 10
Expected Time 0 Property Valuation	$1,000	$1,000	$1,000	$1,000	$1,000	$1,000	$1,000	$1,000	$1,000	$1,000
Expected Return (IRR) @ $1000 Price	7.00%	6.68%	6.61%	6.57%	6.54%	6.51%	6.49%	6.47%	6.45%	6.43%

VALUATION REFLECTING CONDITIONALLY OPTIMAL SALE TIMING
0.50*1294.08 + 0.50*871.96 = 1083.02

Table 4.2 Comparison of scenarios and their average values.

Scenario	Potential Gross Income		Property Value in Year 0 if Sell in	
	Year 1	Year 11	Year 1	Year 10
Optimistic	110.00	164.09	1128	1294
Pessimistic	90.00	79.71	872	706
Average (Expectation)	100.00	121.90	1000	1000

good traditional DCF pro forma should represent. To facilitate the discussion, we've summarized the key aspects of the two scenarios in Table 4.2.

4.2 Scenarios Affect Value

The scenario that happens will affect the property value. We can quantify this effect exactly in the present value as of Time 0, the time of the analysis, assuming the 7% discount rate remains the correct OCC in both scenarios. (This is plausible, since that OCC did not presume any particular future cash flow path, but simply recognized that the future is risky.)

Under the optimistic contingency, the present value of the property as of Time 0 would:

- Be $1128 if it would be sold at the end of Year 1. This includes $55 of operating cash flow for Year 1 plus the reversion of $1152 at the end of Year 1, all discounted for 1 year at 7%.
- Increase the longer we plan to hold the property, reaching Time 0 present value of $1294 for a planned 10-year holding period.

The opposite will occur under the pessimistic contingency. In that case, the present value of the property as of Time 0 would be only $872 if we plan to sell it at the end of Year 1, but would decrease even further the longer we plan to hold onto the property, falling to $706 if we plan to hold it for 10 years.

It is important to note that the traditional single-stream DCF valuation represented by Panel A, based on the unbiased cash flow expectations, gives the same $1000 present value as of Time 0 as the expected present value implied by the 50/50 average of the two scenarios. For example, if we plan to sell at the end of Year 1, the expected present value of the property as of Time 0 is the 50:50 probability times the value of each scenario at the end of Year 1:

$$Expected\ value\ of\ property = (0.50)1128 + (0.50)872 = 1000$$

Moreover, this is true regardless of when we might plan to sell the property (that is, no matter what our valuation analysis time horizon is). For example, if we plan to hold for 10 years, we also get Time 0 present value:

$$Expected\ value\ of\ property = (0.50)1294 + (0.50)706 = 1000$$

It is important to note that the scenario that happens has implications for management decision-making. Investors have the *flexibility* to decide when to sell. They can wait and see which scenario happens, and then make the value-maximizing resale timing decision. Viewed from the present (Time 0), it would make most sense to:

- Hold the property for as long as possible, conditional on the optimistic scenario happening, or at least for the full 10 years in the traditional 10-year horizon analysis, BUT
- Sell the property quickly, conditional on the pessimistic scenario happening, as that will maximize the present value.

This flexibility breaks the symmetry in the present values of each scenario. It leads to an actual, unconditional present value for the investment as of Time 0, differing from the Time 0 expected present value of the two scenarios (the $1000), owing to the effect of management flexibility.

This example is very simplistic, but it makes a general point: investors and managers can choose to act differently in response to circumstances over the course of the investment lifetime, and this can affect the value of the investment. The single-stream, traditional DCF model can hide this fundamental and important fact.

4.3 Flexibility Has Value

We can quantify the value of the project recognizing its flexibility to time the resale. We do this by taking the expected value of the two possible outcomes under their value-maximizing management decisions about the resale timing:

- $1294 for the optimistic scenario (sell in Year 10), and
- $872 for the pessimistic scenario (sell in Year 1).

As those scenarios are equally likely, the present value of the investment in the property, ex-ante as of Time 0, and recognizing management's flexibility to time its resale, is:

$$Expected\ value\ with\ flexibility = (0.50)1294 + (0.50)872 = \$1083 \qquad (4.1)$$

In other words, the investor's ability to time the resale of the asset means that the property with flexibility is worth more than the $1000 present value we estimated using the traditional, single-stream DCF model, even though that model here represents a correct, unbiased expected cash flow projection!

The value of the flexibility itself is the difference it makes to a project:

$$Value\ of\ flexibility = value\ with\ flexibility - value\ without\ flexibility \qquad (4.2)$$

In our present, very simplistic example, this is:

$$\text{Value of flexibility} = \$1083 - \$1000 = \$83 \qquad (4.3)$$

If the investor had no resale timing flexibility, he or she must sell at the end of Year 10 (or any other year fixed in advance); then, the present value of the investment is indeed $1000. But if the investor has the flexibility to make the value-maximizing resale, then the present value of the investment is $1083.

Let's take a moment now to make the crucial point that *flexibility has value*, as the preceding example reveals. This general point is central to this book. If we have flexibility, we can wait and see which scenario happens, and then make value-maximizing decisions. We can thus unlock important value.

This book is all about identifying desirable forms of flexibility and valuing them. It can be useful to know this "extra" value. It can perhaps suggest actions to enable or implement such flexibility. One can consider whether a particular flexibility is worth its cost, if indeed there is any cost to acquire or enable the flexibility. We also note that added flexibility does not always add value (see Box 4.1).

By contrast, we should note that the traditional DCF model tempts users to ignore or downplay the value associated with flexibility in the presence of uncertainty. The traditional DCF model does not allow us to explore possibilities that might exist, or how we might intelligently react to what can happen as the project or investment develops over time. It does not quantify the value implications that flexibility holds for the investment at Time 0, the time of the analysis or decision.

Box 4.1 Does Flexibility Always Add Value?

One of the points of this book is that flexibility is a good thing that current practice overlooks in many situations. The methods we present can help to *quantify* the value of flexibility. This may help designers, developers, investors, and managers to incorporate more flexibility, or to recognize and use that which is already there.

But we don't claim that flexibility *always* adds value. Let's take a simple example. Suppose no automobiles could go faster than 60 miles per hour (MPH). Now suppose we replace them with cars that can go up to 100 MPH. We have thus given drivers more flexibility. They can do everything they could do before (go up to 60 MPH), but now they can also go up to 100 MPH. This will probably make most people better off, as in many circumstances they can safely drive above 60 MPH and thereby save time. But it will also probably result in more deaths. Not everyone will end up better off. Greater flexibility gives people the ability to make things better. But it can sometimes give people the latitude to make things worse. We do not ignore this possibility.

Our main message and focus is that flexibility can have value. We present decision models that show you how to build realistic decision rules for exercising flexibility. The models will show both when flexibility adds value and when it results in less value. You can use such models to help identify decision rules that are more, or less, likely to increase the favorable results from flexibility as compared to the unfavorable results. This can build your intuition about how to design and implement flexibility in real estate projects and investments.

To explore these possibilities of dealing with uncertainty, we have to expand the DCF analysis. In our example, we:

- First represented the uncertainty by scenarios (optimistic and pessimistic cash flows), which took the place of the single-stream, traditional DCF model.
- Then examined the implications within each scenario of the investor's flexibility—in this case, the flexibility *to choose the time of selling the property*.

This is the pattern we use throughout the book: we expand on DCF analyses to quantify the value of flexibility.

4.4 Conclusion

Decision-makers in real estate development and investment projects usually have various types of flexibilities regarding what actions they can take and when to take them. They can and will respond to the actual scenarios as they happen. Recognizing this explicitly in valuation can change our understanding of the value of investments. It can also have implications for the design and management of projects.

This chapter presented a very simplified illustration of these points. In the real world, the future is not nearly as simple as the example in this chapter, and decision-makers may not always respond optimally, either in prospect or when viewed in retrospect. Subsequent chapters will demonstrate more realistic models. But the key point is that we can improve decision-making and fundamental understanding and valuation by explicitly considering, and modeling, uncertainty and flexibility. The remainder of this book presents an approach to help you do that.

5

Future Outcomes Cover a Range of Possibilities

We Can Describe Uncertainties in Real Estate Using Probability
Distributions of Possible Future Outcomes

LEARNING OBJECTIVES

- Understand the meaning of a probability distribution and its shape;
- Understand how we estimate probability distributions of inputs to the DCF model;
- Learn how probability distributions of DCF outcomes differ from input distributions;
- Appreciate the need to work with the entire distribution of uncertainties, as demonstrated by the "flaw of averages."

OUTLINE OF THE CHAPTER

Let's now begin to face the reality of the uncertainties that we inevitably encounter in real estate investment and development. Demand rises and falls; prices and rents do likewise; and governments change taxes, zoning, and other regulations. In short, the future is uncertain. The "forecast is always wrong" in that what actually occurs almost always differs in some way from the pro forma projection.

This reality, this uncertainty, underlies the value of flexibility, the value of the manager's ability to adapt plans to actual circumstances. While a quiet, uneventful life has its attractions, secure, unvarying returns, on average, yield the lowest returns, the risk-free rate. The uncertainty and variability in the market provides the opportunities for higher returns. Skill in understanding and managing change provides the means to take advantage of change. We need to understand and describe the uncertainties in a quantitative manner, so that we can quantify the value of such flexibility. This chapter provides a common understanding of the important ways to describe and quantify uncertainties in real estate.

Flexibility and Real Estate Valuation under Uncertainty: A Practical Guide for Developers, First Edition.
David Geltner and Richard de Neufville.
© 2018 John Wiley & Sons Ltd. Published 2018 by John Wiley & Sons Ltd.
Companion website: www.wiley.com/go/geltner-deneufville/flexibility-and-real-estate-valuation

5.1   Distribution of Future Outcomes

A "distribution" of future possibilities describes the probability, the likelihood, of some situational circumstance. For example, is the market for office space up or down? Will the profit from this investment exceed $10M? In general, some future situations are more likely to happen than others.

The probability distribution of a future variable describes the probability of its possible outcomes over a range—that is, the relative likelihood of occurrence of some value or particular outcome. In a sample or simulation, the relative frequency of the occurrence reflects the probability distribution. The "range" (also known as a "domain") describes all the possible future outcomes or values. The frequency (or "density") indicates the relative likelihood of each possible value on the range. Summing (or integrating) the probability density across the range, by definition, produces a value of unity (1.00). This is because we measure probabilities in relative terms, and the range describes all of the possible outcomes (that is, *something* must happen, which implies the cumulative probability of 1.00).

We often represent probability distributions by graphs. The horizontal axis defines the possible events that can happen, and the vertical axis gives the probability of each such outcome. The distributions can be either continuous or discrete, either curves or bar charts (histograms). We often refer to the "shape of the distribution" as shorthand for more technical names. Two common types of distributions are bell-shaped and skewed, as Box 5.1 illustrates.

The shape of the probability distribution can have important implications both for the value of a project or investment, and for the strategies and decisions we might use to implement or operate the project. For example, for start-up ventures with high chances of failure but great upside potential, we want both the flexibility to exit at low cost if things turn sour, and the ability to cash in fully if the project is a great success. It is therefore important to think about the possible shape of the distributions we might encounter.

The general rule is that we need to work with the entire range of possible outcomes, and not just the most likely cases. For example, consider the skewed probability distribution for the event of fires in any building. It is most likely that the building will not have any fires, somewhat possible for it to have some incidents, and only slightly possible to suffer a total loss from fire. However, we would be unwise in designing a project to focus on the most likely prospects and neglect the possibility of fire. We need to consider the whole distribution of possibilities and act accordingly.

5.2   Quantifying Input Distributions

We need to quantify the probability distributions of future possibilities in order to have the information we need to carry out a quantitative analysis. For investment analysis, this may include variables such as prices, costs, demand, growth rates, yields, etc. There are three ways to obtain information about quantifying the probability distributions of future variables. We can:

- Consult experts for their judgment;
- Base forecasts on perceived trends; and,
- Analyze empirical data statistically for trends and variability.

Box 5.1 Bell-Shaped and Skewed Distributions

Bell-shaped distribution: This is a symmetric distribution, with the greatest probability around the mean, and lower probabilities away from the middle (Figure 5.1a). Such distributions typically result from random processes with continuous possible outcome values, such as the chance deviations from a trend line.

The "normal distribution" is a particular form of the bell-shaped probability distribution. Analysts often use it because it has a standard form and some appealing statistical properties. It is characterized by its mean value and standard deviation. As a reminder, the standard deviation of a distribution is a measure of its range or spread. Technically:

$$\text{Standard deviation} = \sqrt{\text{variance}} = \sqrt{\text{mean of squares of deviations from mean}} \qquad (5.1)$$

We write the normal distribution with the corresponding values as "NormProb(average, standard deviation)." Thus, "NormProb(0, 0.2)" signifies a normal probability distribution with a mean of zero and standard deviation of ±20%.

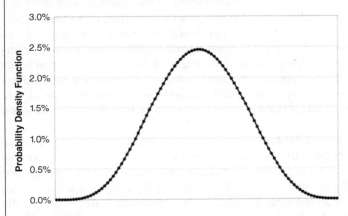

Figure 5.1a Bell-shaped distribution.

Skewed distribution: This type of distribution has the greatest probability closer to one end of the range of possibilities, and the smallest probability at the other end. One "tail" of the distribution is longer than the other. This type of distribution appropriately describes the many kinds of events in which small occurrences are common and big ones are rare. It also occurs when the range is truncated at one end—for example, if values cannot be negative, then a probability distribution of values will have a positive skew (the upside tail is unlimited, but the downside cannot go below zero) (Figure 5.1b).

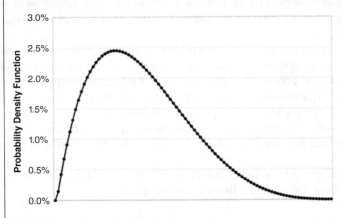

Figure 5.1b Skewed distribution.

We often rely on the opinion of persons who are well informed on a subject. Consider the example in the previous chapter that dealt with two possible scenarios: either an attractive development went forward nearby and boosted the prospective rents, or the development did not occur and rents decreased. Just to demonstrate the analysis, we assumed that each scenario was equally possible, had a 50:50 chance of occurring. In practice, however, we can expect that a developer has access to better, maybe inside, knowledge about the scenarios. In that case, we might accept a developer's judgment that the likelihood of the scenarios was, say, 70:30. We could use this data in the analysis and obtain a more informed, thus better, value of the project. At least, that's what we *think*!

We need to be careful with expert opinions. It is human to bias one's beliefs toward what one wishes were true; what one is familiar with; or one's own vested interests. Experts in many fields often believe they "know" what will happen regardless of persistent evidence to the contrary. Cognitive psychologists refer to this tendency as anchoring: people tend to fixate on their original estimates, and do not use new information to update their original views as much they should. Box 5.2 gives one of many possible examples. Moreover, extensive experiments document cases in which experts are routinely overconfident. Being sure of their knowledge, experts often minimize the range of possible eventualities and estimate probability distributions much too narrowly.

Another way we can obtain information about quantifying the probability of future inputs is by looking at perceived trends. Following trends is a common, instinctive way to forecast the future. Developers perceive that certain markets are "hot" (the ones that have been growing steadily at a good rate), and developers plan and act as if this pattern will continue. We see this all the time in practice. Sometimes the forecasts explicitly refer to a trend: "tourist traffic has been increasing at X percent annually ... and will continue to do so." Sometimes the forecasts are dressed up in a statistical analysis that simply extends the historical trend.

Either way, trend forecasts neglect the fact that trends regularly break. "Trend-breaking" events routinely occur. For example, oil prices drop, the economy of Houston falters, and real estate prices collapse. Or, a real estate boom becomes a "bubble" that bursts. And so on. It can be dangerous to assume that current trends will continue throughout the life of a project. Good analysis needs to make provision for "trend-breaking" events. We need to understand more deeply the dynamics that matter—not just the long-run average trend, but also random volatility as well as tendencies toward, or susceptibility to, cyclicality, mean-reversion, inertia, and "surprise" events or disruptions.

A third way to obtain information about the future is to analyze relevant empirical data. Statistical analysis of historical data on market dynamics is generally the preferable way to obtain the probability distributions for investment analysis, when sufficient data exists. Fortunately, detailed historical data on real estate prices over time are increasingly available in major markets. These enable us to estimate the probability distributions of future real estate prices and rents using statistical analysis. Although history does not repeat, it tends to "rhyme," as the cliché goes.

Statistical analysis can help us understand important dynamic characteristics of the local real estate market. These include such items as the magnitude of:

Box 5.2 Experts Are Often Wrong

Expert forecasts are often wrong, in that they differ remarkably and persistently from what actually happens. Before-and-after graphs comparing what actually happened with prior expert forecasts often produce a "porcupine graph," so called because the forecasts compared to the eventual reality often present an appearance like the quills on a porcupine. Figure 5.2 provides one of many examples. It compares a history of 5-year forecasts of the expected "cap rate" versus the actual cap rate. (The cap rate is the annual income yield on investment real estate asset prices.) The forecasts were based on a survey of experts by the Pension Real Estate Association (PREA), related to the National Council of Real Estate Investment Fiduciaries (NCREIF) average property cap rates. Despite the obvious, steady drop in cap rate between from 2009 to 2016, from 7% to 5%, the expert forecasts kept predicting a return to previous yield rates, but they were consistently wrong!

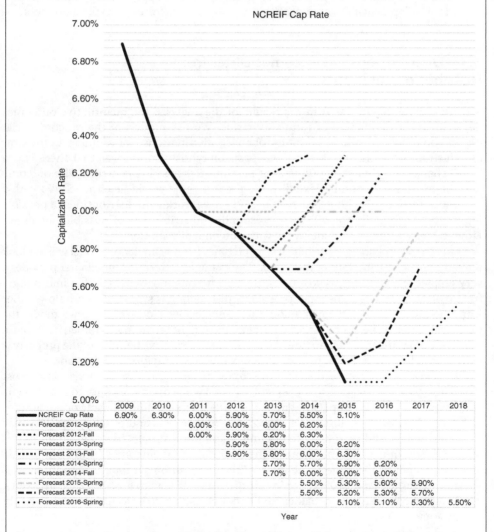

	2009	2010	2011	2012	2013	2014	2015	2016	2017	2018
NCREIF Cap Rate	6.90%	6.30%	6.00%	5.90%	5.70%	5.50%	5.10%			
Forecast 2012-Spring			6.00%	6.00%	6.00%	6.20%				
Forecast 2012-Fall			6.00%	5.90%	6.20%	6.30%				
Forecast 2013-Spring				5.90%	5.80%	6.00%	6.20%			
Forecast 2013-Fall				5.90%	5.80%	6.00%	6.30%			
Forecast 2014-Spring					5.70%	5.70%	5.90%	6.20%		
Forecast 2014-Fall					5.70%	6.00%	6.00%	6.00%		
Forecast 2015-Spring						5.50%	5.30%	5.60%	5.90%	
Forecast 2015-Fall						5.50%	5.20%	5.30%	5.70%	
Forecast 2016-Spring							5.10%	5.10%	5.30%	5.50%

Year

Figure 5.2 Expert forecasts often differ greatly from what actually occurs. *Source*: Pension Real Estate Association, *Expert Forecasts of Cap Rates (Income Yields) of US Investment Property*.

- Volatility (how much outcomes evolve randomly);
- Cyclicality (the tendency of the market to have "boom" and "bust" periods); and
- Mean-reversion (the tendency of extreme observations to be followed by observations closer to the mean), and so forth.

Absent a good reason otherwise, it is usually best to assume that future market prices will tend to reflect dynamic characteristics similar to those that occurred in the past. Quantifying these features in past empirical data can help us understand how flexible management can obtain the greatest value from projects, and thus get the best, most informed project valuations.

For our present purpose, let's simply accept that, when we have good readings on past performance, we can obtain reasonable characterizations of the relevant probability distributions for the parameters used in an investment analysis. Even where we don't have empirical data for a specific local market, we can apply analogy and common sense to develop plausible input probability distributions for many typical projects.

5.3 Distributions of Outcomes Differ from Distributions of Inputs

We are ultimately interested in the results of the analysis, the quantitative outcomes depicted in the simulation of future scenarios. We use models of the outcomes that depend on inputs about the relevant probability distributions. For example, in the simple illustration in Chapter 4, the input probability distribution was that there was a 50/50 chance of either the optimistic or pessimistic scenario occurring. The outcome was that, with resale timing flexibility, the present value would be either $1294 with a 10-year hold, or $872 with a Year 1 resale. When we work with distributions of possible inputs (as we should!), we will get corresponding distributions of possible outcomes. How should we understand and work with outcome distributions?

As a rule, the probability distributions of outcomes from a simulation model will not look the same as the distributions of the inputs. The example in the previous chapter provides a very simple illustration of this possibility. Table 5.1 repeats and extends the key information from that case. Note that the input probability distribution is symmetric: cash flows differ from the projection by an equal amount above or below. However, once we model the manager's decision flexibility on resale timing, the outcomes are not symmetric. Because the investor has the flexibility to time the resale of the property, the value of the property is either above by 29%, or below by 13%, as compared to the pro forma projection.

This fact—that outcome distributions differ from input distributions—is a most important point. Intelligent management will make use of its flexibility to react to circumstances as they develop. Good managers will act to maximize upside opportunities and minimize downside losses. Of course, various physical and other constraints may limit the owners' ability to react to circumstances (for example, to expand their development). But, in general, the shape of the distribution of outcomes from a simulation analysis will not be the same as the shape of the distribution of inputs. For example, it is wrong to assume that a ±10% range in future prices will lead to a ±10% range in profits. The range may be greater or smaller, and it may be asymmetric; as in Table 5.1, it might be +29% and −13%.

Table 5.1 Outcome and input distributions differ.

SCENARIO	CASH FLOW IN		PROPERTY VALUE IN YEAR 0 IF SELL IN	
	YEAR 1	YEAR 11	YEAR 1	YEAR 10
Input Optimistic	110.00	164.09	1128	1294
Input Pessimistic	90.00	79.71	872	706
Input Average	100.00	121.90	1000	1000
Input range around average	10.00	42.19	+128	+294
	-10.00	-42.19	-128	-294
Management realization in Optimistic (Sell Year 10)	110.00	164.09	NA	1294.08
Management realization in Pessimistic (Sell Year 1)	90.00	NA	871.96	NA
Deviation from average	+/- 10%	NA	-13%	+29%

5.4 Flaw of Averages

The "flaw of averages" refers to the idea that we should not base decisions only on the average values of the input parameters. If we do that, we may miss important opportunities or major risks that average values mask. We presented a simple but quantitatively explicit example of this point in Chapter 4. The flaw of averages in general consists of failing to look beyond average conditions, failing to consider scenarios, and thus failing to value options. In the context of DCF valuation, the flaw of averages resides in excessive dependence on the traditional, single-stream cash flow pro forma.

The term "flaw of averages" is a clever pun. It combines the notion of a flaw, that is, a mistake, with the concept of the "law of averages," which is the notion that future events will balance out toward an average. The name thus emphasizes that using average input values to estimate future expected outcome values is a mistake.

The flaw of averages is a generalized extension of the fact that the outcome and input probability distributions typically differ. A particular case of this idea occurs with the mathematical rule called "Jensen's Inequality," which states that, unless a mathematical model (or equation) is linear (that is, only consists of simple additions), the:

$$\text{Actual expected value of function} \neq \text{value of function for average conditions}$$

$$(5.2)$$

A simple example demonstrates this reality. Suppose the mathematical model is

$$\text{Outcome} = x + x^2 \qquad (5.3)$$

And that x is equally likely to be 1, 3, or 5, and thus has an average value of 3. Then:

$$\text{Outcome for average conditions} = 3 + 3^2 = 3 + 9 = 12 \qquad (5.4)$$

But this does not equal the:

$$\textit{Outcome expected value} = \frac{\left[(1+1)+(3+9)+(5+25)\right]}{3} = \frac{44}{3} = 14.67 \qquad (5.5)$$

The overall point is very simple: Unless we recognize and work with the entire distribution of possibilities, we get the wrong answers—and miss hidden opportunities to improve outcomes.

5.5 Conclusion

This chapter discussed probability distributions, setting the stage for the chapters that follow. The chapter's takeaway concepts include the following:

- There are several ways to estimate the probability of inputs to DCF analyses.
- Probabilities for outcomes usually differ from those of inputs: what comes out does not look like what goes in!
- The flaw of averages phenomenon indicates that we get wrong answers if we do not consider the range of inputs.

6

Simulation of Outcomes

Simulation is a Practical, Efficient Way to Explore Uncertainty
and to choose between Alternative Strategies for Managing it

LEARNING OBJECTIVES

- Appreciate simulation as scenario analysis on steroids;
- Understand the procedure of Monte Carlo simulation;
- Appreciate why Monte Carlo simulation is the efficient means to explore uncertainties;
- Appreciate why limited samples are sufficient.

OUTLINE OF THE CHAPTER

6.1   Generating Scenarios
6.2   Real Estate Simulation in a Nutshell
6.3   Simulation Is an Efficient Process
6.4   Number of Trials
6.5   Conclusion

You now have the background to learn about simulation as the essential tool for dealing with uncertainty in making investment and development decisions in real estate. What we call "Monte Carlo" simulation provides the means to analyze and evaluate alternative flexible management strategies.

In general, a simulation is a way to explore what might happen in the real world. It uses some model of reality—physical or mathematical—to run a "what-if" analysis. That is, it provides an answer to the question: What would the outcome of a certain model be if certain input conditions apply?

As we have stressed, we cannot adequately consider uncertainty and estimate the value of flexibility by focusing only on the mean of the outcome distribution. We have to move beyond the traditional, single-stream DCF model. We need to consider the entire distribution of future possibilities. Monte Carlo simulation allows us to do this.

6.1   Generating Scenarios

Think of Monte Carlo simulation as scenario analysis on steroids. It considers many, many scenarios, not just two or three or even a handful. Its major feature is that it draws on probability distributions to generate independent, random scenarios of the future—for

Flexibility and Real Estate Valuation under Uncertainty: A Practical Guide for Developers, First Edition.
David Geltner and Richard de Neufville.
© 2018 John Wiley & Sons Ltd. Published 2018 by John Wiley & Sons Ltd.
Companion website: www.wiley.com/go/geltner-deneufville/flexibility-and-real-estate-valuation

---

Box 6.1 Proper Simulation Software

Good simulation software enables users to specify the kinds of input distributions appropriate to their situation. For ordinary financial analyses, commercial software such as Crystal Ball® or @Risk® have provided this capability with convenient user interfaces. But it is also possible to go quite far using basic spreadsheet software. In this book, we have created the real estate simulations using standard Microsoft Excel® without any special add-ons or extra software. We make the models used in this book available in this book's Companion Website. They can serve as templates or examples for interested readers, and they reveal the "nuts and bolts" behind the analyses described in the following chapters.

---

example, future trajectories of prices, revenues, or resale yields. These probability distributions are our representations of the uncertainty that exists in the real world. From the perspective of the present, the future can contain many possible scenarios, any one—but only one—of which *could* actually occur.

The probability distributions that we specify in the inputs to the model govern the likelihood of occurrence of the outcomes. These distributions are similar to what we introduced in Chapter 5. But we make them more realistic for representing the nature of uncertainty and dynamics in real estate variables, as best we can understand them.

The objective of the Monte Carlo simulation is to obtain representative results, ones that collectively mimic what could happen in reality. In particular, we want to cover the entire range of possible outcomes (or close to it for practical purposes). In Monte Carlo simulation, we refer to each individual, independently generated random future scenario as a "trial." The idea is that each trial has an equal chance of actually happening in the real-world future, as we model it in the simulation. To achieve this, the process for generating scenarios must reflect the appropriate input probability distributions.

Luckily for practitioners, the mechanics for generating trial scenarios are not difficult. The ability to draw samples in exact accordance with a governing input probability distribution (representing the relevant uncertainties and dynamics) is a routine part of modern simulation and standard spreadsheet software (see Box 6.1).

These mechanics use a simple technical process called "random number" generation. This name provides the rationale for linking probabilistic simulation to the Monte Carlo gambling establishments. As shorthand, we routinely drop the "Monte Carlo" label when we refer to probabilistic simulation, which is the only kind of simulation we use in this text.

6.2 Real Estate Simulation in a Nutshell

The Monte Carlo simulation of real estate investment or development projects is a simple repetitive process. The simulation:

- Generates a trial scenario consisting of a future sequence of what might happen based on input probability distributions and a model of the functioning of the project in each period (for example, a DCF valuation over 10 years);
- Calculates the project performance metrics of interest for the project outcome resulting from that scenario (for example, the DCF present value reflecting the future cash

flows in that scenario, or the internal rate of return that the project would yield at a given upfront investment price);

- Repeats this process many times (we usually run at least 2000 trials), thereby generating a "sample" (or a simulation "run") of many outcomes (one for each trial); and finally
- Displays results as graphical and statistical summaries of the entire distribution of the outcomes for the sample (for example, the "target curves" we describe in Chapter 8).

6.3 Simulation Is an Efficient Process

It is important to appreciate that simulation is an efficient process. It is really a remarkable extension of human decision-relevant analytical abilities. Our grandparents could only have dreamed of its capabilities. At first, the task of considering how to deal with all the uncertainties can be scary; there are so many possibilities. So many things could happen in Year 1, and then so many more in Years 2, and 3, and 4 and so on. As Box 6.2 indicates, millions of combinations are possible.

Simulation is able to inform management decisions quickly and efficiently in the context of the huge number of possible combinations by deploying three main features: big-picture focus, speed, and sampling.

- First, we use simulation to build intuition and gain insight into the general nature, or the big picture, of tactical, strategic, and design and planning decisions. We do not specify highly detailed tactics or solutions. For example, the result of a simulation may indicate that management should be flexible about timing the resale of a property. It will suggest guidance on how to make the resale decision, and build intuition about the value implications. The result is not going to specify an exact rule or precise date. Simulation does not tell us exactly what to do in any given circumstance at any specific time; it provides general insight into how to manage real estate uncertainties. This means that simulation models should have a degree of abstraction and simplification. There is genuine practical value in elegance and parsimony.

Box 6.2 Millions of Possible Pathways

To put a number on the relevant complexity of future possibilities, imagine if prices could grow at only five different increments between any two periods (for example, +$2, +$1, 0, −$1, and −$2), always starting from the previous ending level. At the end of the second period, there are many pathways to arrive at any specific final level. For example, we could arrive at a 0 net change by going from 0 to +2 and back down to 0, or by the alternative pathway from 0 to −2 and back up to 0. These pathways make a difference! The overall performance of an investment may be quite different if we have the opportunity to sell at a high point, rather than suffer through a low point.

The number of possible pathways increases exponentially. The five possible outcomes after the first period each lead to five more outcomes by the second period, for a total of 25. Over 10 periods, the total number of pathways will be 5^{10}—that is, nearly 10 million! Moreover, as managers, we could respond to each of these scenarios in many different ways over the years. This means that the total number of combinations of scenarios and reactions can easily become astronomical!

- Second, simulation exploits the computer's ability to execute DCF calculations nearly instantaneously. Standard laptop computers take seconds to produce sufficiently accurate simulations (with thousands of trials) of alternative strategies to manage real estate opportunities under uncertainty. We can therefore generate large samples very quickly—that is, thousands of equally likely, independent scenarios (trials) within a few seconds or less. (And this capability is getting better all the time.)
- Finally, the speed of the computer enables multiple sampling to explore and analyze alternatives and build decision-relevant understanding of the project. We can generate different samples by varying probability and pricing dynamics inputs assumptions or model parameters, such as decision rules or cost assumptions. Doing this sort of analysis in real time is a great way to build intuition and gain insight about a project or investment.

6.4   Number of Trials

In practice, we use 2000 trials as our standard sample size for the example analyses of real estate projects in this book. This is generally quite enough to provide a sufficiently accurate analysis, even if the actual total number of possible combinations is many billions. Larger sample sizes would reflect the sample output distribution more precisely, but take longer to run any one simulation (sample). If the metrics of interest seem unstable in repeated simulation runs, we might increase our sample size to 10 000 trials. Small differences, say 1%, between the estimates of the value of alternatives are probably not economically or managerially significant. We know that the probability data we input into the spreadsheets is not so precise. In any case, the "big picture" perspective does not call for minute detail. We should properly pay attention to major differences in prospective performance and ignore tiny differences (see Box 6.3).

Box 6.3 How Many Trials Are Enough?

It's easy to test to see for yourself how many trials are most suitable for your analysis. Do this by repeating the analysis of alternative management strategies with a range of sample sizes (for example, 500; 2000; 10 000). Then compare the results. Does the simulation with the bigger sample size give you more insight into the choice between alternatives? If the estimated value of the flexible choice is 10% better in one case and 12% (or 9%) better in the other, does it make any difference to your prospective decision? If it doesn't, then you can be satisfied with the smaller sample size.

In general, the standard error of a sample equals the standard deviation in the sample distribution divided by the square root of the sample size (the number of trials). For example, suppose a 2000-trial simulation produces a standard deviation in the project's ex-post internal rate of return outcomes equal to ±5% (that is, 500 basis points in the realized IRRs across the 2000 trials). Then the standard error of the estimate of the *expected* IRR (the sample mean IRR) is $\dfrac{5\%}{\sqrt{2000}} = \dfrac{5\%}{45} = 0.11\%$ (that is, 11 basis points). Classical statistical confidence bounds (equating to approximately 95% probability that the truth lies within the bounds) is conventionally defined as two standard errors, which is, in the preceding example, a ±0.22% range around the simulated sample mean IRR outcome.

6.5 Conclusion

This chapter introduced simulation modeling for real estate investment and valuation analysis. We saw that simulation:

- Can efficiently explore a much fuller and richer range of possible consequences than the traditional, single-stream DCF. It thus realistically reflects uncertainty and management decisions in real estate.
- Uses automated processes to cycle through representative scenarios.
- Delivers simulated future outcome distributions that can give insight into the value of flexibility and how to manage real estate assets under uncertainty.

7

Modeling Price Dynamics

Using Pricing Factors to Model the Dynamics of Real Estate Markets

---

LEARNING OBJECTIVES

- Learn about pricing factors and their role in defining scenarios;
- Learn about random walks describing evolution over time;
- Review dynamics of real estate markets: inertia, cycles, and mean-reversion.

OUTLINE OF THE CHAPTER

7.1 Pricing Factors
7.2 Random Walks
7.3 Real Estate Pricing Factor Dynamics
7.4 Conclusion

This chapter deals with the question of how we should define the input probability distributions and dynamics for the simulation of real estate investments. It covers the

- Concept of pricing factors;
- Random walk model of asset pricing; and the
- Price dynamics that characterize real estate investments.

7.1 Pricing Factors

Pricing factors provide a simple and straightforward way to reflect uncertainty over time in the DCF pro forma. They provide the means to incorporate our estimates of the probability distributions for relevant parameters (such as revenues) in the spreadsheet. Pricing factors are thus a key tool that we use to do the type of simulation analysis described in Chapter 6. What exactly do we mean by a "pricing factor"?

A pricing factor is a ratio that multiplies the original, single-stream pro forma cash flow expectation to arrive at a future cash flow outcome for a given scenario. The idea

Flexibility and Real Estate Valuation under Uncertainty: A Practical Guide for Developers, First Edition.
David Geltner and Richard de Neufville.
© 2018 John Wiley & Sons Ltd. Published 2018 by John Wiley & Sons Ltd.
Companion website: www.wiley.com/go/geltner-deneufville/flexibility-and-real-estate-valuation

is that we take a good (that is, unbiased) original (or "base case") pro forma as a starting point, and we modify its cash flows by multiplying them by the pricing factors.

$$\text{Future scenario cash flow outcome} = \left(\text{unbiased pro forma cash flow}\right) \times \left(\text{pricing factor}\right)$$

$$(7.1)$$

For example, in Section 4.1, we posited an optimistic scenario in which the first year's potential gross income (PGI) would be $110 instead of the pro forma expectation of $100. We could derive this optimistic scenario PGI using a Year 1 "pricing factor" of 1.10. We would multiply the base case expectation of $100 by this pricing factor to arrive at the simulated revenue of $110 for Year 1, in the optimistic scenario.

Likewise, we can define pricing factors for each period in our DCF. In the simulation, in each scenario (each trial), we generate sequences of pricing factors corresponding to the future years in the DCF model. Continuing our example, we could obtain the Year 2 PGI of $115.20, using a Year 2 pricing factor of 1.152. And so on. We generally have a different pricing factor in each future period of a scenario.

Simulation draws on input probability distributions to generate the pricing factors. As a rule, we want the starting (base case) pro forma to represent the mean of the future cash flow probability distributions. (That is, we assume that the base case pro forma is unbiased.) If that is the case, then we want the probability distributions generating the pricing factors to result in zero-mean probability distributions for the pricing factors. (That is, zero mean for the difference from the base case, or a mean of 1.0 for a multiplicative ratio; see Box 7.1.)

To develop a single scenario for an annual frequency model of a 10-year horizon project, the simulation generates a series of 10 future pricing factors, one for each future year. Multiplied by the appropriate elements of the base case pro forma (such as the revenue), the sequence of periodic pricing factors produces a single multi-year scenario. The spreadsheet can then evaluate this scenario as in a traditional DCF, producing PV and IRR metrics, for example. The simulation records any relevant summary results of the DCF analysis (PV, IRR, year of resale, going-in yield, going-out yield, overall average cash flow growth rate, etc.—that is, whatever metrics the analyst might want). Then the spreadsheet generates a new series of 10 pricing factors to develop another scenario, to repeat the process. And so on, 2000 times.

Box 7.1 Build on Existing Knowledge and Practice

It is important to emphasize why the pricing factors should generally be zero-mean probability distributions. Why do we want them to produce expected values that equal the base case pro forma cash flows? The reason is that, as investment and decision analysts, we want to start with the information available in current best industry practice, which includes the use of unbiased DCF pro formas. The simulation analyst should not try to independently start building a cash flow model of the investment from scratch. Rather, the analyst should build on the knowledge of the principal party in the field, the investor. So, we start with the existing pro forma. We note again, however, that this pro forma should be unbiased—a "good," best-practice cash flow pro forma.

It is computationally economical to apply the same pricing factors across the board to all the cash flow components, both revenues and expenses. This is what we do throughout the book, in part for ease of illustration. If warranted in real-world applications, it is not difficult in principle to develop and apply pricing factors separately for each of several cash flow elements in the pro forma, such as revenues and expenses. (In that case, we might want to relabel the factors as "scenario factors" instead of "pricing factors.") However, as we noted in the previous chapter, part of the art of simulation modeling is to simplify reality, to avoid making the model too complex. Therefore, we should avoid any additional feature that doesn't greatly affect the policy and decision implications of our analysis.

7.2   Random Walks

To give you a more concrete sense of pricing factors and to introduce you to the type of pricing dynamics we can use in simulation, we first consider the process known as the "random walk" (RW). The RW process is the classical process for modeling the evolution of stock prices over time.

To develop the RW concept, consider a simulation that is generating pricing factors for a DCF valuation. To be more specific, suppose the input probability function is a normal distribution (discussed in Section 5.1) with mean of zero and standard deviation (volatility) of 20% (NormProb[0,0.20]). The simulation will then calculate the pricing factor (PF) for any Year t t as:

$$PF(t) = PF(t-1) \times (1 + NormProb[0,0.20]) \tag{7.2}$$

where $PF(t-1)$ is the pricing factor for the previous year, and $NormProb[0, 0.20]$ is a random number that Microsoft Excel® draws from the normal probability distribution. Since the mean is zero, this equation generates pricing factors that make prices evolve dynamically and symmetrically around the pro forma expectations. This is consistent with our previous point that we take the base case pro forma to represent unbiased expectations. (Remember, the pricing factors are multiplicative ratios applied to the pro forma, so the price here will be a geometric RW.)

Note that each year's pricing factor deviates from the previous year's pricing factor by a ratio determined by the random number generation. That random number is then "baked into" the new pricing factor level that will be the basis for the subsequent pricing factor for the following year. Future values start from the previous level and differ only by a purely independent random increment. This feature makes this price dynamic an RW stochastic process.

From a practical and economic perspective, the key characteristic of an RW process is that it is "memoryless." That is, changes in the pricing factor from one period to the next are purely random and independent; they are not influenced by anything other than the random number generated for the current year.

Financial analysts often presume that the RW is a good approximation of how stock prices behave in major markets such as New York and London. These stock markets are highly liquid, competitive, and information-rich. Their market pricing is thus very efficient, in that prices rapidly and fully reflect the information relevant for their values.

This makes asset price movements over time reflect only new information (news). This therefore makes the price dynamics memoryless and, hence, well modeled by the RW process.

Figure 7.1 illustrates some RW results based on Equation 7.2. It shows six independent scenarios of pricing factors for 10-year periods, all starting at a base (Time 0) factor level of 1.0. You could think of these as representing six simulation trials. The standard deviation of 0.20 in Equation 7.2 tends to give the pricing factors a "volatility" of 20% per year. Volatility is a measure of the dispersion over time in the pricing factors—the "ups and downs" in values that are a basic characteristic of investment risk (see Box 7.2).

Box 7.2 What is volatility?

In financial economics, the term "volatility" refers to the variation over time in the returns to (or price changes in) an investment asset. We measure it in terms of standard deviation in the returns across time (that is, "longitudinally").

For example, consider a stock whose percentage changes in its price in four consecutive periods are +5%, −3%, 0%, and +8%. We can view this as a "sample" of four random drawings from the probability distribution that governs the stock's returns in each period. The mean of this sample is $\dfrac{(5-3+0+8)}{4} = +2.5\%$, which could be an estimate of the trend of the growth rate per period in the stock's price. The volatility of the price is the standard deviation, which is the square root of the mean of the squares of the differences between the actual price changes and the trend, such as $(5-2.5)^2 = 2.5^2 = 6.25$ in the first period, and so on.

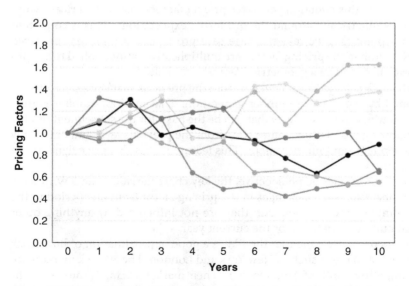

Figure 7.1 Pricing factors for six future scenarios, based on the random walk.

7.3 Real Estate Pricing Factor Dynamics

The dynamics of private real estate markets include other elements, in addition to some degree of RW-type influence. This is for many reasons:

- Real estate markets trade unique whole assets (rather than small homogeneous shares). For example, while one barrel of oil is the same as the next, an apartment with a given floor plan on the third floor facing north is not equivalent to an otherwise identical apartment on the twentieth floor of the same building, facing south with an ocean view. Such differences make it difficult to infer the value of a real estate asset from the prices we observe in other transactions.
- As a result, real estate markets do not process information as efficiently as major public stock exchanges. This makes real estate prices more sluggish or "sticky" than publically traded stock prices.
- The preceding points cause real estate prices to exhibit some inertia, or "autoregression." This means that the return in one year partly reflects the return in the previous year, such that the process is not completely memoryless. News in one period partly gets reflected in the returns in subsequent periods.
- Moreover, real estate prices seem to follow a relatively long and prominent pricing cycle, down markets following up markets, with perhaps as much as ±30% or more in price level amplitude around the long-run trend. This is called "cyclicality."
- Finally, real estate prices tend to exhibit more reversion toward a long-run mean trajectory than stock prices. This is because the value of the building is a major component of the property value. The value of structures depends on their potential replacement cost in the construction industry, which exhibits considerable supply elasticity. In other words, construction prices don't change that much over time (in real terms, net of inflation), and this tends to partly draw real estate prices back

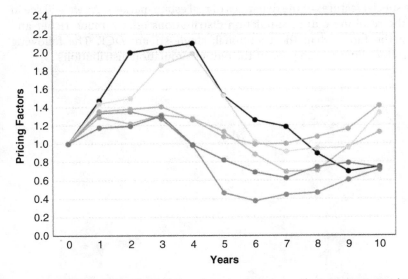

Figure 7.2 Pricing factors for six future scenarios, based on real estate parameters (random walk with autoregression, cyclicality, and mean-reversion).

toward a long-run mean reflecting such costs. (The structure value component of real estate prices, which on average is perhaps about one-half the total property value in the United States, behaves much like the prices of other long-lived capital goods such as motor vehicles, ships, aircraft, refrigerators, etc.)

As a result, the real estate pricing dynamics that we input into our simulations should include autoregression, cyclicality, and mean-reversion, in addition to the RW process. (The RW process also operates in real estate because property markets are not totally inefficient; they do respond contemporaneously to news, to some extent.) When analyzing a stabilized income-generating property, we usually simulate both cash flow dynamics (based in the "space market" for real estate) and asset yield dynamics (based in the capital market). We describe in more detail our probability and dynamics input assumptions in the Appendix at the end of this book.

Figure 7.2 depicts six independent, random, but typical 10-year pricing factor scenarios reflecting our assumed real estate price dynamics. We created this example based on data typical of real estate markets, to model a 10-year cycle, starting in the middle of an upswing. Compare Figures 7.2 and 7.1. Do you notice a visual difference in the patterns? The real estate price scenarios are a bit smoother and less randomly volatile, showing more inertia or momentum, and they appear more cyclical.

7.4 Conclusion

This chapter presented the use of pricing factors as a way to develop representative scenarios based on available data on the historical variations in market prices for real estate. These enable us to account realistically for the price dynamics of real estate investments in our simulation analyses.

Our pricing factors substantially enhance the traditional random walk process, by recognizing the special features of the dynamics of real estate markets. As we will see in later chapters, the resulting output simulation distributions offer a much richer and fuller picture of the future than the traditional, single-stream DCF. The following chapter will introduce how we can present the output simulation distributions.

8

Interpreting Simulation Results

Target Curves and Scatterplots can be used to Graph the Distribution
of the Sample Output

LEARNING OBJECTIVES

- Understand how to interpret the results of a simulation;
- Learn how to construct and interpret target curves;
- See how to use target curves to compare alternatives;
- See how target curves can indicate value at risk;
- Learn how to interpret scatterplots.

OUTLINE OF THE CHAPTER

8.1 Target Curves
8.2 Comparing Target Curves
8.3 Value at Risk
8.4 Scatterplots
8.5 Conclusion

Let's now focus on the output from a simulation analysis. It consists of the outputs of the analyses of many, many (for example, as we've said, 2000) possible future scenarios, the resulting possible outcomes of an investment or development project. How can we make sense of all this information?

We can quantitatively summarize and analyze such output in a variety of ways. Although summary statistics of the sample distribution are helpful for this purpose, we focus in this chapter on a particularly intuitive way in which we can display simulation results, to graph the distribution of the sample output. This chapter describes two important ways to do this: *target curves* and *scatterplots*.

8.1 Target Curves

Target curves are perhaps the most iconic representations of the simulation output. A target curve uses a simple line graph to depict the distribution of the simulated results. It plots the probability of occurrence (on the vertical axis) against some investment performance metric of interest, such as the net present value (NPV) or internal rate of return (IRR), on the horizontal axis.

Flexibility and Real Estate Valuation under Uncertainty: A Practical Guide for Developers, First Edition.
David Geltner and Richard de Neufville.
© 2018 John Wiley & Sons Ltd. Published 2018 by John Wiley & Sons Ltd.
Companion website: www.wiley.com/go/geltner-deneufville/flexibility-and-real-estate-valuation

We can think of a target curve as an estimate or simulation of the underlying, ex-ante probability distribution that the investor faces. Indeed, a target curve represents a sample of the results of a simulation of possible future scenarios or outcomes for the target metric we are focusing on.

We can display target curves two ways: either as frequency distributions or as cumulative distributions. In some situations, for some people, the cumulative representation may be more intuitive. For others, the frequency distributions may be more appealing. The cumulative distribution is just the sum (or integral) of the frequency distribution.

For example, suppose that a target metric of interest is the NPV achieved ex-post by a development project. To make the example simple, suppose that the output NPV of the project has only two values, −$100M and +$200M, and that each of these values occurs an equal number of times in the simulation model. Then the frequency target curve would consist of two vertical columns of equal height with a value on the vertical axis of 50%—one column at the −$100M value on the horizontal axis, and the other at the +$200M value. (The average outcome value would be +$50M, but there would be no column at that value.)

The cumulative target curve depicts the fraction of results that are below any level of performance. In our example, it would be a line at zero on the vertical axis for all values on the horizontal axis below −$100M. It would then jump up to 50% on the vertical axis for all values between −$100M and +$200M (including for the exact value of −$100M). Finally, it would again jump up, now to a value of 100% on the vertical axis for all values at and above +$200M. Figure 8.1 illustrates this example.

More generally, target curves represent continuous distributions. The frequency target curve represents the estimates of the underlying probability density function (PDF), while the cumulative target curve represents the corresponding cumulative distribution function (CDF). Figures 8.2 and 8.3 show realistic examples of what the simulation output distributions can look like. They show outcome frequency distributions for the

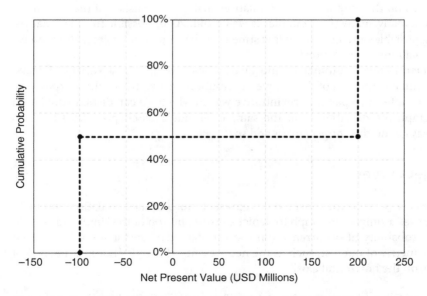

Figure 8.1 Cumulative target curve for a two-state probability distribution.

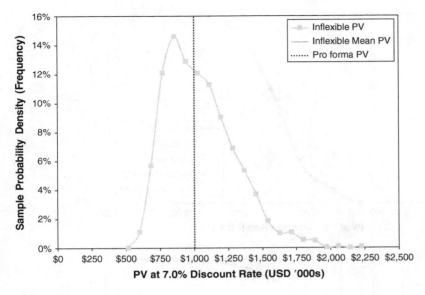

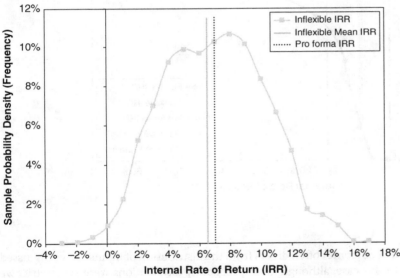

Figures 8.2–8.3

present value (PV) and the internal rate of return (IRR) of a simulation run on the simple rental property investment that we introduced in Chapter 1, using the type of real estate price dynamics inputs described in the previous chapter. The graphs contrast the full range of the simulated outcome possibility distributions (the continuous frequency curves) with the corresponding metrics from the traditional, single-stream pro forma DCF analysis (the dotted black vertical lines).

Figures 8.2 and 8.3 highlight features that we commonly observe when we use simulation to reveal the impacts of uncertainty on investment performance and asset valuation.

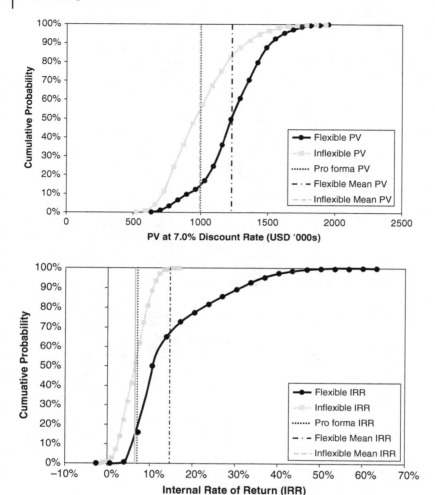

Figures 8.4–8.5

The distribution of outcomes often differs from the distribution of inputs, as we discussed in Section 5.3. In this case, although input probability distributions were symmetric, we observe that:

- The distribution of PV outcomes in Figure 8.2 is not symmetric, even though its distribution of input cash flow uncertainties is symmetrically centered on the base case. Although its average PV is the same as the traditional pro forma PV, the median and modal PV outcomes are significantly below the average, as the value distribution has a positive skew in levels. (There is no possibility of negative value.)
- The average for (expectation of) the distribution of IRR outcomes in Figure 8.3 is significantly below the ex-ante pro forma IRR, although the IRR distribution is symmetric around its average.

8.2 Comparing Target Curves

Figures 8.4 and 8.5 use cumulative target curves to compare the distributions of outcomes for two possible decisions. These alternatives represent different plans or strategies for dealing with uncertain future contingencies in a specific example case. In this instance, the left-hand target curves represent the outcomes associated with an inflexible plan reflecting a traditional DCF. The right-hand curves represent the results associated with a flexible alternative. (These are described further in the chapters that follow.)

The right-hand curves, for the flexible alternative, represent the alternative that most decision-makers would probably view as the better choice. Viewing horizontally for any level of cumulative probability, the right-hand curves indicate better outcomes (higher PV or IRR). Viewing vertically for any target metric outcome, the right-hand curves show a lower probability of lower PV or IRR results—and, thus, complementarily higher probability of higher present value or investment return outcomes.

Cumulative target curves for alternatives sometimes cross each other. We cover such situations in detail later on. In general, such cases imply that one alternative has a broader range of outcomes than the other, and is thus more risky—in the sense that its possible outcomes have a broader dispersion. Such situations typically arise when we compare a risky alternative that has higher average outcomes with a safer choice that has lower probability of losses but also less opportunity for the highest upside outcomes. The better choice might then depend on management's appetite for risk.

8.3 Value at Risk

Value at risk (VaR) is a measure of the possible downside of investments. Bankers, lenders, and investors generally use it as a measure of how bad investments can be in downside outcomes—and of their chances of recovering their loans! We define VaR in terms of the probability of failure. Thus, the 5% VaR represents the upper value, below which there is a 5% cumulative probability. That is, there is a 5% chance that things will turn out that bad or worse.

The cumulative target curve for NPV provides an immediate indication of the VaR at any desired level of probability. For example, to get the 10% VaR, you simply read across from the 10% cumulative probability on the vertical axis to find the intersection with the cumulative target curve, and read downward to find the 10% VaR. Thus, in Figure 8.4, we can see that the 10% VaR for the inflexible case is a PV of about 650, while it is about 900 for the flexible case. The VaR provides a handy measure of downside risks.

8.4 Scatterplots

The comparison of the simulated target curves in Figures 8.4 and 8.5 suggests that the flexible choice, with the curves further to the right, is better. But it is important to realize that flexibility does not always guarantee a superior result.

This is an important point. We need to spend a moment on it, as classical economic models of options frequently neglect this subtlety. Economic models implicitly assume

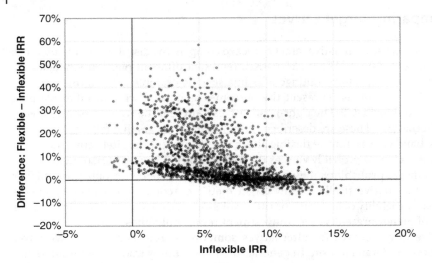

Figure 8.6 Scatterplot of simulated IRR differences.

optimal behavior. However, human beings who implement flexibility do not always behave optimally. Actual managers and investors deploy practical, heuristic, and feasible decision rules that cannot always produce superior results ex-post. In general, good decisions can lead to losses. How often might this happen to us?

Simulation modeling provides a way to explore this important point. It supports a graphical tool—called the "scatterplot"—that is an excellent way to visually understand the range of possible outcomes. It shows how two alternatives differ on some metric in each of the 2000 (or however many) trials composing the simulation run.

Scatterplots consist of dots, each corresponding to the results of one independent, random scenario. The horizontal axis shows the outcome achieved by one choice, typically the inflexible plan. The vertical axis then shows the advantage of the alternative, typically the flexible plan. With this arrangement, any dots above the horizontal axis show when the flexible alternative outperforms the fixed alternative. Conversely, dots below this axis indicate when the inflexible choice performs better. Finally, dots to the right of the vertical axis show when the inflexible investment yields a positive IRR, and dots to its left show when the IRR is negative without flexibility.

Figure 8.6 presents a scatterplot of 2000 simulated random outcomes for a specific case. This example is different from the one shown in previous figures. Figure 8.6 compares flexible versus inflexible approaches to resale timing, along the lines of the situation discussed in Chapter 4 (but here, the model is more sophisticated, as will be discussed in the following chapters). In this scatterplot, the horizontal axis shows the IRR achieved by the inflexible resale timing, fixing the resale at the pro forma horizon Year 10, no matter what. The vertical axis shows the difference between the IRR achieved by having flexible resale timing minus that achieved by the inflexible timing within the same scenario (the same "future history" of pricing factors). (We will present the nature of the flexibility in this analysis in the following chapters.) As you can see, a few dots lie below the horizontal axis, reflecting scenarios in which the inflexible strategy performed better. Some dots are also to the left of the vertical axis, representing scenarios in which the investment led to negative IRRs in the inflexible case.

Box 8.1 Scatterplots and Stochastic Dominance

The concept of "stochastic dominance" helps us compare alternatives with different risks. The notion of "first-order stochastic dominance" (FOSD) is the situation in which one alternative is never beaten by another alternative—that is, B ≥ A in all scenarios. In that case, presumably, any investor with a monotonic value function (for example, always preferring "more" to "less") will prefer the choice that has FOSD over an alternative. This would be true no matter what the risk aversion of the investor, whether he or she is conservative or aggressive, and even if the dominant alternative is more risky than the dominated alternative. FOSD can be seen in a scatterplot of simulation outcomes showing the difference between the two alternatives on the vertical axis. If all the dots are above the zero line on the vertical axis (above the horizontal axis), then FOSD holds, and the dominant alternative is preferred, no matter what the relative variance in their outcomes or the risk aversion of the decision-maker.

In this example, the flexible case beats the inflexible 80% of the time in terms of the IRR outcome. About 15% of the scenarios see the inflexible beating the flexible. In the remaining 5%, the result is identical—which means that, even with flexibility on the resale timing, the property was sold at the end of Year 10, the same as it would be according to the pro forma horizon without resale timing flexibility.

Having flexibility does not guarantee that managers will always use it wisely. And, even when their decision is "wise," in the sense of being very good from an ex-ante perspective, that does not mean that, ex-post, with the advantage of hindsight, it will always have produced the best results. In this context, the scatterplot, and the scenario-by-scenario comparison of the two alternatives that it represents, is a good way to get an intuitive feeling and insight about the relative desirability of different decision rules. In this case, flexible resale timing seems to win, pretty much hands down (see Box.8.1).

8.5   Conclusion

This chapter presented target curves and scatterplots as simple graphical representations of the outcomes of simulation. We will use them throughout the rest of the book.

Target curves come in two equivalent versions. They can either represent frequency of occurrence or the cumulative frequency, which is akin to a representation of cumulative probability. The cumulative curves are simply the summation of the frequency up to a point. Both perspectives represent the same outcome distribution; they just present it in two different ways.

Target curves provide easy visual means to identify preferable alternatives. As a rule, if one curve is always to the right, then it is the preferred case. The cumulative target curve also easily identifies the value at risk of alternatives.

The scatterplot provides a useful indication of the comparative advantage (and disadvantage) of two alternatives.

9

Resale Timing Decision: Analysis

Let's See what happens when we apply the Tools of Flexibility Analysis
to a Classical Investment Decision: when to sell the Property

---

LEARNING OBJECTIVES

- See how realistic simulation can be applied to a common practical decision;
- Understand the resale timing problem and the "stop-gain" rule;
- Understand how to extend the time horizon of the DCF analysis;
- Learn how IF statements enable us to model decision flexibility;
- Understand "trigger" values for the stop-gain rule;
- See how explicit recognition of uncertainty provides important new perspective on traditional DCF valuation.

OUTLINE OF THE CHAPTER

9.1 The Resale Timing Problem
9.2 Extending the Time Horizon of the Discounted Cash Flow Model
9.3 IF Statements
9.4 Trigger Value for Stop-Gain Rule
9.5 Value of Example Stop-Gain Rule
9.6 Conclusion

This chapter shows how we can apply simulation to obtain useful insights and guidance on an important practical problem. It demonstrates the "how" and "why" of flexibility analysis for real estate. It shows how we can do the analysis in a realistic setting, and the results demonstrate by example the value of flexibility for real estate management.

Along the way, we present two methodological additions to the traditional, single-stream pro forma DCF analysis. These are:

- Extension of the time horizon in the DCF model; and
- Use of IF statements.

We demonstrate these additional tools in a very simple, concrete example. But they will be even more useful down the road in more complex development project and management decision analysis.

Flexibility and Real Estate Valuation under Uncertainty: A Practical Guide for Developers, First Edition.
David Geltner and Richard de Neufville.
© 2018 John Wiley & Sons Ltd. Published 2018 by John Wiley & Sons Ltd.
Companion website: www.wiley.com/go/geltner-deneufville/flexibility-and-real-estate-valuation

9.1   The Resale Timing Problem

The question of when and how to decide to sell an investment property is a basic and universal consideration in real estate, as it is in other arenas of investment. Yet, the standard pro forma DCF analysis and valuation of an income-generating property does not address this question. When we limit the analysis to a fixed period, such as 10 years, as is the traditional practice, we act as if this period represents the length of our interest in the property. Indeed, the traditional model explicitly presumes a resale at the end of that period, the liquidation of the investment. But is this realistic? And if not, does this traditional analysis practice matter for valuing the property or understanding investment strategy?

Let's now recognize that prices do go up and down, and that investors generally have the flexibility to decide when to sell. How do we play the game of "buy low, sell high" (or, at least, "sell high")? Flexibility analysis using the simulation modeling we've described in previous chapters is well suited to address this question.

In the investment world, people often think about timing the resale of an asset in terms of a "stop-gain" decision rule. The rule is to sell the asset as soon as its price rises above a pre-specified (trigger) level, no matter what, and not to sell the asset before then.

The idea behind the stop-gain rule is to not be too greedy. In practical terms, the idea is to cash in on your "super-normal" gains and reinvest those profits elsewhere, even if the subject investment might still have some more gain to run up—in other words, the property could still face seemingly bright future prospects.

The stop-gain rule can be rational if you believe that the price dynamics in the asset market are mean-reverting—that once the asset value has pierced some pre-specified high level, then it must surely soon "fall back to earth." To the extent that real estate prices have a strong tendency to go through cycles, that they tend to revert to a mean value, then there is a good chance that a stop-gain rule might be a good investment strategy, a good way to profit from the flexibility that property owners realistically have about when to sell.

Contrarily, if prices do not revert to a mean, if they are truly memoryless, as analysts often assume they are in the stock market, then a stop-gain rule might not be productive, implying that resale timing flexibility might not be as valuable.

Let's explore how the stop-gain rule might work for investing in real estate. We now show how to set up the DCF model to accommodate a stop-gain rule for flexible resale timing for a typical property investment.

9.2   Extending the Time Horizon of the Discounted Cash Flow Model

We have already demonstrated the value of flexibility in the timing of the resale of an asset. In Section 4.3, we considered the case of a rental property whose value depended on whether an attractive complementary development did or did not materialize nearby. In that case, we were able to show that the flexibility to time the resale had significant value. But that example was very simplistic, because we had not yet introduced the use of probability distributions and simulation analysis, which were described in Chapters 5 and 6. We can now make the analysis of resale timing much more realistic.

We need to expand the possible time horizon considered in the DCF model in order to explore fully the general case of resale timing. Indeed, we should not limit the analysis to the 10 years of the conventional DCF analysis. This is a particular instance of a generic issue in handling the analysis of complex choices for managing uncertainty. Different issues require different extensions to the pro forma DCF analysis.

For the analysis of resale timing, an obvious modification to the traditional DCF model is to expand the number of future years in the analysis. In this case, we expand the model from the traditional 10-year horizon to a much larger number, 24 years. (In fact, investors rarely hold investment properties for longer than 24 years, at least in the United States.)

The other crucial addition will be to allow the model to represent a resale before the 24-year horizon, indeed, even before the 10-year horizon in the original traditional pro forma, should the stop-gain rule trigger this decision.

9.3 IF Statements

The key to modeling flexibility to make choices is to embed IF statements in the spreadsheets for the DCF analysis. IF statements are commands that trigger a decision when the spreadsheet encounters pre-specified conditions. They provide the means to automate the process of mimicking the decisions that investors or managers would take. (This is the analog nature of our simulation modeling approach.)

In a sense, IF statements take simulation analysis "to the next level." A simulation without IF statements is passive; it simply describes the outcomes that would occur without any managerial intervention. The IF statements enable the simulation to represent the potentially active managerial or investor interventions. IF statements allow us to capture the outcomes that occur when managers react purposely, meaningfully to events that may occur. And this is how flexibility obtains its value.

An IF statement is a standard command in spreadsheet programs such as Microsoft Excel®. IF statements instruct the analysis to implement management decisions at the proper time. They are remarkable commands that do a lot. They:

- Monitor the development of each scenario over time, period by period;
- Check to see if it is time to implement a predetermined decision; and then
- According to predetermined instructions, alter the inputs to the DCF for all subsequent periods, in effect implementing management instructions to react to specified circumstances.

These abilities allow IF statements to effectively mimic the actions of a human manager or decision-maker following the progress of a project in any future scenario. They thus enable us to create a realistic "what if" analysis, to reflect contingencies: if the scenario develops in this way, then the managers would do such and such, and the outcome would then be so and so.

As an example, suppose we wish to estimate the value of a stop-gain rule to sell on a 20% gain above what had been predicted in the original pro forma. Based on our previous definition of pricing factors, this would be indicated by a pricing factor realization of 1.20 in some year of a given scenario. We would refer to 20% as the stop-gain resale decision "trigger." Suppose that the simulation develops a scenario in which the sequence of pricing factors period by period are as in Table 9.1. The appropriate IF statement checks each

Table 9.1 Example effect of IF statement.

PERIOD	1	2	3	4	5
Simulated pricing factor	1.00	1.12	1.16	1.21	1.23
Result of IF comparison	No	No	No	Yes	No Longer Applicable
Actual entry in DCF	Operating Cash Flows	Operating Cash Flows	Operating Cash Flows	Operating + Reversion Cash Flows	Zero

pricing factor, doing nothing until the simulated pricing factor gets to or exceeds the trigger level (1.20 in this case). It then gives the command to "sell," and this reorganizes the inputs to the DCF to create a sale and value the reversion of the asset at that point.

Importantly, IF statements enable us to consider forms of flexibility far more complex and realistic than those accessible to standard economic equilibrium models of financial options. As we demonstrate in later chapters, this is because they can:

- Respond to complex combinations of past events; and
- Coexist with many different IF statements, so we can easily value simultaneous forms of flexibility. For example, we can "nest" IF statements within other IF statements, such as: IF(current price is above trigger, and IF(we have held the property past some minimum holding requirement)), THEN(sell the property now).

9.4 Trigger Value for Stop-Gain Rule

The stop-gain rule requires the setting of a "trigger" value, the gain at which (and not before which) the resale will occur. For this illustration, we have set this trigger to +20% (that is, a pricing factor of 1.20). In any randomly generated scenario (a Monte Carlo trial), the property will be sold once and only once, in the year when the realized property cash flow outcome first exceeds the original pro forma projected outcome for that year by more than 20%, or in Year 24. We simulate 2000 independent random scenarios for the analysis, each one containing up to 24 future years. Box 9.1 gives details on how to implement this in a spreadsheet.

9.5 Value of Example Stop-Gain Rule

Let's now examine the value of resale timing flexibility under the stop-gain rule. To illustrate, we continue the example of the DCF valuation of the simple rental property we introduced in Chapter 1, and for which we considered the binary scenario analysis in Chapter 4. The DCF model estimates the present value (PV) of the property at a 7% discount rate, or the IRR of the investment assuming a $1000 price.

As we indicated in Section 4.3, the value of the flexibility is the difference it makes to a project:

$$\text{Value of flexibility} = \text{value with flexibility} - \text{value without flexibility} \qquad (4.2)$$

Box 9.1 Programming the Stop-Gain Resale Rule

In case you're interested, here is the structure of the IF statement syntax that we use to program the stop-gain rule in our DCF valuation spreadsheet, in the row that computes the reversion amount:

- IF(a previous year has a reversion amount greater than zero), make this year's reversion amount zero;
- Otherwise, IF(this year's pricing factor is greater than 1.20), make this year's reversion amount the value computed as the next year's net cash flow divided by this year's yield rate reduced by the selling expense factor;
- Otherwise, make this year's reversion amount zero.

The flowchart in Figure 9.1 shows the logic behind this syntax. You can see exactly how we programmed our illustrative decision rule in Microsoft Excel® in this book's Companion Website.

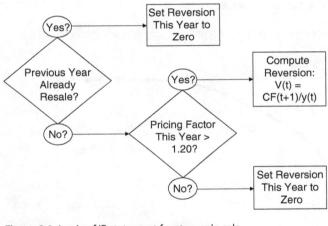

Figure 9.1 Logic of IF statement for stop-gain sale.

To obtain the value of flexibility, we must therefore compare the project with the flexibility against a base case or alternative that lacks the particular flexibility or rule we are evaluating.

In this example, the base case alternative is the situation that assumes that resale always, automatically, and inflexibly occurs in Year 10. This case corresponds to the assumption in the traditional pro forma DCF valuation.

However, the traditional pro forma valuation is unrealistic. It does not take into account the price dynamics in the market place. The traditional pro forma considers only the single-stream future cash flow projection, thereby producing a single PV number (or IRR number at a given price), and a single estimate: "the" PV, or "the" IRR of the investment (ex-ante). In the simulation, we will sample the entire future outcome (ex-post) PV and IRR possibility distributions.

To assess the value of flexibility properly, we must expose the inflexible case to the same independent, random future scenarios as the flexible case. We must compute the outcomes for the two cases, inflexible and flexible, under exactly the same scenarios of pricing factor realizations. We can then compare the results of both the inflexible and

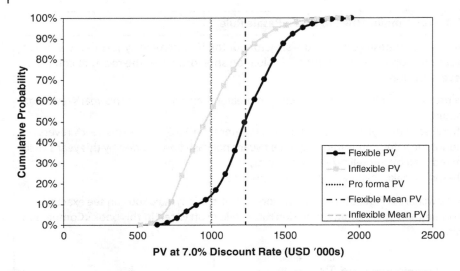

Figure 9.2 Cumulative PV target curve comparison of rental property with and without resale timing flexibility.

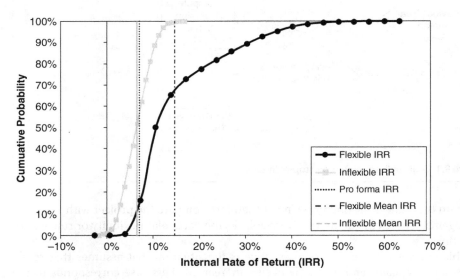

Figure 9.3 Cumulative IRR target curve comparison of rental property with and without resale timing flexibility.

flexible cases, not only against the (single-number) traditional pro forma metrics, but also side by side against each other for the entire distribution of possible (ex-post) outcomes, recognizing the uncertainty and price dynamics that realistically exist.

The target curves in Figures 9.2 and 9.3 show the difference in the distributions of the investment performance outcomes between the flexible and inflexible approaches to resale timing. (These images are identical to Figures 8.4 and 8.5, which we used to explain target curves.) They now demonstrate the value of the flexible stop-gain rule in the case of our rental property investment. Figure 9.2 shows the cumulative sample distributions of the ex-post present value based on the 7% discount rate. Figure 9.3 shows the cumulative sample distributions of the ex-post IRR based on the $1000 price. The inflexible case assumes automatic resale at Year 10. The flexible case implements the stop-gain rule with the 20% trigger, selling the property either before, after, or right at the 10-year horizon of the traditional pro forma. The vertical dashed lines represent the means of the ex-post sample distributions. The vertical black dotted line is the corresponding single number from the traditional pro forma DCF valuation.

Consider first the target curves for the inflexible case. These show the effect of explicitly recognizing uncertainty, without recognizing any management flexibility to time the resale. The simulation reveals the entire range and distribution of possible ex-post outcomes for the property asset investment, as well as the central tendency or expectation of those outcomes. In terms of PV, the mean of the simulated distribution is virtually identical to the traditional pro forma–based PV, $1000. Without recognizing any resale timing flexibility, the traditional approach gives an essentially correct PV, in terms of a single number representing the central tendency of the likely ex-post result. This is because we have assumed that the traditional cash flow pro forma is a "good" pro forma; that is, it presents unbiased expectations of the future cash flows for the property.

But the traditional approach does not give the correct IRR results, as we can see in Figure 9.3, even in spite of the fact that the pro forma contains unbiased cash flow projections. The mean of the simulated ex-post IRR distribution at the $1000 price, assuming the 10-year resale, is not the 7% of the single-stream pro forma, but rather less than 6.75%. This reflects the concave nature of the IRR metric as a function of the cash flows, and reflects the uncertainty that we have modeled of typical real estate pricing factor probabilities and dynamics, as described in Chapter 7. Moreover, the simulation reveals not just a single estimate for the IRR, but the entire range and distribution of possible ex-post IRR realizations. You can think of this as a visual representation of the risk in the investment return. We see that there is about a 90% chance that the actually realized ex-post 10-year IRR could lie anywhere between 2.5% and 11.5% per annum, an approximately symmetrical distribution around a mean of about 6.75%. Thus, the simulation not only explicitly quantifies the expected return but also indicates the investment risk in the return (in the sense of the range in the likely outcome).

Now consider the target curves for the flexible case. These represent the results allowing for flexible resale timing, as implemented by our stop-gain rule with the 20% trigger. This flexibility clearly improves expected value, as the target curves for the flexible case are clearly to the right of those for the inflexible case. The flexible resale rule is much more likely to lead to a more favorable investment result measured by the PV at 7% than the inflexible resale rule. In fact, the stop-gain flexible resale timing provides an average ex-post present value some 25% higher than the traditional pro forma, around $1250 instead of $1000. The result for the IRR is perhaps even more impressive. At the $1000 price, the mean ex-post IRR is around 14%, with a much wider range that is strongly positively skewed, ranging in terms of 90% confidence between roughly 5.5% and well over 30%. (The long, upper-right-hand tail in the cumulative target curve indicates the positive skew.) These findings are interesting in themselves, because, while the simple example rental property from our Chapter 1 pro forma is only an illustration, its numbers are in fact typical of stabilized income-generating investment properties in the United States.

Using a scatterplot like that described in Figure 8.6, we can see that the flexible resale timing (with the 20% stop-gain trigger) beats the inflexible 10-year resale in about three-quarters of the outcomes, while the inflexible beats the flexible in about one-fifth of the outcomes. The few remaining outcomes, where the results are identical, correspond to scenarios in which the stop-gain rule happened to indicate a sale in Year 10, the same as the inflexible rule. In fact, Figure 8.6 is based on the simulation analysis reported in this chapter. If you look back at that figure, you can see that there are some dots below the zero-difference horizontal axis. We therefore do not have first-order stochastic dominance, as per our definition of that term in Box 8.1. However, if you look at the scatterplot of Figure 8.6, you will note that the only outcomes in which the inflexible rule beats the flexible rule are in scenarios in which the investment has performed rather well, at least nearly average and with positive IRRs, mostly upside outcomes and no downside outcomes (no dots below zero in the left-hand tail). Thus, it seems unlikely that any investor would prefer the inflexible rule, even a very risk-averse investor who is mostly very worried about the possibility of extreme downside outcomes.

The scatterplot allows us to see the clear investor preference for the flexible approach, even though that approach does not strictly dominate the inflexible approach (it has greater IRR variance). The much greater variance in the flexible decision rule's IRR distribution as compared to that of the inflexible rule's is due to the positive skew in the IRR distribution (which appears prominently in Figure 9.3), and is therefore not an apples-to-apples measure of risk for comparison with the variance in the inflexible rule's IRR distribution.

9.6 Conclusion

This chapter applies simulation to a specific, concrete example that is realistic and contains useful and practical implications for decision-makers. The question of timing the resale of investment property is universal and fundamental.

This chapter showed how we can explicitly recognize and model uncertainty and flexibility. Procedurally, this requires us to extend the conventional DCF analysis and to implement IF statements in the spreadsheet to enable us to model a possible type of active management of the property.

The results of the analysis demonstrate that the simulation tool we are presenting does indeed enhance the traditional DCF valuation model. In this analysis, flexibility increased the expected present value by 25% (from $1000 to $1250). In the following chapter, we will discuss what this means.

10

Resale Timing Decision: Discussion

Let's think about Additional Insights we can get from Simulation

---

LEARNING OBJECTIVES

- See how simulation can explore the sensitivity of results to assumptions;
- Appreciate how real estate cycles impact the value of timing flexibility;
- Understand the difference between private value and market value;
- Appreciate how flexibility analysis through simulation can give sophisticated investors significant market advantage.

OUTLINE OF THE CHAPTER

10.1 Sensitivity Analysis
10.2 When to Use the Stop-Gain Rule
10.3 Implications of Flexibility for Property Valuation
10.4 Conclusion

Now that we are almost halfway through the book, it is a good time to take a break from the math and graphs and think about some of the contextual issues in using simulation to explore our alternatives for flexible management of real estate.

10.1   Sensitivity Analysis

Simulations of flexibility provide us with masses of data. We can analyze this information to gain additional insights beyond investment performance targets such as PVs and IRRs.

For example, simulation analysis allows us to see the effect of resale timing flexibility on the various metrics of investment performance. Since the simulation keeps track of when the IF statement indicates that it is desirable to sell, we can see how this flexibility affects the average holding period for the property. How frequently does the simulation say we will hold the property for more than 10 years? Or for less than 5 years? In our example with a 20%-trigger stop-gain resale rule, detailed analysis of the results indicates that the average holding period for the investment is just barely less than the 10 years assumed in the pro forma. The median holding period is between 7 and 8 years. We hold the investment all 24 years in the potential horizon in just over 10% of the scenarios. These statistics mimic typical property investment holding behavior in

Flexibility and Real Estate Valuation under Uncertainty: A Practical Guide for Developers, First Edition.
David Geltner and Richard de Neufville.
© 2018 John Wiley & Sons Ltd. Published 2018 by John Wiley & Sons Ltd.
Companion website: www.wiley.com/go/geltner-deneufville/flexibility-and-real-estate-valuation

the United States, which gives us some confirmation that the 20% stop-gain rule might in fact not be too different from what many investors actually do. (Of course, this presumes, as we believe, that our input price dynamics assumptions are based on solid knowledge and empirical evidence about the nature of commercial property price dynamics in the United States.)

By rerunning the simulation, we can furthermore carry out a sensitivity analysis. We can explore how different assumptions or specifications of the flexibility would change the results. For instance, we could add more conditions to the resale rule, such as requiring a minimum hold or setting a maximum hold of less than 24 years, or requiring additional simulated conditions to exist or not exist for the resale.

In our case, we explicitly tested different trigger levels. The result was that the 20% trigger level we examined seems to be quite good, although its performance nearly equals any trigger level between 15% and 25% in terms of the PV and IRR target curves. The insight we can derive from this sensitivity analysis is that flexibility in timing the resale for this example is beneficial, adding value and improving investment return performance, and that it's not worth much argument about the exact trigger level roughly around +20%.

We can also slightly modify the simulation to explore variations of the timing rule. Thus, we also explored a stop-loss decision rule. Such a rule triggers us to sell as the price goes down. However, that rule does not work well for our real estate case. The stop-loss rule locks in the loss implied by its trigger level, even though mean-reversion, or even just random volatility, causes the property's prospects to tend to improve after a down period.

10.2   When to Use the Stop-Gain Rule

The stop-gain rule is a logical resale decision rule for real estate because the price dynamics for real estate display cycles and mean-reversion. These drive the value of stop-gain rules. Price dynamics without these factors—dynamics that more typify stock markets—do not allow the stop-gain rule to add value to the asset (holding the discount rate constant), although the stop-gain rule can still improve the IRR performance of the investment (at a given price).

Further analysis of the simulation model allows us to note that the value of the stop-gain rule depends on when (at what point of the cycle) we apply the rule. In our simulation model, we allow the cycle to vary randomly and uniformly between 10 and 20 years in length, and with a starting phase that also varies uniformly across all phases (peak, trough, and every phase in between). In other words, our analysis is agnostic in terms of where we presently are in the market cycle as of Time 0, the time of the investment decision (and of the PV analysis).

But in the real world, market participants often have a good impression about where they are in the relevant property market cycle, or at least, they should be able to have such an impression. This is especially possible if there is good data about current pricing in the market and some history about market pricing trends, such as histories of rents or vacancy rates, and property transaction price indices or historical data on yields and capital flows in the market.

The simulation model allows one to see the points in the cycle where the stop-gain rule adds the most value. It depends on the length of the cycle period, but, in general, the rule is pretty robust, no matter where you are in the market cycle. Even at those points in the cycle where the flexible rule performs worst, the 20% stop-gain resale provides a mean ex-post PV not much below that of the inflexible 10-year resale.

10.3   Implications of Flexibility for Property Valuation

Let us return to a rather intriguing point that we glided over in the previous chapter: the finding that the value of the property with the flexibility seems to be greater than the property's market value. Specifically, the simulation indicated that the mean ex-post PV of the property investment with the stop-gain rule was around $1250, based on the market OCC of 7%. This valuation is about 25% more than the $1000 estimate of the market value from the traditional DCF valuation model based on the 7% OCC and the single-stream cash flow projection that is the unbiased expectation of the property cash flows. (And we noted that $1000 is also the mean ex-post PV at the 7% OCC in the simulation with forced resale at Year 10.)

Is the property really only worth $1000? Wouldn't $1250 be a better estimate of its value, ex-ante? This $1250 is the mean of the ex-post present value results (at the 7% discount rate) that are possible with a plausible representation of resale decision timing flexibility (assuming our simulation reflects realistic property price uncertainty and dynamics). If 7% is indeed an accurate estimate of the OCC (as discussed in Chapter 2), the property seems to be worth more than its $1000 market value, estimated using the traditional DCF valuation model. What are we to make of this?

A key point to recognize is that, while the flexibility simulation analysis is relevant for potential investors, it is not a model of the equilibrium price, or market value, of the property. The value resulting from the flexibility analysis relates to the *private* value of the property, as we defined this term in Chapter 2. The market value could well be the $1000 we originally estimated. If so, then that means, from the private or investment value perspective of an investor who will follow the stop-gain decision rule (with the 20% trigger), a purchase of the property at the market value price would present a windfall value (positive NPV) of $250. Briefly put, a smart investor could use flexibility to outperform the market!

However, in this regard, it is important to consider that the investor's ability to profit from the resale flexibility according to our stop-gain rule is not certain. It depends on several factors. Will the investor be able to:

- Implement and have the discipline to adhere to the 20% stop-gain decision rule? This will require sufficient information to be able to judge (at least approximately) when the current market for the property breaches the effective equivalent of the "20% trigger."
- Carry out such a resale decision discipline, which may involve selling quite early, or holding on quite long? In fact, it might be inconvenient to sell just whenever the market happens to breach the 20% trigger. What will the investor do with the proceeds at that time? Might the investor need to cash out on the value of the property sooner? There is some loss of flexibility when you commit to a strict rule, no matter what that rule is. The relevant decision environment is not just this one property in isolation,

but other business and investment considerations that the investor may have. (On the other hand, the automatic, inflexible resale at Year 10 implied by the traditional pro forma might be just as, or even more, unrealistic or difficult to implement.)

These considerations bear upon why the market equilibrium price could well differ from the $1250 value.

We should also consider the other side of the deal: the party who *buys* the property from the investor when the stop-gain rule is triggered for the resale. What makes the rule work is mean-reversion in the property market. This suggests sales only when prices are relatively high, likely to trend downward, or at least likely not to trend abnormally upward going forward from the sale date for at least a few years. In fact, in real estate investment markets, we do observe a positive correlation between transaction volumes and sale prices. But if everyone adopted the stop-gain rule, we would never see any sales when prices are down (which is counter-factual), and sellers, triggering their stop-gain rules, should have difficulty finding buyers when prices are high (which is counter-factual). Widespread adoption of the stop-gain rule would seem to be incompatible with the property market functioning as smoothly as it usually does, unless there is substantial disagreement among investors about where they are in the cycle. This suggests that, in the real world, many investors have trouble with at least one of the bullet points presented in the preceding list.

Finally, it is important to recognize that the mean of a target curve is only one aspect of the performance of the investment. The investor may also care about other features of a target curve, such as the downside tail or the upside tail. And the investor may care about other metrics besides the present value, such as the IRR. In the present example, as you can see from Figures 9.2 and 9.3 and our discussion of the scatterplot in Figure 8.6, the stop-gain decision rule produces good results from those other perspectives as well. But this will not always be the case.

With these considerations in mind, the suggestion is that a sophisticated investor might use flexibility to identify and exploit hidden value that most other investors do not appreciate—and, therefore, which the market does not recognize or price. The traditional DCF pro forma could correctly identify $1000 as the current market value of our subject property. But flexibility analysis using simulation reveals the potential for significant profits. It suggests that we could buy the property for $1000, and yet obtain an asset worth $1250 to us (in a private valuation sense), provided we have the flexibility, discipline, and information necessary to carry through with a particular investment resale strategy.

Flexibility analysis thus has important practical implications for real estate business strategy and tactics. That's the reason for this book. That's why we're presenting this modeling and analysis. Perhaps, in time, all real estate investors will understand and exploit flexibility analysis, and the profit gap between private and market values may disappear. Until then, those who understand and can analyze the value of flexibility should have a significant advantage.

10.4 Conclusion

The discussion in this chapter places flexibility analysis using simulation in a larger context. From a tactical perspective, it indicates how we can use simulation to explore assumptions and details of plans to manage our risks in our uncertain world. Strategically, it emphasizes that sophisticated investors can use flexibility to identify and exploit hidden value that the market may not recognize or price.

11

Development Project Valuation

This Chapter Looks at Valuation of Development Projects From an Investment Perspective, Considering Uncertainty, Flexibility, and Time-to-Build

---

LEARNING OBJECTIVES

- Understand the differences between investment in existing assets and investment in development projects: development projects also involve "time-to-build" and construction costs;
- Appreciate why opportunity cost of capital (OCC) for construction costs is lower than for investment in existing assets;
- See how these differences change the net present value (NPV) valuation framework for investment in development projects;
- Understand the fair valuation of land for a development project;
- Appreciate how development projects can be more profitable, but also riskier, than investments in otherwise similar existing assets.

OUTLINE OF THE CHAPTER

11.1 Time-to-Build Difference between Development Projects and Existing Assets
11.2 Lower Opportunity Cost of Capital for Construction Costs
11.3 Illustrative Example
11.4 Residual Value of Development Land
11.5 Investment Risk in Development Project
11.6 Conclusion

Until now, we've focused our analysis on an existing productive asset—archetypically, a rental property. Such assets represent the bulk of real estate investment in many countries, and they are, in some sense, the primal or underlying asset of real estate. They provide productive services for long periods, evidenced by the rental income flow that they do, or could, generate. (Some assets are owner-occupied, but that doesn't mean they aren't providing valuable benefits for their occupants.) The production of profitable income-generating, "stabilized" assets is the purpose and reason for being of the real estate development industry. ("Stabilized" means that they are operating normally, at near full occupancy most of the time.)

We now shift attention to development projects, to the process of creating built assets—that is, of creating stabilized assets, like our example in the preceding chapters.

All stabilized real estate assets physically consist of two parts; these are the:

- Land that provides the location and site; and
- Structures that constitute the built space necessary to produce value.

Flexibility and Real Estate Valuation under Uncertainty: A Practical Guide for Developers, First Edition. David Geltner and Richard de Neufville.
© 2018 John Wiley & Sons Ltd. Published 2018 by John Wiley & Sons Ltd.
Companion website: www.wiley.com/go/geltner-deneufville/flexibility-and-real-estate-valuation

In the United States, on average across all the existing real estate assets (including old and new buildings), about half of the total property asset value is attributable to the structure, and about half to the land. The land is neither produced nor consumed, but we must build the structure (and the structure will ultimately depreciate to zero value). We refer to the construction process that produces a built real estate asset as a real estate development project. Beginning with this chapter, and for the remainder of this book, we focus on development projects.

11.1 Time-to-Build Difference between Development Projects and Existing Assets

Development projects are particularly interesting and important. They represent the visible physical and economic process of creating value. They bring new real estate assets into the world. They transform financial capital into physical capital.

Real estate development projects are also capital intensive, as construction usually represents a large fraction of their total cost. Since real estate structures tend to be very long-lived, development makes a major, long-lasting impact on the physical and social world, for better or worse. It is important to do development projects as best we can, for environmental, social, and economic reasons.

From an economic and management perspective, there is an essential difference between a development project and an existing built real estate asset. This is the difference between when you pay for and receive the asset. With an investment in an existing asset, you pay the price and obtain the productive asset now, simultaneously. With a development project, however, there is a gap. You pay for the construction of the asset over time and obtain its value only upon its completion and stabilization.

With an existing asset, the timing of the investment decision is essentially the same as the timing of receipt of the net present value (NPV) of the investment, the value of the asset minus the cost (price) you pay for it. In other words, the investor experiences the benefit (the value of the built asset) and the cost (the price to buy it) together, at the same time. In contrast, with a development project, there is a "time-to-build" period between the timing of the investment decision (the commitment of the land and the investor to the construction project) and the receipt of the benefit or purpose of the investment—the productive, stabilized built asset.

When valuing a development project, we start the clock when the developer decides to invest in the project and commits the land to its construction. We define this as "Time 0" for the development. (Note that the developer may already own the site before starting the development project, but commitment of the land still incurs the opportunity cost of the land, as the opportunity to sell the land at its then market value is foregone at that time.) The project thus incurs part of the development cost (part of the cost of the investment), particularly the cost of the land, up front, at Time 0.

The project incurs much of the investment cost after Time 0. This consists of the cost of building the structure (or structures, if the project involves more than one building). It is only at the end of the construction process, which we label as "Time T," that we have fully paid for the development (or the first phase of it) and receive the newly built asset (or its first phase).

This gap between the start of the project and the completion of construction, the "time-to-build" between Time 0 and Time T, complicates the computation of the NPV of the investment in the development project, compared to that of the simple purchase of an existing built asset. Part of the complication lies in the fact that it is appropriate to apply different rates of the opportunity cost of capital to the construction costs and to the built asset, because they have different levels of risk.

11.2 Lower Opportunity Cost of Capital for Construction Costs

In general, the opportunity cost of capital (OCC) appropriate for construction costs should be quite a bit less than the OCC of the built property. This is for two reasons:

- Construction costs tend to be relatively stable; and
- We can better mitigate their risks.

In short, lower volatility means lower OCC, but let's explore this issue further.

There is typically less uncertainty about future construction costs than about future real estate values. In most countries, the "price elasticity" of supply of construction goods and services, which consists largely of labor and materials, is quite high at any time. ("Price elasticity" refers to how production changes with changes in prices. Economists define it as the percentage change in quantity divided by the percentage change in price.) This means that a small change in price will evoke a relatively large change in the quantity supplied.

High price elasticity of supply tends to keep construction prices stable. This is because, when demand for construction increases, the supply increases apace, and the resulting competition among construction suppliers keeps prices from rising much. Vice versa, when demand falls, construction firms lay off workers, stop ordering materials, and drop out of the business. This reduction in supply prevents construction prices from falling much. Cyclical variations in margins are a minor part of construction costs, and long-term trends, such as keeping up with inflation, do not create volatility.

In contrast to construction costs, much of the value of the built asset lies in its location value, the land component, the supply of which is very constrained (inelastic). This causes real estate prices to vary considerably with changes in demand, unlike construction prices.

Furthermore, to the extent that there is uncertainty or risk in the construction costs within a given project, these risks are largely specific to the particular project. (This is referred to as "idiosyncratic" risk.) Surprises in construction costs likely relate more to technical issues than to market or financial issues. And the contractor may provide a guaranteed price contract, relieving the developer of most of such technical risks. (Cost overruns due to change orders from the developer don't count as price increases, because the developer is receiving greater "quantity" of construction product in return.) Because of these considerations, there is little *covariance* between developer's construction costs and financial market returns in the capital markets (see Box 11.1). This means that, in their overall investment portfolios, investors could diversify away any such idiosyncratic construction cost risks that may exist. In the capital market, investors would thus not require an extra ex-ante return premium for assets whose cash flows mimic construction costs. This makes the OCC of construction costs low.

Box 11.1 What is covariance?

"Covariance" is a statistical concept referring to how two things move together, or not. If construction costs and real estate prices both vary a lot over time, and furthermore if construction costs always tend to be high when real estate prices are high, and vice versa, then the two have high covariance.

 If both construction costs and real estate prices vary a lot over time, but not together, that is, if when construction costs are high, real estate prices are as likely to be low as high, then they have little covariance, even though they each have plenty of "variance."

 And if construction costs and real estate prices do move together, but the construction costs don't move much (the magnitude of construction price changes is small, construction has little variance), then again, the covariance is low.

At this point, students sometimes protest. They say, "But construction is really risky; developers need to treat construction cost with great caution!" Their first instinct is to want to apply a higher OCC rate to construction cost to reflect the high risk. How does this observation fit with the argument that the OCC for construction costs should be lower?

 The explanation for this seeming contradiction lies in the fact that we are dealing with two different meanings of "risk." Thus:

- Construction is "risky" in the sense that it is a large fraction of the total value of the project, and it is a negative element in the profit (NPV). This means that, if you underestimate construction cost by much on a percentage basis, you can drastically cut into the project profits. We certainly agree that developers need to treat construction cost with caution. The analysis needs to be careful not to underestimate the magnitude of the expense of construction when analyzing the profitability of the development project. In the NPV framework that we are here employing, this translates into "Don't underestimate the present value of the construction cost."
- But, such "risk," defined as profit sensitivity to cost, is not what determines the OCC for investments in the capital market. Recall that the OCC is the discount rate that is relevant for translating future money values to present money values. The capital markets determine this rate in the manner described earlier in this section.

In an NPV (investment profit) analysis of a development project, we are working toward a present value of construction cost, starting from a projection of what that cost will be at a future date when it is time to pay for it, which is when the construction cash outflow will occur. It is in this situation that we should view both the risks and thus the OCC (discount rate) from the capital market perspective, and hence as being lower.

 To demonstrate that it is correct to use a lower OCC for construction costs, consider the consequence of applying a larger discount rate to these costs. We would end up with:

- A *lower* present value magnitude at Time 0 of future construction cost paid at Time T;
- A smaller construction cost amount to subtract in calculating the NPV of the project as of Time 0; thus
- Making the project appear more profitable; which is
- Just the opposite of what we want to do to reflect the risk of construction!

Thus, the economic perspective that the OCC on construction costs should be relatively low actually confirms and *implements* the instinct to recognize the riskiness of construction costs when designing and planning a development project from an investment perspective.

Consistent with this, it is reasonable to assume a construction cost OCC rate of around 3%, for example, if the real estate OCC rate is around 7% (as we have been assuming in the previous chapters). This 3% rate is what we will assume for our illustrative simple development project.

11.3 Illustrative Example

To better understand how investments in development projects differ from investments in existing assets, let's explore a simple example. We compare two investments:

- *Rental investment*: The property from the Chapter 1 case ($1000 PV pro forma with resale in 10 years);
- *Development investment*: A project to create that same stabilized rental property, combining land and construction costs, over a 1-year time-to-build.

This illustrative development project is as simple as it could be, but contains the essential differences between investments in development and investments in existing built assets. Specifically in this case, the differences are that the development:

- Does not receive the net cash flow of the rental in Year 1 because the building is not already complete;
- Has to pay for construction at the end of Year 1, at the end of the time-to-build; and
- Combines two elements, land and construction, with only the land component being paid for up front at Time 0.

Apart from these differences, the example investments are identical. They have the same net cash flows over time and the same growth rates. Note, however, that the OCC for construction and built real estate differ, as discussed in the previous section. Table 11.1 summarizes the relevant parameters for the valuation of the projects. (We will use upper case to refer to the two alternatives as if they are the names of two specific, real investments: "Rental" and "Development.")

Table 11.1 Essential parameters for the example investments.

END OF YEAR:	YEAR 0	YEAR 1	YEAR 2	YEAR 3...	GROWTH	OCC
RENTAL						
Built Property Cash Flow ($)	0	50	51	52...	2% / year	7% / year
Built Property Value ($)	1000	1020	1040	1061...	2% / year	7% / year
DEVELOPMENT						
Land Cost ($)	310	0	N/A	N/A	N/A	N/A
Construction Cost ($)	0	663	N/A	N/A	2% / year	3% / year
Built Property Cash Flow ($)	0	0	51	52...	2% / year	7% / year
Built Property Value ($)	N/A	1020	1040	1061...	2% / year	7% / year
Development Project Profit ($)	N/A	357	N/A	N/A	N/A	15% / year

Now let's explore the value at Time 0 of the Development (that is, at the end of "Year 0") that delivers a property worth $1020 after 1 year at the end of Year 1. (Recall that all values and cash flows are quoted "in arrears"—that is, as of the end of the year.) The Time 0 value of the asset the development project will produce is:

$$\text{Present value of future built property} = \frac{\$1020}{1.07} = \$953 \qquad (11.1)$$

This differs from the $1000 value of Rental at Time 0. This is because the Development does not benefit from the net cash flow in Year 1 ($50), which has a present value at Time 0 of $50/1.07 = $47. Indeed, at Time 0, we have:

$$\text{PV}(\text{Development}) = \text{PV}(\text{Rental}) - \text{PV}(\text{Year 1 net cash flow}) = \$1000 - \$47 = \$953 \qquad (11.2)$$

The Development in effect makes a "forward purchase" of the Rental property. This purchase is worth less at Time 0 than the Rental, which is an immediate purchase of the already-productive asset. Development is worth less because it does not benefit from the net cash flow over the "time-to-build" period.

Now let's consider the construction costs. What is their PV as of Time 0? We might suppose that, if paid at Time 0, these costs would be, for example, $650. But supposing construction costs also grow at 2%, the bill for Year 1 construction will be 1.02*650 = $663. To obtain the Time 0 present value of the construction costs, we need to discount them using the construction cost OCC of 3%. Thus:

$$\text{Present value of construction cost} = \frac{\$663}{1.03} = \$643 \qquad (11.3)$$

We can thus calculate the NPV of the Development at Time 0 exclusive of land cost. It is the residual—the difference between the PV of the benefit (the forward purchase of the built asset) minus the cost (the PV of the construction cost):

$$\text{NPV}(\text{Development}) \text{ at Time 0} = \$953 - \$643 = \$310 \qquad (11.4)$$

11.4   Residual Value of Development Land

This residual value of $310 in Equation 11.4 is the economic value of the land, with two caveats. This calculation presumes that the:

- Project is the highest and best use (the so-called "HBU"—the project that has the maximum feasible residual value) for this site; and
- Timing is "ripe" to undertake the project (it is better to build now than to wait and speculate on further growth in land value).

In these conditions, $310 is what we could expect to sell the land for. So, $310 represents the market value of the land, and therefore the opportunity cost of not selling the land but instead undertaking the development project. (That is, $310 is what we're foregoing at Time 0 by doing the development project instead of selling the land.) This land price provides expected returns sufficient to compensate for the investment risk in the project, since we have computed the $310 residual by discounting the future cash flows at their OCCs.

Under the above assumption about the land market value, what are the implications of alternative prices? If we could obtain the land for:

- *Less than $310*, then the project would present the investor with a positive NPV (evaluated at fair market prices), suggesting super-normal profit for the buyer/developer (but sub-normal profit for the land seller).
- *More than $310*, then (at least in the view of the landowner) the project is either not the highest and best use for this land site, or else the time is not yet "ripe" for launching the project. It would be better to wait and continue holding the land available for future development.
- *Exactly the market value of $310*, then NPV = 0 for the development project net of the land cost, which is the classical criterion sufficient to make the investment acceptable from the standpoint of market value. Price equal to market value indicates that an investment is fairly priced from the perspectives of both sides—that is, the investment provides just the market OCC rate of return, ex-ante.

11.5 Investment Risk in Development Project

We can use the computed market value of the development project to estimate its investment risk. We can do this by first determining the expected return to the investment in the project when the investor pays market value. In our case, the expected profit at the completion of the construction project at the end of Year 1 is:

$$\text{Expected profit when development completed} = \$1020 - \$663 = \$357 \qquad (11.5)$$

Therefore, the return on investment, at the market value (fair) price, is:

$$\frac{Profit}{Investment} = \frac{(357 - 310)}{310} = \frac{47}{310} \sim 15\% \qquad (11.6)$$

Assuming the project is the HBU and the land is ripe for development, this 15% must be the economic OCC for the investment in the land. (The land is what enables the development project.) This 15% OCC thus reflects the amount of investment risk that is in the project, as the capital market perceives and "cares about" (prices) such risk (as reflected in asset market values).

The development project thus has quite a bit more investment risk than an otherwise similar existing built asset, or than what the asset that is being constructed will have once it is complete:

$$\text{Development OCC} \sim 15\% > 7\% \text{ Rental OCC} \qquad (11.7)$$

To obtain a more precise estimate of the difference in risk, we should subtract the risk-free rate from each OCC in order to estimate their risk premiums (see Section 2.5). Assuming the risk-free rate to be 2%, just slightly less than the 3% construction cost OCC, we obtain:

$$\text{Development risk premium} \sim 13\% > 5\% \text{ Rental risk premium} \qquad (11.8)$$

This implies that, as far as the investment marketplace is concerned, the development project has $\frac{13}{5} = 2.6$ times the amount of investment risk as an investment in an otherwise identical already existing (stabilized) built asset.

The reason development projects typically have more risk is fundamentally because of the *leverage* that is inherent in development projects. *Mathematically, a development project is essentially equivalent to an investment in an existing stabilized asset using borrowed funds.*

To illustrate this concept, suppose we could borrow money for 1 year at an interest rate of 3%. Then, at Time 0, we could borrow $643 and combine that borrowed money with $310 of our own money to purchase a 1-year forward claim on a rental property for $953. (We have already seen that this is the value of such a forward claim on a property that is today worth $1000, including the present value of its Year 1 expected cash flow of $50, which the forward claim would not provide.) Then, in 1 year, if all goes well, we will take ownership of the rental property that we expect to then be worth $1020. We will then owe and pay back 1.03 × 643 = $663 on our loan. Thus, we will have an expected net at Year 1 of: $1020 – $663 = $357. Not coincidentally, this exactly equals the expected profit from the development project. In other words, the development project is mathematically equivalent to the forward investment in the existing property using borrowed money. That is, development is a levered position in the fully operational real estate asset.

As we know from finance theory, leverage magnifies both the risks and returns of investments. Note in particular that the development project in this example is *not* riskier because the development is speculative (not yet leased). The example assumes that the asset to be built will yield exactly the same operating cash flow as the existing stabilized (fully leased) building. We assume, in effect, that the development is pre-leased. Speculative development (without pre-leasing) would add even more risk.

The type of leverage that is in the development project is referred to as "operational leverage." The type of leverage that would be in the purchase of a stabilized income property using borrowed money is referred to as "financial leverage." Operational leverage is inherent in development projects. You can't avoid it, because it is in the nature of the construction process. Financial leverage, on the other hand, is a choice made by the investor, relating to the capital structure chosen for the investment (or for the firm making the investment).

11.6   Conclusion

This chapter introduced the essential economics of real estate development projects. In particular, it compares development to investment in otherwise identical existing built property assets. We saw that the essential difference between the two is in the timing of incurring the costs and benefits of the investment. This has implications regarding the different levels of investment economic risk between the benefit (the to-be-built asset) and the cost (the construction).

We have seen how these considerations lead development investments to be inherently riskier than built property investments, owing to the effect of operational leverage. We have also seen how land value derives from the present value of the highest and best use development project for the site, as the residual between that value and the present value of the construction costs.

We have demonstrated these points concretely by extending the simple numerical example of the rental property presented in Chapter 1, showing how we can quantify the economic features mentioned in the preceding text.

12

Basic Flexibility in Development Projects

The Most Basic Flexibility in Real Estate Development is the Option
to Choose whether and when to Build

LEARNING OBJECTIVES

- Review call (and put) options as defined by economists;
- Understand land as a call option on development;
- Appreciate call (and put) options as forms of flexibility;
- See implications regarding uncertainty and flexibility in project evaluation;
- Understand the value of flexibility to develop (or not).

OUTLINE OF THE CHAPTER

12.1 Review of Call (and Put) Options
12.2 Land as a Call Option on Development
12.3 Drivers of Option Value
12.4 A Practical Example of a Call (and Put) Option
12.5 Flexibility and Scenario Analysis for Development Projects
12.6 Conclusion

Flexibility is a way to manage and profit from uncertainty. It is the main theme and construct we introduce in this book. So far, we have discussed this in the context of existing built real estate properties. Beginning now and for the rest of the book, we view flexibility in the context of development projects. Indeed, these involve many different kinds of decisions concerning timing, scope, and composition. Development projects thus offer great opportunities for using flexibility to advantage, probably more so than investments in stabilized properties.

This chapter introduces flexibility in development by focusing on the simplest and most common type of flexibility, the decision of whether or not (in effect, the decision of when) to develop, when the outcome is uncertain (which is to say, essentially, always). Along the way, we discuss the relation of flexibility to economic options, focusing on what we can learn from the mainstream financial perspective on options.

Flexibility and Real Estate Valuation under Uncertainty: A Practical Guide for Developers, First Edition.
David Geltner and Richard de Neufville.
© 2018 John Wiley & Sons Ltd. Published 2018 by John Wiley & Sons Ltd.
Companion website: www.wiley.com/go/geltner-deneufville/flexibility-and-real-estate-valuation

12.1   Review of Call (and Put) Options

We focus on call options because they illustrate the main features of financial options, of which there are many different kinds. A call option provides an investor the:

- Right without obligation; to
- Obtain an "underlying asset," such as a share of common stock; upon
- Payment of a "strike price" (or "exercise cost").

For example, a call option on shares in ABC Corporation at a strike price of $100 allows you to purchase shares for that price, even when (if) ABC's price in the stock market rises above $100.

A most important point here is that options derive their value from the flexibility they provide their owners. This is inherent in the "right *without obligation*" nature of options. An option gives its holder the *flexibility* to do something (or *not*), at the owner's discretion, without the *obligation* to do it. The flexibility to "do the right thing in the circumstances" enables the owner of an option to avoid bad situations and benefit from good ones. This asymmetry in outcomes contingent on circumstances is key to the value of options in dealing with uncertainty.

A call option on buying shares will thus never have negative value (so long as we use it rationally). You either:

- Buy the asset because it is profitable to do so; or
- Do not exercise your right to buy the asset, with no gain but also no loss.

In the case of call options on shares, it is obvious and easy to avoid negative values for options. You can observe the market price of the stock, and you know the exact cost of the option's strike price. You would never pay a strike price greater than the current value of the stock. If ABC's stock price were $90, then you would not exercise your option to buy the stock for the $100 strike price. If you wanted ABC stock, you would buy it for $90 on the market instead of through your option at $100. (In this sense, having a call option is "all gain, no pain.")

This is not to say that you can't lose money with options. In the case of traded options, you have to buy them, which means you have to make an upfront investment to obtain the option. But if, for example, the value of ABC stock goes down after you buy your call option on it, then the value of your call option will also go down and ultimately could expire worthless if ABC stock price never goes above the option strike price.

To close out this section, we note that a put option is the converse of a call option. It is the "right without obligation" to "sell (or dispose of) an asset" at a given price. Put options enable you to close out a deal that looks unprofitable. Insurance is a form of put option: in case of fire insurance, for example, the insurance company pays you an amount that is independent of (and above) the then-current (post-fire) value of the house. The ability to default on a mortgage, if it is "non-recourse," thereby giving the borrower limited liability, is also a put option. You give up an asset (the collateral property) in return for getting rid of a liability equal to the present value of the mortgage balance (which presumably by then is greater than the current market value of the property).

12.2   Land as a Call Option on Development

Economists have long recognized that real estate development projects are essentially similar to the exercise of a "call option." The ownership of the land provides the *right without obligation* to undertake the development project. In the case of the real estate development project:

- The underlying asset (what you get by exercising the option) is the value of the completed built property;
- The exercise cost of the option (what you pay to get that asset) is the construction cost of the project. This cost does not include the cost of the land itself because the land is what provides the option.

The value of the land for development is the value of the option. (In Section 11.4, we saw how we can compute that value as the simple residual of the built value minus the construction cost, at the time when it is optimal to exercise the option.)

There's an important difference between land as a call option for development and call options for buying company shares. The market values of widely traded assets (such as company shares, barrels of oil, and other commodities) are regularly available and easily observable. However, the value of a development is not obvious. Built properties are unique, and no one can know the exact market value of any given property at any given time (see Box 2.1). Developers thus may sometimes make unprofitable decisions that are "irrational," at least in retrospect. They may misread the signals and be too quick to build, in some cases, or perhaps too slow in others.

In modeling flexibility in real estate development projects, we need to be realistic regarding the actual use of flexibility in practice. Our models must allow for the representation of suboptimal exercise of flexibility. Indeed, a feature of our method of modeling options is that it allows the exploration of practical management decision rules to see which best minimize the possible unfavorable outcomes. The practical simulation modeling we present in this book thus differs from the theoretical option valuation modeling often studied in economics. Economic models generally assume optimal exercise behavior. We use a more direct analog model of plausible exercise decision behavior.

12.3   Drivers of Option Value

Understanding developable land as a call option brings profound and important insight to the evaluation of development projects. Indeed, understanding gleaned from economic option valuation theory offers two important lessons for us:

- The greater the uncertainty, the more valuable the option;
- Delaying the use of options can be valuable.

The idea that options are more valuable when there is more uncertainty may at first seem counter-intuitive. We normally prefer sure assets to risky ones; in fact, we demand a risk premium in our expected return to make it worth our while to hold risky assets, which is equivalent to marking down their value. What is going on here?

The reason for why call options are more valuable when there is more uncertainty comes from that "all gain, no pain" point we made earlier, about the payoffs from options being asymmetric. To see this, think about the possible value of a call option on ABC at the $100 strike price bought when ABC is selling at $100. If ABC shares are not very volatile, ranging in value only between, say, ±$5 from $100, then the maximum value of the call option range is only $5. If, however, the shares are highly uncertain, ranging in value between ±$40 from $100, then the maximum value of the call option is up to $40. In the latter case, the downside in the stock is eight times what it was in the former case, falling to as low as $60 instead of to only $95 from the starting value of $100. However, in either case, the downside on the call option is the same. If ABC shares fall, you simply won't exercise the call option, and you'll walk away with the same amount—zero. Because the call option is not concerned about the downside, only the upside drives its value. Hence, the greater the volatility, the greater the value of option, and of the flexibility it enables.

Flexibility is thus valuable in the management of real estate assets because of the inherent uncertainty surrounding long-term assets. Flexibility is particularly valuable in development projects because they inherently have greater risk than stabilized rental properties (as we saw in Section 11.5).

The second lesson about call options relevant here is that delaying their use may be desirable. It is not necessarily best to exercise them the moment they show a profit. For example, suppose the market price of shares of ABC is rising, and they are now at $105. Exercising the option to buy them for $100 would yield an immediate profit of the difference, $5. Is now the time to cash in? Maybe, but maybe not. If the market price rises further to $110, the value of exercising the call option would double to $10. Maybe you should wait. The point is that we need to think carefully about the timing of the use of options.

The message for the valuation of development projects is that we need to pay close attention to our choices in the timing of development. Effective valuation of development projects should consider both their uncertainty and timing.

In any case, the call option model of land value and development projects powerfully highlights the importance of considering uncertainty and flexibility in the analysis. In the rest of this chapter, we focus only on the threshold type of flexibility, the ability to time the project. In subsequent chapters, we cover other types of flexibilities that reside in the design and management of development projects.

12.4 A Practical Example of a Call (and Put) Option

Bentall 5 ("Bentall Five") is an office tower in downtown Vancouver, Canada (see Figure 12.1). Its development offers a fascinating example of the use of an option in real estate. The design of Bentall 5 featured the flexibility to buildout the tower in two vertical phases. Developers could build the first phase of 22 floors and then decide whether and when (if ever) to add on the additional five floors. They thus had "the right, but not the obligation" to expand the tower vertically. This was the call option built into the project. You can think of it like a component of "land" value that existed once the first 22 floors were complete.

To create the flexibility to expand the tower vertically, the designers had to make sure that the bottom phase met all the requirements to construct and sustain the potential top phase. That is, they had to provide the strength to carry extra load, enough shafts for access, etc. The cost of the additional strength, of the loss of rentable space due to

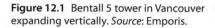

Figure 12.1 Bentall 5 tower in Vancouver expanding vertically. *Source*: Emporis.

additional shafts through the floor plates, etc., represent the price the developers had to pay for the call option (in effect, to create the additional "land" value).

We can view the flexibility to decide whether and when to complete the top phase of the building in two ways. The call option on expansion is equivalent to a put option on further development. That is, the flexibility to cap off the tower at the lower height enables the developers to reduce the total cost of the investment relative to the full 27 floors if they thought the incremental asset consisting of the top phase would be unprofitable. Viewing the design in this way, the price for the put option is essentially the same as the price for the call option; it is the extra cost associated with making the lower building suitable for vertical expansion.

This relationship between a call option to expand and a put option to forego an element of a project is an example of "put-call parity." The essence is that we can often view the same flexibility in development in two ways. Just as the ability to expand a project (call option) is the converse of the ability to reduce its size (put option), so the potential to decide when to accelerate a development (call option) implies the opportunity to decide to postpone further work (put option). Expressed most simply: the option to *do* something is also the option to *not do* it.

In actuality, the developers of Bentall 5 completed the first phase in 2002. They added the second phase 5 years later, in 2007. We do not know whether they started out optimistically and then retrenched when the Vancouver real estate market turned unfavorable in the early 2000s (exercised their put option), or if they planned cautiously at first and subsequently extended their project opportunistically (exercised their call option).

The essential point here is that the flexibility appears to have served the developers well. It really doesn't matter how you label it.

12.5   Flexibility and Scenario Analysis for Development Projects

The Bentall 5 example is a concrete, real-world case of a particular and dramatic call option specifically designed into the project. Now let's return to the basic, widespread type of flexibility in development, the land call option that is the focus of this chapter.

Let's consider a highly simplified numerical example. It's similar to the one we used to introduce the concept of the interaction of uncertainty and flexibility for an existing rental property in Chapter 4. There, the basic type of flexibility was the resale timing decision. Here, with the development of a new building, it is the call (or put) option on the project itself: in any given period, we have the flexibility to do the project or not. We simply extend and elaborate on the development example from Chapter 11, the construction of our simple rental property. Table 12.1, reproducing Table 11.1 for convenience, summarizes the project in terms of the traditional, single-stream, DCF pro forma.

To illustrate the essential point, we construct an overly simplistic world consisting of only two possible scenarios, as in Chapter 4. We also assume that the option to build will expire after 1 year. This is sufficient to illustrate how the interaction of uncertainty and flexibility adds value.

As in the Chapter 4 example, we suppose that uncertainty in the relevant future consists of only two mutually exclusive scenarios, one optimistic and the other pessimistic, with equal probability of either occurring. At Year 1, the developer will learn which scenario will actually occur. (You could suppose the scenarios concern the announcement of whether the government will or will not build a complementary project, such as a new subway or metro line.) In the optimistic scenario, the completed asset will be worth 50% more than in the pro forma, or $1530. In the pessimistic scenario, the outcome will be symmetrically the opposite, the asset being worth half or 50% less than the pro forma, or $510 (see Table 12.2).

Suppose first that the developer has no flexibility. The project must be implemented in Year 1, no matter which scenario happens. Since the construction cost is in any case

Table 12.1 Essential parameters for the example investments.

END OF YEAR:	YEAR 0	YEAR 1	YEAR 2	YEAR 3...	GROWTH	OCC
RENTAL						
Built Property Cash Flow ($)	0	50	51	52...	2%/year	7%/year
Built Property Value ($)	1000	1020	1040	1061...	2%/year	7%/year
DEVELOPMENT						
Land Cost ($)	310	0	N/A	N/A	N/A	N/A
Construction Cost ($)	0	663	N/A	N/A	2%/year	3%/year
Built Property Cash Flow ($)	0	0	51	52...	2%/year	7%/year
Built Property Value ($)	N/A	1020	1040	1061...	2%/year	7%/year
Development Project Profit ($)	N/A	357	N/A	N/A	N/A	15%/year

Table 12.2 Comparison of decision with and without flexibility.

DECISION CASE	EX-ANTE MEAN	NO FLEXIBILITY		FLEXIBILITY	
VALUE ITEM	(PRO-FORMA)	OPTIMISTIC	PESSIMISTIC	OPTIMISTIC	PESSIMISTIC
T=1 Project Value	$1,020	$1,530	$510	$1,530	$510
Less Construction	$663	$663	$663	$663	$663
T=1 Net Value	$357	$867	($153)	$867	($153)
Probability	N/A	0.5	0.5	0.5	0.5
Actual Outcome	$357	$867	($153)	$867	$0
T=1 Expected Value	$357	$357		$433	
Discount rate	15%	15%		15%	
T=0 Valuation	$310	$310		$377	

the same ($663), the profit in the two possible outcomes will be symmetrically opposite as compared to the pro forma expected profit of $357. As Table 12.2 shows, the net value would be a profit of $867 in the optimistic scenario, and a loss of $153 in the pessimistic scenario. With equal probability, this gives us an expected Year 1 value for the project as of Time 0 equal to $357. (The "ex-ante" column refers to values as of Time 0, the "present" time for the valuation.) If we reduce this future value to its Time 0 equivalent by discounting at the 15% OCC rate previously described in Chapter 11 for the project, we get the present value equal to $310, as previously computed in Chapter 11. (Compare the bottom line in Table 12.2 with the Year 0 column in Table 12.1.)

Now consider the situation in which the developer has the flexibility to decide *not* to build in Year 1, after learning how the future turns out. In effect, suppose the developer has a call option on the project, and can choose in Year 1 whether to exercise it or not. Or, equivalently, you could assume that the developer has a put option to abandon the project, and can choose in Year 1 whether to exercise it or not. If the optimistic scenario materializes, the developer will do as projected in the pro forma—that is, build the project. In that scenario, the developer will collect $867 profit in Year 1. But if the pessimistic scenario occurs, the developer will exercise the right to not build the project, accepting a zero outcome in that case rather than incurring the $153 loss. As the present value of zero is zero, the Time 0 valuation of the project with this type of flexibility is not the aforementioned $310, but rather $377—with rounding, computed as:

$$\frac{(0.5)867+(0.5)0}{1.15}$$

Thus, we see how flexibility in the presence of uncertainty can add value to a development project. In this case, the flexibility is the ability to abandon the project (or, equivalently, not to exercise the option to build the project). The result is qualitatively similar to what we saw in Chapter 4, in that the flexibility, combined with the uncertainty, results in a value superior to the single-stream, pro forma valuation based purely on the (correct, unbiased) expectation.

12.6 Conclusion

This chapter introduced the basic concept of options, including the call option and its counterpoint, the put option. It has discussed how we can evaluate developable land as a call option on the project that we could develop on the land.

We have also noted that we can view the call option and put option on development projects as the opposite sides of the same coin in a sense, depending simply on one's starting perspective. The option to "do" something is equivalent to the option to "not do" the same thing.

We also demonstrated how options become more valuable. And we provided a simple numerical example quantifying the value of the basic and common type of flexibility represented by the land development option.

Finally, we also discussed a dramatic real-world example of an option literally designed and built into the top of a skyscraper in Vancouver.

13

Option Dichotomies

We Introduce a Typology of Flexibility in Development Projects

---

LEARNING OBJECTIVES

- Understand the difference between defensive and offensive options;
- Understand the difference between Options "on" and "in" the project;
- Understand the difference between Timing and Product options.

OUTLINE OF THE CHAPTER

13.1 Three Dichotomies for Thinking Generally about Development Options
13.2 Defensive versus Offensive Options
13.3 Options "On" and "In" Projects
13.4 Timing Options versus Product Options
13.5 Conclusion

This chapter suggests some ways to think generally about options in real estate development projects. Specifically, we present a three-way typology to place these options into an overall context.

13.1 Three Dichotomies for Thinking Generally about Development Options

As we noted in Chapter 3, the terms "flexibility" and "option" overlap considerably in the context of this book. Developers have certain types of flexibilities that do not fit the technical economics definition of an "option." An example is the resale timing flexibility of an existing property we explored quantitatively in Chapter 9. But we can view most of the types of development flexibility that we focus on in this book as options, at least conceptually, pretty much as we defined them in Section 12.1.

At this stage, we introduce three general ways to think about options in development projects. The idea is to help us think about what we can use options for, how we can

Flexibility and Real Estate Valuation under Uncertainty: A Practical Guide for Developers, First Edition.
David Geltner and Richard de Neufville.
© 2018 John Wiley & Sons Ltd. Published 2018 by John Wiley & Sons Ltd.
Companion website: www.wiley.com/go/geltner-deneufville/flexibility-and-real-estate-valuation

implement them, and what they consist of. It is helpful to discuss these issues in terms of dichotomies, of contrasts between opposites along different dimensions. We suggest three contrasts:

- Defensive versus offensive options;
- Options "on" versus options "in" the project; and
- Timing options versus product options.

13.2   Defensive versus Offensive Options

From the perspective of investment or project management, we can often think of options in real estate development as being either "defensive" or "offensive" in nature. Specifically:

- Defensive options help to protect against downside circumstances and outcomes, if things turn out worse than anticipated.
- Offensive options allow the developer to take advantage of upside opportunities, if things turn out better than expected.

Relating to the concepts we introduced in Section 12.1, offensive options are often call options. They allow the developer to obtain something, provided the circumstances are right, that would not have otherwise been possible. For example, the ability of the Bentall 5 project developers in Vancouver to build an additional five floors on top of their building, when/if the market would provide sufficient demand, is an offensive option that we could view as a call option.

Defensive options are often like put options. They allow the developer to avoid a loss, at least at the margin. For example, if the original Bentall 5 planners had intended to build the full 27-story building, then the ability to pause or stop at 22 floors if demand did not turn out as strong as they had anticipated, is a defensive option that we could view as a put option. (The developers could "sell" the top five floors for a certain NPV of zero, rather than the negative NPV they would get if the incremental value of the top five floors would be less than their incremental construction cost.)

As is so often the case, in the Bentall 5 project, the call option on the top five floors was also a put option on them, depending on perspective and on which design is made as the original "base plan." Were the developers starting out planning to build a:

- 22-floor building with the call option to add five floors? or a
- 27-floor building with the put option to reduce the size if desirable?

The ability to look at the same thing from two different angles can usefully help designers and decision-makers build intuition and understanding about possibilities for flexibility.

It is helpful to think of defensive options as "insurance." While they do not provide traditional insurance policies, they fulfill the same function. They enable developers to avoid losses, at the cost of preparing the option (such as designing in the ability to reduce the size of a building). Placing options in this context helps us to recognize that an option that we do not use is not "wasted." We do not complain to our life insurance broker that he wasted our money because we did not die last year! When you buy insurance, you buy "protection"—that is worth something even if you never end up cashing in on it.

We can also think of "offensive" options in the same light. In this case, they provide "opportunity"—to take advantage of upside opportunities when and if they are present. (Section 15.6 expands on this concept.)

13.3 Options "On" and "In" Projects

In the field of engineering systems design, the concept of options "on" versus options "in" a project refers to whether the option is on the system as a whole ("on" the project) or concerns some detailed portion of the system ("in" the project). When it concerns some constituents of the project, it typically refers to some elements of technical design. The Health Care Service Corporation (HCSC) building in Chicago provides a classic example of options "in" a project. The technical elements that enabled the owners to double the height of their 30-floor building years after it opened consist of such things as stronger columns and footings, extra elevator shafts, etc. (see Figure 13.1).

In the case of real estate development, a useful way to view this concept is that options:

- "On" the project apply to the entire project, or to a large component of it as a whole;
- "In" the project apply at a more specific or granular level within the project or inside its major components.

Thus, the option to choose the timing of when (and whether) to begin the overall project, or a major phase of the project, would be an option "on" the project (or "on" a phase of the project). The option to time the start of a project, discussed in Chapter 12, is the most basic example of an option "on" a real estate development project.

In contrast, an option "in" a project might be the ability to pause and restart the project at any time after it has already begun (in effect, the ability to delay the completion of the project after it has begun). The ability to switch the type of building on a particular site from one use to another (such as from rental apartments to condominiums, or from office space to lab space) is another example of an option "in" the project.

Figure 13.1 Vertical expansion of the HCSC building in Chicago (center of images). Phase 1 (left) and Phase 2 (right). *Source*: Goettsch Partners and Wittels and Pearson.

The distinction between options "on" versus "in" can be rather fuzzy and ambiguous, and does not necessarily matter. As with the case of puts and calls (defensive and offensive options), the usefulness of the concept is not negated, and can even be enhanced, by the ability to look at design features from either or both perspectives.

13.4 Timing Options versus Product Options

The final dichotomy that can be useful for conceptualizing development options is between "timing" options and "product" options. Timing options are about *when* to build, while product options are about *what* to build. Timing options provide the developer with flexibility to decide the time when to start or complete a project, or some component of it. Product options give the developer flexibility about what type or size (density) of structures to build.

As with the other dichotomies, the timing/product dichotomy also includes some overlap in practice, even though the conceptual distinction is useful. For example, the vertical expansion option in the Bentall 5 development was certainly a product option. It gave the developers flexibility to decide the final size and height of their real estate product (the office building). But this option also included timing flexibility, as the developer could delay indefinitely (or at least for several years) the decision to exercise the call option (the expansion to 27 floors).

Note that timing options can have different degrees of flexibility. Some may only exist over a limited time, perhaps because planning permissions may expire. Others might be subject to uncertain limitations. For example, the governmental authorities might exercise some right to change zoning regulations describing permissible use (this was a concern for HCSC). In some cases, developers may effectively have the right to exercise their timing option at any time.

In general, timing options can be subtle. For example, in the field of financial options, analysts speak of "European," "American," and "Bermudan" options. You can only exercise European options at one point in time, and, if you don't, you lose them forever. You can exercise American options at any time (at least until an expiration or maturity date, if the option is not perpetual). You can exercise Bermudan options at several possible times, but not at just any time. The point is that timing options can differ.

13.5 Conclusion

This chapter invites you to think generally about flexibilities in terms of:

- *Use*: Are they for exploiting new opportunities (offensive) or insuring against downside events (defensive)?
- *Application*: Do they apply to the whole project ("on"), or to some parts of it ("in")?
- *Type*: Do they refer to the product, or merely to its timing of its start or completion?

The following two chapters will explore in more depth the two major option types: product and timing options.

14

Product Options in Development

We Discuss Three types of Product Options

LEARNING OBJECTIVES

- Understand the concept of base plan;
- Introduce product expansion flexibility;
- Understand the difference between horizontal and vertical expansion flexibilities;
- Introduce product mix flexibility.

OUTLINE OF THE CHAPTER

14.1 Concept of Base Plan
14.2 Product Expansion Flexibility
14.3 Product Mix Flexibility
14.4 Conclusion

This chapter introduces you to three types of flexibilities concerning the scale or type of products (buildings) that development projects produce. These concern horizontal and vertical expansion, and flexibility in the mix of product.

14.1 Concept of Base Plan

In general, expansion options reflect the ability of the developer to add an additional quantity of built space to a "base plan" of the project. The base plan refers to the initial plan for the complete project, what the developer intends to build with a high degree of commitment. It is the reference point for our analyses.

For definitional clarity and analytical convenience, we focus on the notion of expansion options as being those that enable developers to add more total real estate product (greater amounts of built space), beyond that in the base plan.

Developers may, of course, exercise flexibility to abandon parts of the base plan. This possibility, a type of defensive option, is inherently part of the way we define the production timing options to be described in Chapter 15.

Flexibility and Real Estate Valuation under Uncertainty: A Practical Guide for Developers, First Edition.
David Geltner and Richard de Neufville.
© 2018 John Wiley & Sons Ltd. Published 2018 by John Wiley & Sons Ltd.
Companion website: www.wiley.com/go/geltner-deneufville/flexibility-and-real-estate-valuation

14.2   Product Expansion Flexibility

We can view expansion flexibilities as call options "in" the overall project. Or, they could equivalently be viewed as options "on" whatever is the additional product entailed in the expansion. As with all call or offensive options, they enable the developer to take advantage of better-than-anticipated circumstances in the relevant real estate markets (as described in Section 12.1).

   We now introduce the two basic types of expansion options: horizontal and vertical. A horizontal expansion consists of building more structure across additional land, increasing the overall "footprint" of the development. A vertical expansion adds extra floors to one or more structures, without expanding the footprint, increasing the floor area ratio (FAR) of the project. (FAR is a measure of the density of construction.) Both vertical and horizontal expansion options may exist in some projects. One of the original designs for the Court Square Two project in New York City envisaged this possibility (see Figure 14.1). With a horizontal expansion option, developers obtain ownership or control over extra land, but set it aside and hold it in reserve (or "banked," as it is sometimes called), without immediate plans for development in the original project base plan. (They may develop it to a low-intensity use, such as parking or open space.) The cost of this extra land is the cost of obtaining the horizontal expansion option.

| Court Square Two: Phase I | Court Square Two: Phase I & II |

Figure 14.1   A flexible design for Court Square Two, New York City. *Source*: courtesy of Kohn Pedersen Fox (2005), in Pearson and Wittels, "Real Options in Action: Vertical Phasing in Commercial Real Estate Development" (masters thesis, Massachusetts Institute of Technology, 2008).

With a vertical expansion option, developers design buildings to allow them to add floors to the existing structure, generally while maintaining the functioning of the original lower floors. The cost of enabling such vertical expansion, in the form of both incremental construction costs and loss of building efficiency in the lower floors (less rentable space due to need for greater shafts and common spaces), is the cost of the vertical expansion option. The Bentall 5 project, described in Chapter 12, is an example of such an option, at least in the manner in which it was actually built. Another famous example is the Health Care Service Corporation (HCSC) building in Chicago.

You can see that the expansion option is like a call option because it allows the project to obtain assets that were not part of the base plan. Expansion options represent adding to the quantity of the project. Thus, they are "offensive" in nature. They enable developers to strike opportunistically to obtain a greater upside than they envisioned in the base plan, which they already viewed as being sufficient and complete. Expansion options generally become relevant and valuable in scenarios in which the real estate market turns out to be more favorable than developers expected when they settled on the base plan, or when the development has an extremely long time horizon. (For example, in the case of the HCSC building, the project was owned by the user/occupant of the building as their corporate headquarters, so the "developer" could have a virtually unlimited time horizon.)

We will note some basic considerations for modeling expansion options in Chapter 23, after we have discussed the modeling of project phases in Chapter 22. For the moment, let us simply note that, despite the cost of giving a structure the strength to carry eventual heavier loads, expansion options may actually reduce initial capital expenditures because they permit developers to build only for immediate requirements (see Box 14.1).

Box 14.1 Do expansion options really cost more?

Expansion options typically involve incremental costs in the development project up front, in order to enable the option to exist later. For example, to create the flexibility to double the height of its Chicago building, HCSC had to pay for more structural steel and stronger footings to carry the possibly eventual load.

However, we need to be careful in how we think about such costs. Paradoxically, these incremental costs may actually save money in the short run! How is this possible?

Developers may at least partially offset the incremental cost of the necessary upfront investment to create the option by the possible savings they can obtain by reducing the scale of the initial buildout in consideration of the future expansion possibility. For example, if you knew you could never expand a certain building, you might design it to an optimal height of 45 stories. But knowing you can expand it to 45 stories (or even more) later, you might satisfy yourself with an initial height of only 30 stories, the amount of space needed in the short term. While the vertically expandable 30-story building would cost more to construct than a non-expandable 30-story building, it might cost less than the alternative non-expandable 45-story building. Similarly, you might buy 45 acres if you knew that was all you could ever get, but you might buy only 30 acres now if you could also obtain an option to acquire an adjacent 15 acres more.

14.3 Product Mix Flexibility

Product mix flexibility consists of the option to change the mix of product types in a development. Also referred to as a product "switching" option, we can view this type of flexibility in two ways.

In the case of a project producing many small-scale structures or built units, it is most appropriate to think of this option as the flexibility to vary the proportion of different types of buildings or units. For example, a housing development might involve some proportion of its output as condominiums and some as rental units, or some as upscale three-bedroom units and some as lower-priced efficiency apartments. The option in this case would enable the developer to change the proportions from those in the base plan.

In the case of a project producing one or a few large structures, product mix flexibility is more like a discrete option to convert the structure from one type to another just prior to (or conceivably even during) the construction process. For example, the architect might have designed the building so that it could be readily finished out as either office space or lab space, or as apartments or extended-stay hotel rooms.

Product mix flexibility is interesting, in that it essentially involves a combination of the call and put options. Switching the previously planned product mix from Type A to Type B is the simultaneous exercise of a call on B and a put on A. The product switching option enables the developer to avoid downside outcomes in the market for either alternative type of structure, and/or to take advantage of upside outcomes for either type. The switching option is both offensive and defensive; it pushes the target curve to the right all along the curve, both in the downside and upside tails (and therefore in the middle).

The value of product mix flexibility depends heavily on the correlation between the markets for the alternative types of real estate products. The lower the correlation, the more valuable is the switching option, other things being equal (including the volatilities). The option has value only when one alternative turns out to be more valuable than the other. The likelihood of this is greater when there is less chance that the prices of the two alternatives move together. In the extreme, if the correlation were 100%, then the switching option would have no value; you would always stick with the alternative that appeared best to begin with (and which would presumably therefore be included in the base plan).

14.4 Conclusion

This chapter introduced three types of product options that build upon the developer's original base plan:

- Horizontal and vertical expansion options, which are essentially like call options, and are effectively offensive options in the project.
- Product type switching option, to change from a base plan product type or product type mix, which is really a combination of the call and put options, and can act both offensively and defensively within the project.

15

Timing Options in Development

Now we Turn to the Types of Timing Options

LEARNING OBJECTIVES

- Review project start-timing flexibility, the delay option;
- Introduce project production timing flexibility;
- Understand the difference between the two forms of production timing flexibility—modular production and phasing;
- Understand parallel and sequential phasing;
- Characterize options as defensive or offensive according to their simulation target curve results.

OUTLINE OF THE CHAPTER

15.1 Project Start-Timing Flexibility (the Delay Option)
15.2 Project Production Timing Flexibility
15.3 Modular Production Timing Flexibility
15.4 Phasing Timing Flexibility
15.5 Types of Phasing
15.6 Recognizing Defensive and Offensive Options in Simulation Results
15.7 Conclusion

Broadly speaking, timing options are more common in development projects than are product options. Almost all development projects have at least some basic type of timing option. Here, we consider three types of timing options. For purposes of conceptual understanding, and to build your analytic intuition, the timing options we consider here effectively take the product as given. It is useful to distinguish relatively "pure" types of options. In reality, timing options will, of course, often exist simultaneously with product flexibility.

After discussing the types of timing options, this chapter concludes with a demonstration of how one can characterize options as defensive or offensive by what they do to the shape of the cumulative and frequency target curves in the results of a Monte Carlo simulation.

15.1 Project Start-Timing Flexibility (The Delay Option)

In Section 12.2, we introduced the most basic and common type of timing option in real estate, the call option on development that resides in land ownership. From the perspective of land valuation presented in Chapter 12, fee simple or freehold ownership of

Flexibility and Real Estate Valuation under Uncertainty: A Practical Guide for Developers, First Edition.
David Geltner and Richard de Neufville.
© 2018 John Wiley & Sons Ltd. Published 2018 by John Wiley & Sons Ltd.
Companion website: www.wiley.com/go/geltner-deneufville/flexibility-and-real-estate-valuation

land provides the right without obligation to develop the land at any time in perpetuity (contingent on planning permissions, of course).

In principle, the landowner has flexibility to start the project at any time. As with all options, the start-timing option for a project faces a favorable asymmetry in its future payoffs ("all gain, no pain"). As long as the landowner/developer has not yet triggered the option (has not started development), he or she can either take advantage of upside realizations in the real estate market by starting the project in such good conditions, or can wait out downturns before starting the project.

Although the start-timing option is essentially a call option on the construction of a property asset, we can view it as a delay option on the development project. From the perspective of the developer, flexibility in starting a project often involves delaying from an initially planned start date.

In practice, developers need to do a lot of preliminary work before they can start a project, more so with more complex projects. The preliminary work may include assembling several land parcels and purchasing or gaining control of the site. They must also get the project designed and specified, first at a broad level and then in more detail. They may need planning permission, approval of zoning changes, and various other permits. They then have to put construction documents out to bid, and line up construction financing. All of this requires significant time and money, so the developer typically views the date of completion of such preliminary work as the planned start date for the project.

In reality, however, the preliminary work in most cases does not *require* developers to start construction immediately when the preliminary work is complete. To some degree (and with more or less planning and enabling), the start date can remain flexible beyond the initial first possible (and likely planned) start date. The longer the delay, the more effort that the developer must make to maintain the viability of the specific plans for the project. However, in principle, the delay can be virtually indefinite in many cases, if delay makes economic or other type of sense.

Delay may indeed make sense if the market conditions are not currently as good as when the developer envisioned and planned the project. In this case, the delay option is effectively a defensive option. It allows investors in the project to reduce their losses during a downturn. This is typically the realistic, practical nature of flexibility in starting projects. This is why developers usually view (and refer to) it as the "project start-delay option." In fact, it is essentially the same thing as the development call option that we introduced in Chapter 12. But, as we have seen, options can be viewed from two perspectives—the option "to do" something, or the option "to not do" it.

15.2 Project Production Timing Flexibility

Real estate development projects create products in the form of one or more building structures. Once the development project has started, there may exist various ways and approaches to vary the timing of the production of this output. There will generally be an initially planned production schedule, a base plan. Production timing flexibility is the ability to deviate from this base plan.

If the project is simply to produce one building, then there may not be much flexibility in the production timing. Most easily, it may be possible to vary the speed of the construction.

Figure 15.1 Harvard University's Allston Science Complex, delayed 6 years. *Source: The Crimson,* June 14, 2012 (https://s3.amazonaws.com/thumbnails.thecrimson.com/photos/2012/06/14/ 113909_1277855.jpg.800x530_q95_crop-smart_upscale.jpg).

Builders could increase or decrease overtime work, or include construction at night or in cold weather, or not, with a trade-off in terms of cost and completion date. But once started, it rarely makes economic sense to stop the construction of a single building, except in extreme cases, especially for large buildings. In such cases, owners will sometimes pause construction after the foundation is complete, or temporarily "cap" one or two stories of a high-rise to await conditions more desirable for completion. For example, following the 2008 financial crisis, Harvard University capped its billion-dollar project to build a new science complex, and did not resume work until about 7 years later (see Figure 15.1).

In the case of multi-building development projects, ranging from tract housing developments to large residential or mixed-use projects, there is often much more scope to modulate the rate of production of the buildings after the overall project has been started. In effect, developers can delay the full buildout or completion of the project beyond the originally planned production schedule (or, in some cases, accelerate it ahead of the original schedule). Viewed from the perspective of the base plan schedule, such production timing flexibility represents an option "in" the project. If it involves only the ability to pause the process or stretch out the time to construct the project, thereby delaying the completion (possibly even ultimately abandoning parts of the project), then we would consider this a purely defensive type of flexibility, cutting the losses or reducing the magnitude of investment costs exposed to loss. If the production timing flexibility also involves some ability to accelerate the project, then we could view that aspect as an offensive option, enabling the profiting from earlier or better-than-expected demand conditions.

While the variety of types of production timing flexibility in the real world is potentially very rich and nuanced, we focus in depth on two somewhat stylized and archetypical types: modular production and phasing.

- *Modular production* means that, in principle, the developers can pause and restart projects where they left off, at any time, effectively anywhere in the project.
- *Phasing* means that the project contains two or more phases, with some flexibility in the start times of at least one of the phases.

Modular production would generally provide much greater timing flexibility than project phasing. But the two types of flexibilities are not necessarily mutually exclusive. A given phase could contain some modular production flexibility. But, in the pure cases, to distinguish for analytical purposes, modular flexibility means there is no need for phasing, and phasing would not envision being able to pause or leave incomplete any phase once its construction has begun.

15.3   Modular Production Timing Flexibility

With modular production, the idea is that, once developers have started a project, they can stop or pause it (or some phase of it) at almost any point, and then may resume it later from that point. They may also be able to permanently abandon the project at the stop point. Modular production timing flexibility requires some specialized design and planning for the project, and will not be possible in all multi-building projects.

An example of modular production timing flexibility is a large tract housing development built consecutively on a contiguous grid pattern, which is serviceable for any scale of project completion. The developer would neither pave streets nor sell lots in the next block until buyers had bought up the previous blocks. Modular production flexibility would mean that the developer could decide not to sell any units in a given year, but then could resume the original schedule in any subsequent year. Developers must usually build some amount of infrastructure at the beginning of the project in order to enable at least a portion of the overall project to proceed to buildout (see Box 15.1).

Modular production seems most feasible "horizontally," applying to buildings or groups of buildings. But modern design and construction techniques offer some possibilities for "vertical" modular production. These make it possible to build out the scale and configuration of an individual building with flexibility in the timing of completion. (For example, there are techniques for inserting "pods" into a building frame.)

Box 15.1 Bardhaman planned community

The 2008 plan for the Shrachi "Renaissance Township" community in Bardhaman, West Bengal, India, envisaged the construction of about 5000 housing units over 260 acres. It is a good example of the modular development of housing. As common in India, and indeed in Singapore and many other countries, developers build out the product only when buyers have committed substantial money for their units.

15.4   Phasing Timing Flexibility

"Phasing" (or "staging") flexibility differs from modular production in two important respects:

- First, the overall project is divided into just a few discrete, substantial physical parts;
- Second, developers should complete each phase once they start it.

Large developments typically only have two or three "phases" or "stages," although very large projects can have many more. Each phase consists of certain planned buildings, together with their related infrastructure and grounds. The phases may be quite different from one another, or very similar. The key point is that each phase represents a largely self-contained development project in itself. Once the project has completed a phase, that phase can operate at full, or at least normal, rates of productivity or serviceability.

For example, a first phase might include a first series of houses, or apartment blocks, or a parking garage linked to a hotel and office building. Second and possibly subsequent phases might simply be more of the same, or they might include different real estate products that are complementary to the previous phase(s), such as condominiums or a shopping center.

The second defining characteristic of a "phase" as distinct from modular development is that, once developers have started to build a phase, they pretty much have to complete it. A phase is an integrated complex that cannot function well unless it is all there.

Phasing thus does not provide as much production timing flexibility as pure modular development. This is because the phases are discrete or "lumpy," and must be completed once started.

The distinction between phasing flexibility and the expansion options described in Chapter 14 can be fuzzy in practice, but it is meaningful at a conceptual level, and useful for design and planning purposes and analytical consideration. It can allow us to gain insight about the value of project flexibility. We noted that the key distinction in principle is that the expansion option is not part of the base plan, and is not as likely to be realized, at least not in the foreseeable near- to medium-term future. Another important difference between project phasing and expansion options is that the latter require some early investments to enable the expansion option. The creation of an expansion option requires an upfront investment, either in additional land or in structural strength and other physical design requirements of the building. Phasing, on the other hand, usually does not require any upfront cost. It is simply a way of designing, organizing, and programming the production of the base plan.

15.5   Types of Phasing

Phases within a project can be either parallel or sequential in their temporal relationship with each other. By definition, developers can build parallel phases in any order, or simultaneously. They are not temporally dependent. An example might be "Housing Block A" and "Housing Block B" fronting roads providing simultaneous access to both sites. The developer might choose to build both phases simultaneously if the housing market is very strong, making it likely to sell the combined quantity of houses sufficiently quickly. Or, the developer could choose to first build Housing Block A and hold off on starting House Block B until later (or vice versa). This would be prudent if the housing market seems just strong enough to absorb rapidly only one of the two phases' buildings.

With sequential phases, on the other hand, there is a temporal order and dependency between the phases. We *cannot* start "Phase 2" until we have at least started "Phase 1" and have taken it to some stage of completion. Perhaps we cannot start Phase 2 until Phase 1 is physically complete, or possibly near full operation. (The former situation suggests physical dependency, while the latter suggests economic dependency.) A physical reason for sequencing might be that you can't get to the site of Phase 2 until at least the infrastructure of Phase 1 is complete. An economic reason might be that a planned retail center may not be viable until the surrounding housing units fill up and provide the necessary market for the retail center.

In terms of analysis and valuation methodology, parallel and sequential phases require different approaches. We should model:

- Parallel projects either as separate, independent projects, or else as horizontal expansion options; and
- Sequential phases as compound options—that is, options on options. We show how to simulate sequential phasing in Chapter 22, in which we explore the phasing option in more depth with a numerical example.

15.6   Recognizing Defensive and Offensive Options in Simulation Results

Offensive and defensive options each lead to different types of results in terms of their impact on the nature of the risk and return performance faced by investors in the project. The difference shows up dramatically in simulation analysis, in the shape of the target curves representing the distribution of possible future performance outcomes of investments.

As we described in Chapter 8, target curves provide a useful way to visualize the output from a Monte Carlo simulation. They depict either the cumulative or frequency distribution of the simulation results for a metric of interest to investors, such as NPV or IRR.

The target curves output by a simulation typically reveal interesting characteristics of the types of flexibilities that we have been describing. Most notably, the way the flexibility affects the shape of the target curve reveals the extent to which it is essentially a defensive or offensive option (or perhaps both). With the target metric on the horizontal axis (such as NPV or IRR), and probability on the vertical axis, defensive options truncate the left-hand tail of the target curve—they cut the downside. Conversely, offensive options extend outward to the right the right-hand tail—they boost the upside. Either of these changes will work to increase the mean of the distribution of possible outcomes— in effect, the ex-ante mean. A pure defensive option, such as a delay option, which only truncates the left-hand tail, will also reduce the standard deviation or dispersion in the possible project outcomes, which is usually viewed as reducing the investment risk (particularly when the target metric is the IRR).

The timing options described in this chapter largely tend to be defensive. The product options described in the previous chapter tend to be more offensive. Some types of flexibilities, such as the product mix flexibility described in Section 14.3, can move the

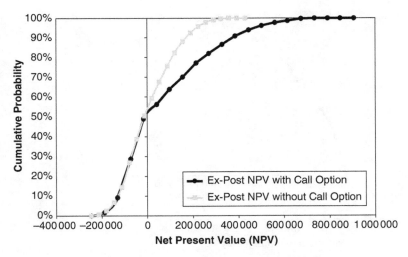

Figure 15.2a General effect of "call" options on development project as seen in cumulative target curves.

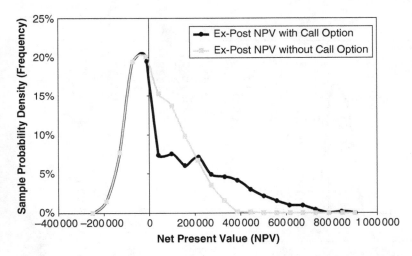

Figure 15.2b General effect of "call" options on development project as seen in frequency target curves.

entire target curve to the right. (Recall that the product type switching option can be viewed simultaneously as a call on one alternative and a put on the other.)

Using generic output from an example simulation, we can illustrate the characteristic differences in target curves between defensive (put) and offensive (call) options. Figures 15.2a and 15.2b indicate call option type flexibility as seen in both the cumulative and frequency target curves (for the same simulated outcomes). Figure 15.2a is the cumulative curve, and Figure 15.2b is the frequency curve. You see how the call option shifts the performance distribution to the right in the better outcomes, increasing the chance of better outcomes, making greater upside possible for the project.

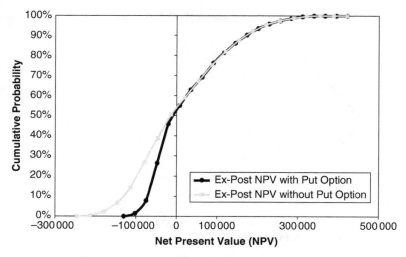

Figure 15.3a General effect of "put" options on development project as seen in cumulative target curves.

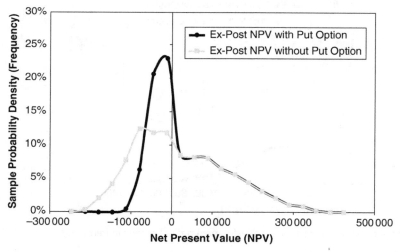

Figure 15.3b General effect of "put" options on development project as seen in frequency target curves.

Complementarily, Figures 15.3a and 15.3b indicate put option type flexibility, again seen in both the cumulative and frequency target curves. Here, you can see how the put option protects and chops off the downside, shifting the left-hand tails of the curves to the right. Defensive flexibility enables performance outcomes in the downside scenarios that are not as bad as without flexibility.

15.7   Conclusion

This chapter presented the several types of timing flexibility in development projects: start delay, modular production, and phasing (in both parallel and sequential forms). It sets the scene for our demonstration in the remaining chapters of how we can analyze each of these types of flexibilities.

We also suggested some perspectives that can be incisive for building useful intuition about flexibility, including how target curves of investment performance produced by simulation analysis can explain the concept of defensive and offensive options.

In the following chapter, we will introduce an example development project, patterned on an actual project in the real world, that will allow us to demonstrate, at a more concrete and realistic level, how we can simulate real estate development project flexibility value for the various types of options described in this and the preceding chapters.

16

Garden City: An Example Multi-Asset Development Project

We Present the Traditional DCF Valuation Spreadsheet Model
for the Example Development Project We use in the Rest of Book

---

LEARNING OBJECTIVES

- See example spreadsheet DCF model of a development project that produces multiple assets over several periods of time;
- Understand how to deal with the timing of the development process;
- Understand how to deal with flow of revenues from several assets over time;
- Consider the base case evaluation of the overall project;
- See assessment of project economics, including OCC and NPV.

OUTLINE OF THE CHAPTER

16.1 Overview of Multi-Asset Development Project
16.2 Structure of a Realistic Multi-Asset Spreadsheet Pro Forma
16.3 Cash Flows for the Example Pro Forma
16.4 Temporal Profile for Base Case
16.5 Expected Economics of the Garden City Project
16.6 Conclusion

Chapters 11 and 12 introduced the basic economics of real estate development. They covered the essential elements of investments in development projects: land commitment, time-to-build, forward purchase, leverage, uncertainty, and flexibility. They also showed how flexibility can add value to such projects. But the example in Chapter 12, though intuitive, was quite simplistic. We need to see how to evaluate flexibility to manage uncertainty in more realistic situations.

This chapter introduces and explains a pro forma spreadsheet model of a realistic development project, which will enable us to explore and estimate the value of flexibility in subsequent chapters for a project that produces multiple assets over several periods. Although simplified, the project and its spreadsheet DCF model are complex enough to demonstrate important basic points about modeling and valuing flexibility. Furthermore, we have noted that simplification is part of the art of simulation analysis. We think that the balance of simplicity and complexity in the example case introduced in this chapter may be about right to aim for in many practical simulation analyses. The example introduced here will enable us in subsequent chapters to quantitatively explore

Flexibility and Real Estate Valuation under Uncertainty: A Practical Guide for Developers, First Edition.
David Geltner and Richard de Neufville.
© 2018 John Wiley & Sons Ltd. Published 2018 by John Wiley & Sons Ltd.
Companion website: www.wiley.com/go/geltner-deneufville/flexibility-and-real-estate-valuation

the types of flexibilities that we introduced in Chapters 14 and 15. The project, which we call "Garden City," is a simplified representation of an actual, typical, medium-scale housing development project.

16.1 Overview of Multi-Asset Development Project

Garden City is an upscale, urban housing development project. Its base plan design is to produce 850 for-sale residences of two types—some in high-rise buildings, and some in townhouse-style, single-family homes. Developers expect a market consisting of wealthy households wanting to buy high-quality housing units. Figure 16.1 shows the project. The land site covers $106\ 000\,\text{m}^2$ (or 10.6 hectares, equivalent to 26 acres).

We assume that developers have agreed to buy the permitted land site for the project for \$200 M. However, we do not necessarily assume that this value is exactly the current market value of the site. (In other words, as is typical, at the given price, the NPV of the project net of the land price might not be exactly zero.)

The Garden City project has an overall density of approximately 2.0 floor area ratio (FAR). This implies approximately $212\ 500\,\text{m}^2$ floor area of built space, not including

Figure 16.1 Concept of the Garden City project.

basement space and underground parking garage areas in a platform that will cover the entire site. Consistent with the intended market, the housing units in Garden City are large, averaging $250\,m^2$ (approximately $2500\,ft^2$).

16.2 Structure of a Realistic Multi-Asset Spreadsheet Pro Forma

Let's now begin to walk through the project pro forma so that you understand in some depth both the:

- Mechanics of a multi-asset development project DCF spreadsheet; and
- Economics of the Garden City project.

This will be worth your while, as we use this example project for most of the remainder of this book.

The pro forma in Table 16.1 represents the base plan and the base case DCF for the Garden City project. Our example analysis considers the project from Time 0 (the end of "Year 0" or beginning of "Year 1"). This lets us explore the consideration of flexibility during the planning process, involving the design, evaluation, and investment decision phase of the project.

The "base case" refers to the best, unbiased estimates of the project cash flow expectations as of Time 0. This is reflected in the Table 16.1 pro forma underlying the investment decision analysis for the project. It is comparable to the single-stream DCF pro formas we discussed in the previous chapters.

We use the terms "base case" and "base plan" somewhat interchangeably. However, the "plan" focuses more on the timing of the construction quantities, while the "case" focuses more on the net cash flow expectations. In any case, the two are tightly interconnected.

This pro forma for multi-asset development differs from the pro formas presented earlier in this book in an important respect. In addition to presenting the cash flows of the project, it displays the planned timing of the different physical elements associated with the development. It shows how the developers plan to produce the 850 housing units over 9 years (although they will complete almost all the units within 7 years). To make it easier to read the pro forma, we have differentially shaded these elements in the computer spreadsheet table:

- The physical amounts of real estate products are the lighter shaded rows; and
- The implied cash flows are the darker shaded rows.

The project involves three types of construction:

- *Infrastructure*—including the underground platform containing the parking garage and basement shells; and
- *Two types of housing products*—high-rise and townhouse. For pedagogical purposes, to allow greater generality, we label them simply as "Type A" and "Type B," and we make them exactly equal in planned quantity (to help facilitate drawing general conclusions—for example, about the value of a switching option—although, in the real world, the exact quantities of the two types would likely differ).

Table 16.1 Pro forma base plan and base case for Garden City.

#	EX ANTE PRO-FORMA PRICE FACTORS	UNITS	TOTALS	YEAR 0	YEAR 1	YEAR 2	YEAR 3	YEAR 4	YEAR 5	YEAR 6	YEAR 7	YEAR 8	YEAR 9	YEAR 10	YEAR 11
	Type A			$1.000	$1.020	$1.040	$1.061	$1.082	$1.104	$1.126	$1.149	$1.172	$1.195	$1.219	$1.243
	Type B			$1.000	$1.020	$1.040	$1.061	$1.082	$1.104	$1.126	$1.149	$1.172	$1.195	$1.219	$1.243
	Construction Cost			$1.000	$1.020	$1.040	$1.061	$1.082	$1.104	$1.126	$1.149	$1.172	$1.195	$1.219	$1.243
	Product Mix: Type A Units Proportion			0.500	0.500	0.500	0.500	0.500	0.500	0.500	0.500	0.500	0.500	0.500	0.500
	DEVELOPMENT PROJECT PLAN	**UNITS**	**TOTALS**	**YEAR 0**	**YEAR 1**	**YEAR 2**	**YEAR 3**	**YEAR 4**	**YEAR 5**	**YEAR 6**	**YEAR 7**	**YEAR 8**	**YEAR 9**	**YEAR 10**	**YEAR 11**
1	Total Sold	Residences	850		144	392	138	96	62	10	8	0	0	0	0
2	Land Cost	USD '000s		$200,000											
3	Infrastructure Quantities	Residence Equivalent	240		80	80	80	0	0	0	0	0	0	0	0
4	Infrastructure Construction Costs	USD '000s	$156,080		$51,000	$52,020	$53,060	$0	$0	$0	$0	$0	$0	$0	$0
5	**Type A**														
6	Total Sold	Residences	425		72	196	69	48	31	5	4	0	0	0	0
7	Total Started	Residences	425		0	72	196	69	48	31	5	4	0	0	0
8	Total Completed	Residences	425		0	0	72	196	69	48	31	5	4	0	0
9	Type A Revenues	USD '000s	$558,738		$30,600	$115,566	$146,076	$137,124	$66,419	$38,256	$18,522	$4,261	$1,914	$0	$0
10	Type A Construction Costs	USD '000s	$287,806		$0	$23,409	$88,876	$89,639	$40,368	$27,802	$12,923	$3,295	$1,494	$0	$0
11	Type A Profits	USD '000s	$270,932		$30,600	$92,157	$57,200	$47,485	$26,051	$10,454	$5,599	$965	$421	$0	$0
12	**Type B**														
13	Total Sold	Residences	425		72	196	69	48	31	5	4	0	0	0	0
14	Total Started	Residences	425		0	72	196	69	48	31	5	4	0	0	0
15	Total Completed	Residences	425		0	0	72	196	69	48	31	5	4	0	0
16	Type B Revenues	USD '000s	$558,738		$30,600	$115,566	$146,076	$137,124	$66,419	$38,256	$18,522	$4,261	$1,914	$0	$0
17	Type B Construction Costs	USD '000s	$287,806		$0	$23,409	$88,876	$89,639	$40,368	$27,802	$12,923	$3,295	$1,494	$0	$0
18	Type B Profits	USD '000s	$270,932		$30,600	$92,157	$57,200	$47,485	$26,051	$10,454	$5,599	$965	$421	$0	$0
19	Net Annual Cash Flows	USD '000s	$385,784	-$200,000	$10,200	$132,294	$61,339	$94,971	$52,103	$20,907	$11,198	$1,931	$841	$0	$0
20	NPV @ 18.0% Discount Rate		$24,711												
21	IRR		22.57%												
22	**Project Economics**		**Time 0 PV**												
23	Built Asset Revenues		$882,588 =PV[V]		$61,200	$231,132	$292,151	$274,249	$132,839	$76,512	$37,043	$8,521	$3,829	$0	$0
24	Construction Costs		$657,910 =PV[K]		$51,000	$98,838	$230,813	$179,278	$80,736	$55,604	$25,845	$6,591	$2,988	$0	$0
25	Implied Land Market Value		$224,678 =PV[V]-PV[K]												
26	Implied Mkt OCC (as IRR)		18.01% =PV[v]-PV[K]	-$224,678	$10,200	$132,294	$61,339	$94,971	$52,103	$20,907	$11,198	$1,931	$841	$0	$0

"Infrastructure" is the construction necessary to begin the project. It includes the various components relating to the service and underground platform of the site. Developers must start the infrastructure before any construction of the housing buildout can begin. However, they do not need to complete the infrastructure entirely before the housing construction can start. According to the base plan, infrastructure construction is to occur during the first 3 years of the project in equal amounts per year. In terms of the quantity units of construction, our example spreadsheet accounts for all construction in approximate equivalents of the finished housing space. This is a simplification to aid our use of the example for pedagogical purposes. By this measure, the total required infrastructure amounts to 240 housing units worth of construction, and thus Table 16.1 shows 80 units of infrastructure built in each of Years 1, 2, and 3.

The base plan projects the production of an equal amount of each type of housing, built on the same schedule. The developer can build either type of housing product on the same underground platform, but the two types are physically different. They are thus likely to appeal to somewhat different markets of buyers. These two markets are positively correlated, but they are not identical. If the market for Type A housing is strong, the market for Type B housing will probably also be strong, and vice versa, but not necessarily. When we come to dealing with uncertainty, we can expect that the quantity and timing of their demand, sales, and construction will tend to differ.

The base plan projects Year 2 as the start of the construction for both Type A and Type B housing. This is 1 year after the start of construction for the infrastructure, and before its completion. As the spreadsheet indicates, it projects the start of 72 units of housing of each type for Year 2, another 196 are to begin in Year 3, and so on. The base plan anticipates a total production of 425 units of each type of housing in the complete project by the end of Year 9.

16.3 Cash Flows for the Example Pro Forma

For our illustrative purposes, we assume simplified, stylized projections of revenues and costs in the base case pro forma. As of Time 0, the estimates are for expected average:

- Construction costs of $625 000 per housing unit or equivalent; and
- Sales revenues from the housing of $1 250 000 per unit.

The base case pro forma projects all revenues and costs to grow at 2% each year for all types of construction and housing. It thus projects the cost of the planned 80 housing units (equivalent) of infrastructure construction in Year 1 to be $51 M, as in row 4 of the Table 16.1 pro forma. This is found as:

$$Infrastructure\ Cost\ in\ Year\ 1 = 80\left[\$0.625M(1.02)\right] = \$51M \qquad (16.1)$$

The extra 2% is because Year 1 is 1 year in the future as compared to the Year 0 pricing estimation base year.

The sales process works as follows. The developer sells units in a given year at the then prevailing price. Customers pay for the unit in three equal annual installments. The developer starts construction in the year after the sale, and completes those units in the following year. Thus, for any given housing unit whose sale happens in Year t,

Table 16.2 Extract from Garden City pro forma.

ROWS	ELEMENT	YEAR 1	YEAR 2	YEAR 3
6	Total Quantity Sold	72	196	69
7	Total Quantity Started	0	72	196
8	Total Quantity Completed	0	0	72
9	Type A Revenues	$30,600	$115,556	$146,076
10	Type A Construction Costs	0	$23,409	$88,876
11	Type A Profits	$30,600	$92,157	$57,200

its construction would start in Year t+1 and end in Year t+2. Construction is thus ongoing, and the developer incurs construction costs for the units sold during Years t+1 and t+2.

The developer receives revenue from the sale equally across all 3 years. The purchaser pays one-third of the unit price:

- Up front as a pre-construction deposit in Year t;
- Upon construction commencement in Year t+1; and
- Upon completion in Year t+2.

Thus, the revenues from pre-sales at least partly finance the construction. This is common of such projects in emerging market countries, but may also occur in mature economies. It lowers the debt burden or equity cash investment for the developer.

The developer is contractually bound to start and complete construction in Years t+1 and t+2, respectively, for any unit sold in Year t. Thus, for example, we see that the pro forma projects (starting in lines 5 and 12) the:

- Sale of 72 units each of Type A and Type B in Year 1;
- Start of their construction in Year 2; and their
- Completion in Year 3.

Now let's see how this works out in detail in the pro forma. To make the discussion easier to follow, we have extracted relevant portions from the spreadsheet and presented them in Table 16.2. This refers to Type A housing, whose projections are identical to those for Type B housing.

The projected sale of 72 units of Type A housing in Year 1 ultimately generates revenues of:

$$Sale\ of\ Type\ A\ housing\ in\ Year\ 1 : 72\big[\$1.25M(1.02)\big] = \$91.8M \tag{16.2}$$

This revenue will arrive one-third ($30.6M) each in Years 1, 2, and 3. We can see this amount in row 9 under Year 1. As with the infrastructure costs, the 1.02 factor reflects 1 year of projected price growth to Year 1. This average price of [$1.25M(1.02)] applies to all units sold in Year 1, and hence to the revenue received from them across all 3 years—including the latter 2 years, by which time the then-current new-sale price may have changed for the units sold later.

In Year 2, the projected sale of Type A units will ultimately generate:

$$Sale\ of\ Type\ A\ houses\ in\ Year\ 2 = 196\big[\$1.25M(1.02)^2\big] = \$254.898M \tag{16.3}$$

The buyers will pay one-third of this ($84.966 M) in Year 2. Thus, the:

$$Total\ Type\ A\ revenue\ for\ Year\ 2 = \$84.966M + \$30.6M = \$115.566M \qquad (16.4)$$

This is indicated in row 9 under Year 2.

The construction costs for the Type A units each year are in row 10. In Year 1, there is no cost, because no housing units are yet under construction. (The project is incurring construction costs in Year 1 for infrastructure, as noted earlier, indicated in row 4 of Table 16.1.) The cost of the housing units sold in Year 1 start in Year 2. We assume that housing construction costs occur equally in the 2 years required for each unit's construction. Construction costs occur according to the price level prevailing whenever the construction occurs. Unlike the prices for housing, a sales contract does not lock in cost of construction. Thus, for the 72 units of Type A housing construction occurring in Year 2, half of their total per-unit construction cost of $625,000(1.02)^2$ will occur in that year:

$$Housing\ construction\ cost, Year\ 2 = \frac{72\left[\$625\,000\left(1.02\right)^2\right]}{2} = \$23.409\ M \qquad (16.5)$$

This is indicated in Table 16.2, row 10, under Year 2. The construction cost for Year 2 is multiplied by the 1.02^2 factor, because there is 2 years' worth of price appreciation between the Time 0 pricing base year and Year 2. The construction cost for Year 3 will be subject to a 1.02^3 growth factor.

The overall bottom-line net cash flow for the project, within each year, reflects:

- Installment revenues received from sales of Type A and Type B houses;
- Minus the construction costs for the number of housing units of each type actually under construction during that year; and
- Minus any infrastructure construction costs still occurring during the year.

Thus, for example, looking at the project's bottom-line net cash flow in row 19 of the full spreadsheet (Table 16.1), we have, for Year 2, the expectation of $132.294 M, found as the sum of the:

- Net revenue from the sales of Type A housing, a profit of $92.157 M;
- Plus the equal projection for the Type B housing;
- Minus the $52.020 M infrastructure construction cost;
- To arrive at the net bottom line of $132.294 M.

16.4 Temporal Profile for Base Case

It is informative to recognize the distribution of effort and cash flows over time. We can pull this information out easily from the pro forma and display it in bar charts.

Figure 16.2a presents the pro forma temporal profile (schedule) of construction quantities for the project—the base plan. It shows the planned annual amount of project construction for the base plan each year. This temporal profile is typical of many multi-asset housing development projects. The quantity of construction usually starts slowly and builds rapidly up to a peak in the early/middle part of the project, and then

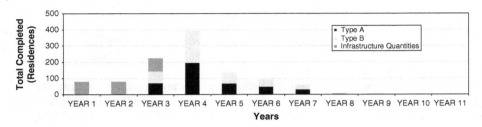

Figure 16.2a Pro forma temporal profile of project construction.

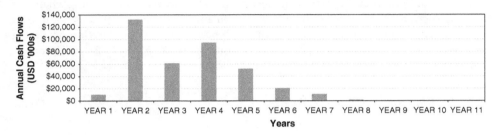

Figure 16.2b Expected net cash flow gross of land cost.

tails off toward the end. (We consider other temporal profiles in Chapter 23.) The chart indicates the three different types of physical construction: infrastructure, and Type A and Type B housing. As noted, the base plan envisions equal quantities and timing for the two types of housing.

The physical production profile of the base plan underlies and determines the temporal profile of cash flow in the base case of Figure 16.2b. This consists of the installment sales revenues minus the current production costs, including for infrastructure in the early years. The cash flow profile differs a bit from the physical production profile for two reasons. Partial revenues from installment plan sales anticipate the cost of construction of the housing by a year and evens out the corresponding revenues over 3 years, while the construction costs occur only over the latter 2 years. We must also subtract out infrastructure costs during the early years. Nevertheless, the expected cash flow profile in the pro forma follows the physical production profile approximately.

16.5 Expected Economics of the Garden City Project

We can analyze the investment economics of the Garden City project in the manner we described in Chapter 11. The idea is to calculate the implied value of the initial investment in the site, and thus to estimate the NPV and OCC for the development investment.

We are assuming that the Garden City project is the highest and best use (HBU) of the site, and that the project is "ripe" for immediate development. (This means that it makes sense to exercise now at Time 0 the development call option as described in Chapter 12, rather than holding the land site for future speculation.)

In this case, the implied value of the land is the difference between the present values of the development assets and of the construction costs, in both cases discounted at appropriate rates reflecting the risk of the cash flows. For illustrative purposes, we continue to assume the same OCC that we employed in Chapter 11—that is, we use annual rates of 7% for built assets (the housing units once completed), and 3% for construction costs. Applying these discount rates to the Garden City project, we obtain the following results (see Time 0 present values in lines 23–25 in Table 16.1):

- Present value of housing sales (rows 9 and 16 of pro forma) = $882.588 M (row 23). This is the present value of the "benefit" of the project, of the real estate assets to be produced, controlling for time and investment risk (presenting the 7% expected return).
- Present value of construction cost (rows 4, 10, and 17) = $657.910 M (row 24). This is the present value of the opportunity cost of the construction investment, controlling for time and risk—that is, the present value of the "cost" of the project (discounted at 3%), not including the land cost.
- The implied value of the land is then: $224.678 M = 882.588 M – 657.910 M. For Garden City, this is the maximum bid price that a developer could pay for the land to achieve a project NPV of at least zero. This is the equivalent of the amount defined in Equation 11.4. Assuming the developer is typical of the most competitive developers for this type of project, then this amount would be the market value of the land, as it provides the developer with sufficient expected returns, considering the investment risk involved. (For example, we saw in the simple example in Chapter 11 that this implied an expected return on the development project of 15% per annum.)

We do not need to know the OCC rate for the development project itself in order to compute this NPV and land valuation, provided we know the OCC rates for the benefits and costs of the built real estate assets and the construction costs (7% and 3% in our case). However, once we have computed the project Time 0 valuation as discussed in the preceding text, we can then "back out" the implied OCC rate for the project. This is the internal rate of return (IRR) that we calculate from the implied valuation of the land and the project's future net cash flow expectations (row 26 in Table 16.1). For Garden City, this is 18.01%.

Typical industry practice employs a slightly different procedure. It posits an OCC rate for the development project, often as an ex-ante "hurdle rate," to be achieved in order for the project to be considered worthwhile. In principle, such a hurdle rate should equal the OCC rate that we just computed, in terms of a going-in IRR expectation, given a price for the land. For a project like Garden City, a hurdle rate of 18% would indeed be reasonable. In the Table 16.1 pro forma, we assumed an 18.00% hurdle rate to obtain the project NPV of $24.711 M (row 20, Time 0). This positive NPV represents a gain over the given land price of $200 M. We can view this as indicating that the $200 M price for the land is modestly below its market value. (It could be that the price was negotiated earlier, when expectations were lower, or before some value had been added to the site by the developer's actions—such as production of project designs and obtaining of land assemblage and construction approvals—the costs of which are now sunk.)

An alternative interpretation of the positive NPV is that the developers of Garden City are uniquely able to design and profitably execute the best possible development for this land site. In that case, they need not share with the landowner all of the added value that they can uniquely create on the site. This difference, the positive NPV from a market value perspective, provides the developers with a modest "super-normal" profit (sometimes referred to by economists as "entrepreneurial profit").

Putting this into perspective, the super-normal profit here is relatively modest. The $24.7 M is only about 12% of the land price, or less than 3% of the gross PV of the project benefits. Row 21 in Table 16.1 provides another way of seeing this. The IRR for the project at the $200 M land price is about 22.6%, modestly higher than the posited 18% economic OCC hurdle rate.

16.6 Conclusion

This chapter presented the spreadsheet DCF valuation model of the typical example multi-asset development project that we use in subsequent chapters to demonstrate the modeling of uncertainty, and the valuation of flexibility for such a project. The model and discussion in this chapter are typical of current best practice in the real estate development industry.

We also discussed the basic economics of the project at the level of a traditional, single-stream DCF pro forma analysis, consistent with the presentation in Chapter 11 (focusing on unbiased expectations and market valuations).

17

Effect of Uncertainty without Flexibility in Development Project Evaluation

We Re-analyze the Garden City Project by Reflecting Uncertainty Without Flexibility

---

LEARNING OBJECTIVES

- Understand how to model uncertainty in multi-asset development projects using pricing factors;
- Understand the valuation of development projects under uncertainty;
- Discover how real estate pricing probability and dynamics inputs impact simulated project performance without flexibility.

OUTLINE OF THE CHAPTER

17.1 Modeling Uncertainty for the Multi-Asset Development Project
17.2 Generating Random Future Scenarios
17.3 Outcomes Reflecting Uncertainty for the Multi-Asset Development
17.4 Effect of Different Probability Inputs Assumptions
17.5 Conclusion

While the preceding chapter provides a good description of current best practice in the analysis of multi-asset real estate developments, that analysis is incomplete. Current best practice does not sufficiently or explicitly consider the uncertainty and flexibility that exist in reality. The Garden City pro forma and DCF evaluation reflect a single-stream cash flow model analogous to that described for an existing rental asset in Chapters 1 and 2. Its single cash flow projection represents, at best, the expectation of future cash flows from the project. Table 16.1 is merely the ex-ante mean of the future outcome probability distributions governing the possible ex-post investment performance of the project. These average values do not reveal the range of uncertain outcomes that could happen; they do not fully reflect actual uncertainty.

This chapter improves the DCF pro forma–based spreadsheet for Garden City. It builds on the basic model and analysis to reflect uncertainty explicitly. We do this using Monte Carlo simulation, as introduced in Chapter 6. This is the first step toward allowing us to value flexibility in the development project. We first realistically introduce uncertainty into the traditional model without flexibility. Then, starting in the next chapter, we will also include flexibility. To build your intuition, it is useful to start with an understanding of the effect of uncertainty without flexibility. Then you will be able to see better the effect of flexibility itself.

Flexibility and Real Estate Valuation under Uncertainty: A Practical Guide for Developers, First Edition.
David Geltner and Richard de Neufville.
© 2018 John Wiley & Sons Ltd. Published 2018 by John Wiley & Sons Ltd.
Companion website: www.wiley.com/go/geltner-deneufville/flexibility-and-real-estate-valuation

The model and results discussed in this chapter thus provide a benchmark for valuing flexibility in multi-asset real estate developments. The following five chapters show how to do that for the various types of flexibilities that we described in Chapters 14 and 15.

17.1 Modeling Uncertainty for the Multi-Asset Development Project

We model uncertainty for multi-asset projects along the lines presented in Chapter 7, using pricing factors to represent uncertainty in the future values that matter. The main difference is that we should recognize that each of the assets in the project might reflect different pricing dynamics.

Recall that pricing factors are ratios that represent deviations from the ex-ante expectations of cash flow values that are in the base case pro forma. In the case of the Garden City project, the base case pro forma is the single-stream cash flow projection presented in Table 16.1 (reproduced in the top part of Table 17.1). We apply pricing factors to the base plan using Equation 7.1:

Future Scenario Cash Flow Outcome = (*unbiased pro forma cash flow*)×(*pricing factor*)

$$(7.1)$$

We use the computer to generate a set of pricing factors to represent a future scenario for the project—a possible "future history" of how the relevant real estate markets could evolve, as reflected in relevant prices. Analysts base the pricing factors on probability distributions and dynamical assumptions as described in Chapter 7 (such as cyclicality, to reflect what they know and believe about the markets and costs relevant for the project; see the Appendix at the end of the book for more depth).

In the case of multi-asset development projects, we generally need to have different pricing factors for each of the important assets and construction processes. This is because these are likely to vary independently to a degree. For example, when the real estate market goes up, the demand for larger residences might increase faster than the demand for smaller units—and vice versa when the market goes down. Technically speaking, it is unlikely that the future realizations of uncertainties in different real estate markets are perfectly correlated, although they are likely to be positively correlated.

In the Garden City project example, we have three major different elements in terms of markets, and therefore in terms of price dynamics. These elements are the:

- Market for Type A housing;
- Market for Type B housing; and
- Cost of construction (which reflects the construction market and the project).

We therefore generate three different, separate series of pricing factors for each future scenario—one for each of these three elements.

We need to exercise judgment in developing pricing factors for the different elements of a complex project. As we have already noted, an important principle in simulation modeling is the desirability of keeping the model sufficiently simple. We don't want to lose sight of the forest for the trees! So, we try to focus only on the most

Table 17.1 Garden City base case (top) and example random future scenario pricing factors and resulting outcome (bottom).

		UNITS	TOTALS	YEAR 0	YEAR 1	YEAR 2	YEAR 3	YEAR 4	YEAR 5	YEAR 6	YEAR 7	YEAR 8	YEAR 9	YEAR 10	YEAR 11
	PROJECT BASE CASE														
1	Total Sold	Residences	850		144	392	138	96	62	10	8	0	0	0	0
2	Land Cost	USD '000s		$200,000											
3	Infrastructure Quantities	Residence Equivalent	240												
4	Infrastructure Construction Costs	USD '000s	$156,080		$51,000	$52,020	$53,060	$0	$0	$0	$0	$0	$0	$0	$0
5	**Type A**														
6	Total Sold	Residences	425		72	196	69	48	31	5	4	0	0	0	0
7	Total Started	Residences	425		0	72	196	69	48	31	5	4	0	0	0
8	Total Completed	Residences	425		0	0	72	196	69	48	31	5	4	0	0
9	Type A Revenues	USD '000s	$558,738		$30,600	$115,566	$146,076	$137,124	$66,419	$38,256	$18,522	$4,261	$1,914	$0	$0
10	Type A Construction Costs	USD '000s	$287,806		$0	$23,409	$88,876	$89,639	$40,368	$27,802	$12,923	$3,295	$1,494	$0	$0
11	Type A Profits	USD '000s	$270,932		$30,600	$92,157	$57,200	$47,485	$26,051	$10,454	$5,599	$965	$421	$0	$0
12	**Type B**														
13	Total Sold	Residences	425		72	196	69	48	31	5	4	0	0	0	0
14	Total Started	Residences	425		0	72	196	69	48	31	5	4	0	0	0
15	Total Completed	Residences	425		0	0	72	196	69	48	31	5	4	0	0
16	Type B Revenues	USD '000s	$558,738		$30,600	$115,566	$146,076	$137,124	$66,419	$38,256	$18,522	$4,261	$1,914	$0	$0
17	Type B Construction Costs	USD '000s	$287,806		$0	$23,409	$88,876	$89,639	$40,368	$27,802	$12,923	$3,295	$1,494	$0	$0
18	Type B Profits	USD '000s	$270,932		$30,600	$92,157	$57,200	$47,485	$26,051	$10,454	$5,599	$965	$421	$0	$0
19	Net Annual Cash Flows	USD '000s	$385,784	-$200,000	$10,200	$132,294	$61,339	$94,971	$52,103	$20,907	$11,198	$1,931	$841	$0	$0
20	NPV @ 0.0% Discount Rate	USD '000s	$24,711												
21	IRR		22.6%												

EX POST PRO-FORMA PRICE FACTORS

	YEAR 0	YEAR 1	YEAR 2	YEAR 3	YEAR 4	YEAR 5	YEAR 6	YEAR 7	YEAR 8	YEAR 9	YEAR 10	YEAR 11
Type A	0.797	0.801	0.920	1.112	1.187	1.281	0.823	0.597	0.604	0.596	0.651	0.664
Type B	0.801	1.207	1.087	1.316	1.382	1.304	0.932	0.686	0.629	0.649	0.710	0.804
Construction Cost	1.029	1.108	0.995	0.968	0.941	1.070	0.955	1.109	1.014	1.013	0.917	1.001
Product Mix: Type A Units Proportion	0.500	0.500	0.500	0.500	0.500	0.500	0.500	0.500	0.500	0.500	0.500	0.500

		UNITS	TOTALS	YEAR 0	YEAR 1	YEAR 2	YEAR 3	YEAR 4	YEAR 5	YEAR 6	YEAR 7	YEAR 8	YEAR 9	YEAR 10	YEAR 11
	PROJECT OUTCOME (SCENARIO)														
1	Total Sold	Residences	850		144	392	138	96	62	10	8	0	0	0	0
2	Land Cost	USD '000s		$200,000											
3	Infrastructure Quantities	Residence Equivalent	240												
4	Infrastructure Construction Costs	USD '000s	$159,612		$56,492	$51,766	$51,354	$0	$0	$0	$0	$0	$0	$0	$0
5	**Type A**														
6	Total Sold	Residences	425		72	196	69	48	31	5	4	0	0	0	0
7	Total Started	Residences	425		0	72	196	69	48	31	5	4	0	0	0
8	Total Completed	Residences	425		0	0	72	196	69	48	31	5	4	0	0
9	Type A Revenues	USD '000s	$572,580		$31,733	$109,886	$143,808	$137,780	$77,901	$45,909	$21,347	$3,073	$1,142	$0	$0
10	Type A Construction Costs	USD '000s	$282,551		$0	$23,295	$86,018	$84,323	$43,176	$26,549	$14,337	$3,340	$1,513	$0	$0
11	Type A Profits	USD '000s	$290,028		$31,733	$86,591	$57,791	$53,456	$34,724	$19,360	$7,010	-$267	-$371	$0	$0
12	**Type B**														
13	Total Sold	Residences	425		72	196	69	48	31	5	4	0	0	0	0
14	Total Started	Residences	425		0	72	196	69	48	31	5	4	0	0	0
15	Total Completed	Residences	425		0	0	72	196	69	48	31	5	4	0	0
16	Type B Revenues	USD '000s	$664,387		$36,936	$129,295	$169,447	$162,437	$88,668	$50,703	$22,090	$3,500	$1,313	$0	$0
17	Type B Construction Costs	USD '000s	$282,551		$0	$23,295	$86,018	$84,323	$43,176	$26,549	$14,337	$3,340	$1,513	$0	$0
18	Type B Profits	USD '000s	$381,836		$36,936	$106,000	$83,429	$78,114	$45,492	$24,154	$7,753	$160	-$201	$0	$0
19	Net Annual Cash Flows	USD '000s	$512,252	-$200,000	$12,176	$140,825	$89,966	$131,570	$80,216	$43,514	$14,763	-$107	-$572	$0	$0
20	NPV @ 18.0% Discount Rate	USD '000s	$89,674												
21	IRR		32.6%												

important elements. For example, in the case of Garden City, we model only a single pricing factor series to apply to all three different types of construction—the infrastructure and the two types of housing. In effect, we assume that a single construction market exists for all three types, which seems reasonable. We thus generate only three sets of pricing factors, each set corresponding to one of the three elements listed in the previous paragraph.

We generate the pricing factors for Type A and Type B housing based on probability distributions that reflect typical real estate market price dynamics common to both types of housing. Additionally, the pricing factors for each type will include some independent elements to reflect "idiosyncratic" risk and sub-market-specific pricing. Thus, the pricing deviations from the pro forma assumptions will tend to be positively—but not perfectly—correlated between Type A and Type B housing. In some scenarios, the market for Type A will be up when the market for Type B is down, and vice versa.

The price dynamics for construction costs are generally rather different from those of real estate assets. This is reflected in the fact that the OCC for construction costs is usually lower than that for real estate investments (see Section 11.2). Construction price indices are typically much more stable than real estate price indices, and only slightly correlated with them. This might be less true in rapidly urbanizing, emerging market countries, where real estate development might represent a large share of the national aggregate demand for basic materials such as steel and concrete and for basic unskilled labor. Nevertheless, even in such circumstances, it is likely that construction costs are far less volatile than real estate prices, and not very highly correlated with them. This is what we assume in our analysis of the Garden City project.

17.2   Generating Random Future Scenarios

Table 17.1 contrasts the single-stream pro forma for the Garden City base case with the results from a single randomly generated future scenario. The top panel is the base plan and base case pro forma, exactly as we presented in Table 16.1. The bottom panel shows one random result of applying pricing factors to this base case.

Note that the base plan projects a fixed schedule of construction, unit sales, and completions spanning from Year 1 through Year 9. Because we are not yet modeling any flexibility in the timing or product of the project, we are maintaining this base plan schedule for the production of housing units in any future scenario.

But there is uncertainty in the future real estate markets, as revealed by the pricing factors. These derive from the random number generation process in the spreadsheet. The middle part of Table 17.1 shows one set of these factors, representing a single scenario. It presents three series of pricing factors—corresponding to construction costs, and Type A and Type B housing. Each series reflects the randomly generated pricing factors for each of the 9 years in the base plan. Each pricing factor reflects some independent, purely random element, but also reflects both stochastic (random realizations generated across time) and deterministic systematic effects across time (such as cycles), as well as the correlations between the markets. For example, returns (changes) for one market in one period may contain elements of returns from other periods or other markets.

We multiply the pricing factors in the middle part by the base case original pro forma cash flow amounts in the top panel to arrive at the scenario outcome cash flow amounts shown in the bottom part of Table 17.1. For example:

- Multiplying the $51M base case infrastructure cost in Year 1 from row 4 in the top part of the table;
- Times the randomly generated construction cost pricing factor in Year 1 (1.108) from the middle part of the table;
- Yields $56.492M—the ex-post-realized Year 1 infrastructure cost cash outflow amount in row 4 in the bottom part of the table.

(Note that comparison of revenues from housing sales, after the first year, is not so straightforward. This is because the revenues in any year reflect a blend of pricing across the 3 years of the installment payment plan.)

The bottom part of Table 17.1 is just one, illustrative, randomly generated future scenario for the Garden City project. In Monte Carlo terminology, it is one "trial." It happens to be a favorable outcome as compared to the base case because it results in an ex-post NPV of $89.674M, as compared to the base case of $24.711M, and an ex-post IRR (at the given $200M price) of 32.6% as compared to the base case projection of 22.6%.

In general, some outcome scenarios are more favorable than the base case pro forma, and some are less favorable. They reflect the pricing factors generated based on the real estate pricing probability distributions and dynamics input into the spreadsheet simulation model, and these fluctuate in some sense around the mean reflected in the base case.

The input probability and dynamics assumptions reflect the realistic real estate market pricing dynamics that we discussed in Chapter 7 (and which are discussed in more depth in the Appendix at the end of this book). These price dynamics include the random walk, autoregression, mean-reversion, and cyclicality discussed in Chapter 7. We also introduce idiosyncratic noise, which is a characteristic of individual real estate asset prices, and is one source of the lack of perfect correlation among different real estate products (see Section A.2 in the Appendix). As usual, we run the simulation model to generate several thousand independent random scenarios and analyze the distribution of results across the outcomes of all those trials.

17.3 Outcomes Reflecting Uncertainty for the Multi-Asset Development

Figures 17.1–17.4 show the results of modeling uncertainty for the Garden City project. They show the project's future investment performance across 2000 randomly generated scenarios in the Monte Carlo simulation. All the charts reflect the same sample distribution, the same "run" of the simulation model. The focus is on two target metrics, the achieved ex-post NPV and IRR of the project, as indicated on the horizontal axes in the charts. We compute the NPV using 18% as the discount rate, reflecting the "hurdle rate" for the project as described in Section 16.5 (but which should, in principle, approximate the market OCC, as in fact is the case in this example, since we estimated the project OCC to be 18.01%). We compute the project's realized IRR based on the given $200M purchase price for the land.

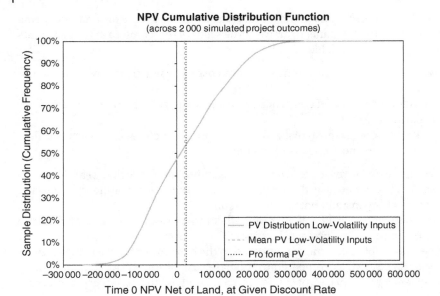

Figures 17.1–17.2

As noted in Chapter 7, any individual "run" of the simulation model (a single "recalculation" of the spreadsheet with many scenarios) produces a sample distribution of the possible future outcomes of the project. Such sample distributions of outputs are effectively estimates, as of Time 0, of the underlying ex-ante probability distribution governing the project's future investment performance. Normally, Time 0 is the time we plan to begin construction. Each time we run the simulation model, we generate a different sample, and no two runs will produce identical target curves. We strive for a

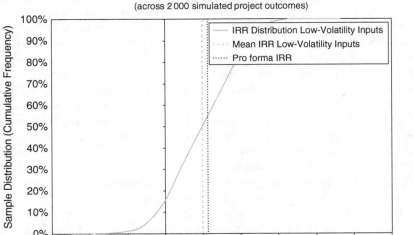

IRR Cumulative Distribution Function
(across 2 000 simulated project outcomes)

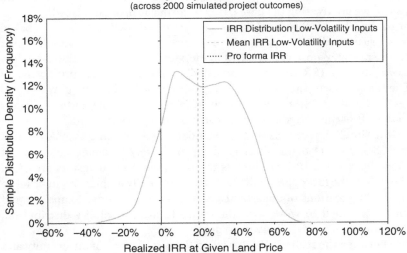

IRR Frequency Distribution Function
(across 2000 simulated project outcomes)

Figures 17.3–17.4

sample size large enough that the target curves are quite stable for practical purposes, between simulation runs.

We depict the results graphically using either cumulative or frequency target curves (Chapter 8). The graphs in Figures 17.1–17.4 quantify and qualify the future uncertainty. They greatly enrich the picture provided by the classical single-stream pro forma and by the traditional economic analysis of the project that was described in Section 16.5. That traditional approach is, at best, only a depiction of the average, or probabilistic, expectation of the future, based on estimates of the ex-ante means of the cash flow probability distributions as reflected in the pro forma.

Regarding the NPV of the project (net of the given $200M land price), Figures 17.1 and 17.2 suggest that the future outcome probability has a slight positive skew around an expected value that is essentially the same as the single-stream pro forma NPV. (The right-hand tails are slightly longer than the left-hand tails.) This is the same type of result as we noted in Chapter 8 regarding investments in existing assets. There, we were looking at the PV distribution, because we were valuing an existing built asset; and here, we are looking at the NPV distribution, because we are subtracting out land and construction costs to value a development project. Without any flexibility in the implementation of the project, the probability distribution has the same general characteristics for the money-valued target metric. This is because present values are linear functions of future cash flows, which mathematically makes the mean of a distribution of future PVs equal to the PV of the mean of the future cash flows.

In Figures 17.1 and 17.2, the dashed, gray, vertical line is essentially at the same value as the dotted black line of the traditional pro forma NPV for the project, as reported in Chapter 16. The dashed, gray, vertical line is the sample mean of the simulation output distribution for the run depicted in the chart. As noted, there will always be some minor variation in sample statistics around true values. The sample mean NPV and the pro forma NPV are very close, and not statistically significantly different. In principle, we expect these two NPVs to be the same, owing to the linearity of the present value function, and because our random cash flow pricing factors are neutral and centered around the base case, since we are treating the base case pro forma as being unbiased.

Also, similar to the Chapter 8 results, the ex-post (realized) IRR distribution (based on the given land price) tends to be symmetric, as Figures 17.3 and 17.4 reveal. But, just as in Chapter 8, the mean ex-post-realized IRR in the Monte Carlo simulation is slightly below the 22.6% going-in IRR that was indicated in the traditional pro forma of Chapter 16. The sample mean IRR is about 20%. Notice that the dashed, gray, vertical lines in Figures 17.3 and 17.4 (the sample mean IRR) are noticeably and statistically significantly to the left of the dotted black vertical lines (the pro forma IRR).

Furthermore, the simulation reveals that the standard deviation in the achieved IRR is approximately 23%. It suggests that there is an approximately 5% chance, 5% value at risk, that the actually realized IRR will be less than negative 16%. Investors are often interested in the tails of the future possibilities. As we repeatedly emphasize, in order to appreciate fully the implications of uncertainty, and especially in order to analyze and evaluate flexibility, we need to work with the entire future probability distribution. This is what the simulation model allows us to do.

The difference between the realistic IRR based on the distribution of uncertainty and the IRR based on a single average case is a typical result. It reflects the "flaw of averages" point made in Section 5.4: the average of a non-linear function does not necessarily equal the value of that function evaluated at the average. (On average, houses don't burn down, but the mortgage lender still requires you to buy fire insurance.) In the absence of flexibility, the IRR, as a function of the NPV, curves downwards (it is concave).

The scatterplot of the Garden City simulation results demonstrates this curvature (Figure 17.5). It shows the IRR as a function of the NPV of the project. Each point in the graph indicates the Garden City IRR and NPV results for one of the 2000 simulated future scenarios. The NPV result is on the horizontal axis, and the IRR result is on the vertical axis. The points, of course, spread out randomly, including a few outliers, but the central shape of the "cloud" is that of a curve that bends downwardly over the NPV

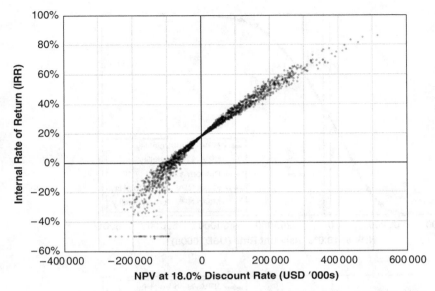

Figure 17.5 Garden City simulation results reflecting uncertainty without flexibility: IRR as a function of NPV.

values on the horizontal axis. This is why, and how, the expected IRR is less than the pro forma IRR of the expected cash flows. This biases the pro forma IRR, which is the IRR of the average cash flows, to be greater than the average of the probability distribution of the ex-post IRRs, the more so the greater the uncertainty in the future cash flows.

17.4 Effect of Different Probability Inputs Assumptions

The results shown in Figures 17.1–17.4 derive from pricing factors that reflect input assumptions about real estate price dynamics. The authors believe that these are realistic and that they reflect typical real estate markets. We present and discuss our specific input assumptions in the Appendix. But real estate price dynamics differ over time and across different real estate markets. And no one ever knows the exact "true" price dynamics assumptions to input into the simulation model.

We should thus always be "humble" in using and presenting simulation analyses. We should always recognize that they will contain error, and we should never ignore common sense. We should consider how other assumptions might affect results.

To illustrate such a sensitivity analysis, we repeat the simulation of the Garden City project, assuming higher volatility in our real estate market pricing dynamics. Specifically, we ran the analysis using annual volatility in the real estate market of about 23%, measured for existing property assets without leverage. We label this as a "high-volatility" assumption. We compare it to the previous results, which we obtained using a "low-volatility" assumption of around 17%. Both these assumptions are within the plausible range for the volatility that individual property assets experience.

Figures 17.6–17.9 contrast the results of the high- and low-volatility assumptions. The high-volatility inputs assumption results in project performance output distributions

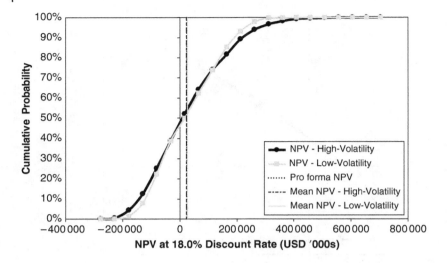

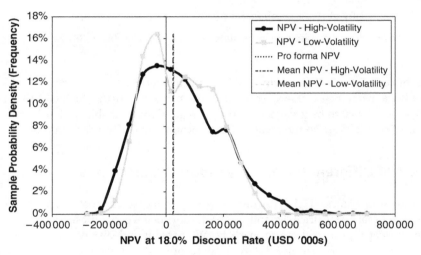

Figures 17.6–17.7

that are slightly more spread out, reflecting greater investment risk (other things being equal). This is seen in the greater range or spread in the target curves (they are "flatter" over the range of output values on the horizontal axes). However, the effects of the alternative assumptions are not terribly large. There is no effect on the mean NPV, and only a slight effect on the mean IRR. (The thin, black, dashed line representing the mean outcome with the high-volatility assumption is slightly to the left of the thicker, dashed, gray line representing the mean of the low-volatility assumption.) In principle, greater volatility reduces the mean IRR, due to the previously noted concavity effect (and the "Jensen's Inequality" rule, discussed in Section 5.4). Increasing the input volatility assumption increases the sample standard deviation of the realized IRR, which we could view as a measure of investment risk, from about 23% to about 27%. This

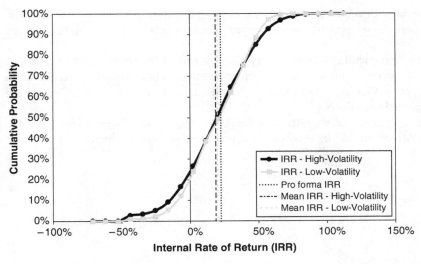

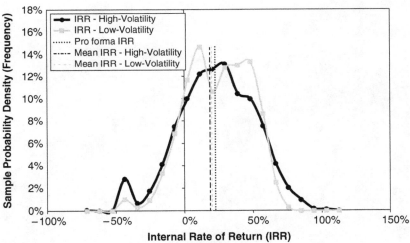

Figures 17.8–17.9

spread is around the mean realized IRR of approximately 20% under the low-volatility assumption and 19% under the high-volatility assumption. (Recall that the pro forma IRR is 22.6%.)

17.5 Conclusion

This chapter showed how we can analyze future uncertainty by embedding the traditional DCF pro forma of our example Garden City development project into a Monte Carlo simulation spreadsheet model. We discussed the nature of the resulting simulation for the development project, including the typical target probability distributions, and the effects of varying input assumptions about the nature of the uncertainty.

The results we see with our Garden City example reflect the general principles about the relationship between uncertainty and basic investment performance metrics—such as the implication that expected IRRs are less than the pro forma IRR based on the project's expected cash flows.

In the following chapters, we introduce flexibility into our simulation of the value the Garden City project under uncertainty, which we explored in this chapter.

18

Project Start-Delay Flexibility

We Model the Value of the Most Basic and Widely Available Development Project Option

---

LEARNING OBJECTIVES

- Learn how to calculate the value of the flexibility to delay the start of the development project;
- Consider the developer's delay decision rule;
- Understand the value of option as modeled in a realistic example project.

OUTLINE OF THE CHAPTER

18.1 Project Start-Delay Option
18.2 Option Exercise Decision Rule
18.3 Defining "Profit" in the Decision Model
18.4 Value of Start-Delay Flexibility in the Garden City Project
18.5 Conclusion

Now that you have seen how our example development project performs under realistic uncertainty without flexibility, it is time to begin to see the effect that flexibility can have. Remember, the real benchmark for judging the effect of flexibility is not the traditional, single-stream pro forma, but rather the project recognizing uncertainty but without flexibility. This chapter begins a series of five chapters in which we introduce specific types of flexibilities, one at a time, into the simulation model of the investment performance of the Garden City project under uncertainty that we described in the last chapter.

In this chapter and the next, we will focus on the most basic type of flexibility that exists most widely in development—the flexibility to delay the start of project. We use the results of this analysis to gain intuition about the nature of the value that project start-delay flexibility adds to the project, from an investment perspective.

We will introduce a key feature of the model: the developer's decision rule regarding how, or when, to trigger the option. We begin to explore the effect of such decision rules in this chapter, and will explore the topic further in the following chapter.

Flexibility and Real Estate Valuation under Uncertainty: A Practical Guide for Developers, First Edition.
David Geltner and Richard de Neufville.
© 2018 John Wiley & Sons Ltd. Published 2018 by John Wiley & Sons Ltd.
Companion website: www.wiley.com/go/geltner-deneufville/flexibility-and-real-estate-valuation

18.1   Project Start-Delay Option

Chapter 15 presented the option to delay the start of a project at a general level. We noted there that this delay option is an example of the broader concept of production timing options. The overall start-delay option reflects the fundamental development call option that land ownership entails, as described in Chapter 12. In general, landowners have broad discretion about when, and whether, they choose to start a development project on their land. We provided a very simple numerical example of this option in Section 12.5. That example was overly simplistic, considering only a single period of time and binary scenarios with instantaneous construction. Now, our more realistic Garden City example project and simulation model will allow us to explore this option much more completely and realistically (although still with sufficient abstraction so as not to lose sight of the forest through the trees).

As described in the preceding chapters, we generally view call options as "offensive" options, enabling without mandating the landowner to profit from a favorable circumstance. However, we made the point in Section 12.4 that call options and put options are really two sides of the same coin, and the option "to do" is also the option "to not do." With this in mind, we noted in Section 15.1 that, in practice, by the time developers have done the necessary preparation work to be able to start a development project, the timing flexibility that exists is typically viewed as a "delay" option, which is essentially a defensive type (put) option. In other words, in practice, developers plan to start the project "right away" unless they choose to exercise their option to postpone starting it.

This is the perspective from which we model the option to delay the start of our Garden City example project. We presume that the developer has completed the preparations for the project, and could start the project immediately as per the base plan schedule—or could elect to postpone the project. We assume that the decision-maker can consider the current market conditions and decide whether to begin the project in any year—or, alternatively, hold off for another year and reconsider at that point. Once the developer starts the project, it must be completed according to the base plan schedule, without any delay beyond the initial start delay.

Thus, for analytical clarity, the only type of flexibility we consider in this chapter is the option to delay the start of the project. We ignore any other timing or product options. For practical as well as technical modeling reasons, we put an upper limit on the delay at 15 years, after which, if the project still has not been started, we assume that it will be permanently abandoned (for a land resale "salvage value" equal to one-half the original land purchase price).

18.2   Option Exercise Decision Rule

To specify the option to delay the start of the project, we must program a decision rule into our simulation model. The decision rule specifies the conditions that will trigger the delay option. In other words, in any given scenario, the decision rule will determine in which year the developer will start the project (or, potentially, will abandon it permanently if the project has not been started by Year 15). We can program this decision rule to be almost anything we want it to be (within reason). How shall we think about what it should be?

Formal economic analyses of options model the situation mathematically and attempt to solve for explicit formulas to define the optimal decision rule. However, as noted at the outset of this book, such formal economic models rely on several simplifying assumptions that are unrealistic and overly restrictive for practical application to real estate development projects. (For example, they typically assume that the price dynamics process of the asset market is a pure random walk. While this is a decent approximation for the stock market, it is not very accurate for real estate markets. See Section 7.2.)

We take a different approach in our simulation of the value of flexibility. We allow the asset price dynamics to be much more complex and nuanced (see Section 7.3). And we do not presume optimal or even necessarily rational behavior on the part of the decision-maker. Rather, we pose an intuitive and likely realistic model of the actual decision-making process. (The rule we adopt does share with the formal economic models the basic intuition that the decision to delay is based on lack of apparent and sufficient profitability for the project.)

One can model decision rules to exercise options in many ways. Note, however, that we can only properly base decision rules on what has happened; we cannot know the future—see Box 18.1. In the present chapter, we consider what we will call our "Aggressive Developer Rule." (We will consider a different rule in the following chapter.)

The Aggressive Developer Rule models very optimistic developers who hardly ever delay starting the project. According to this rule, the developer will start the project (that is, doesn't trigger the delay option) unless *all* the following three conditions hold:

- The development would be unprofitable at the prices indicated by the current year's pricing factor realizations; *and*
- The development would also be unprofitable at the prices indicated by the previous year's pricing factor realizations; *and*
- The profitability of the development is less (worse) under the current year's pricing factor realizations than under the previous year's pricing factor realizations.

This Aggressive Developer Rule makes it inherently difficult to *not* start the project. It sets up a bias against delaying the project. The developer holds off on starting the project only if several indicators are "flashing red"—that is, only if the housing market has been sufficiently bad as to depress housing unit sales profitability below the base case for 2 years in a row, and, furthermore, if the market is getting worse.

Box 18.1 The decision rule can't use a "crystal ball"

An important point concerning decision rules: any realistic decision rule can only refer to information available as of the time of the decision. It cannot imply that the decision-maker has a "crystal ball." Thus, decision rules can check the pricing factor realizations for the current and previous years in the scenario, information that would realistically be available as of the decision time for the current year. But decision rules cannot depend on pricing factor realizations in later years within the scenario.

Such a decision rule might well approximate the behavior of some developers. After all, developers do tend to be an optimistic lot. Furthermore, there can be serious practical and organizational impediments to delaying a project that is ready to start.

18.3   Defining "Profit" in the Decision Model

At this point, it will be worth our while to elaborate briefly on a key aspect of the decision rule to trigger the option. Such rules usually are based on some measure reflecting the profitability of the project at a given time (a potential trigger decision time) within the realized, randomly generated future scenario. The relevant profitability can be measured and implemented in the spreadsheet model in various ways. In a very sophisticated approach, one could program a decision-maker's forecast of the future IRR of the project based on current and past realizations in the scenario.

Our philosophy is to lean more toward simplicity. One technique that we employ in this regard is that we measure "profitability" only relative to the base case. That is, we work with the pricing factors, and not directly with the implied money values in the scenario. The scenario money values are simply the money values in the base case multiplied by the pricing factors. If, in a given period, the relevant revenue pricing factor is less than the relevant construction cost pricing factor, then profitability relative to the base case is negative in that period. This is the definition and measure of profitability that we employ to govern the option implementation decision.

This definition of profitability is easy to program from a technical perspective. Perhaps more importantly, it also reflects the principle we first suggested in Section 7.1 when we were introducing pricing factors. We want to defer to the existing knowledge and expertise in the field, about the investment project that we are modeling. We want to build on the knowledge that the principal parties have about the project, as reflected in the pro forma that they have developed. Of course, this pro forma should be unbiased, not in itself inclined toward either optimism or conservatism. Given this, and given that the investor's pro forma is viewed as representing an economically justified project (as discussed in Chapter 11), we want to benchmark the relevant definition of "profitability" on that pro forma, just as we want the pricing factors to have a zero-mean probability distribution (mean ratio of 1.0).

18.4   Value of Start-Delay Flexibility
in the Garden City Project

Now let's explore the effects of start-delay flexibility in our example Garden City development project with the Aggressive Developer Rule. Our perspective, as always, is primarily that of the investor in the project. How does this type of flexibility affect the expected value and returns for the project, as well as its risk from an investment perspective?

Of course, the results of our analysis apply only to our specific Garden City example project. Our main purpose is to demonstrate a methodology and a perspective, not to

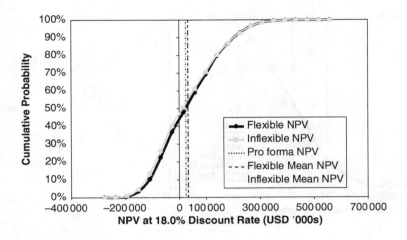

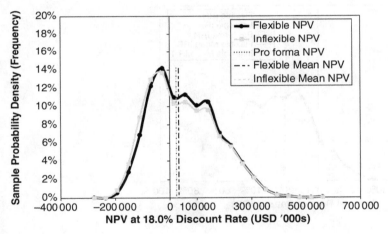

Figures 18.1–18.2

derive fully general conclusions. However, we have constructed the Garden City example to be a typical multi-asset development project. The numbers in it are typical, and
the simulated price dynamics reflect typical real estate market dynamics. The results of
our analysis should, therefore, be suggestive for many such projects, particularly at a
broad-brush and qualitative level. This makes them interesting beyond only demon-
strating an analysis methodology.

In this section, we compare the simulated investment results of the Garden City project with start-delay flexibility versus without flexibility (the latter essentially being the
benchmark we presented and discussed in Chapter 17). The comparison is always made
on the same simulated future realized scenarios. We compare the results with those of
the inflexible development plan. Both analyses are otherwise similar. They assume the
18% hurdle discount rate and the $200 M land price.

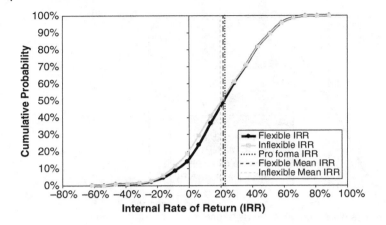

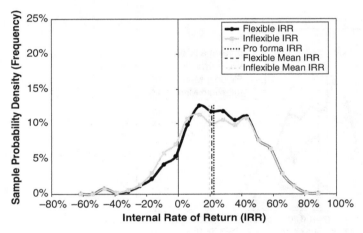

Figures 18.3–18.4

Figures 18.1–18.4 compare the target curve results for the two cases, in terms of cumulative and frequency outcome distributions, for the NPV and IRR performance metrics. Notice that the delay option adds some value, even though the Aggressive Developer Rule is biased toward not delaying the project. Specifically, this delay option increases the:

- Mean ex-post NPV of the project by about $8 M (from approximately $25 M in the inflexible base case to approximately $33 M). This is 4% of the $200 M land price. This is worthwhile, as the expected NPV is a metric that is arguably quite relevant for evaluating the land.
- Mean ex-post IRR by about 175 basis points, from under 20% to over 21%. (A "basis point" is one-hundredth of a percent, a common unit in the investment industry for referring to returns and especially to "spreads," or differences between two returns.) Yet, the standard deviation of the simulated IRR falls slightly from about 24% to under 23%. Thus, the expected return is increased, and its risk is decreased.

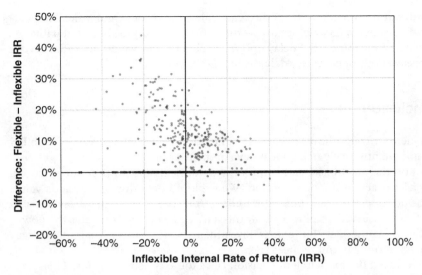

Figure 18.5 Scatterplot of IRR outcomes for start-delay flexibility (Aggressive Developer Rule).

- These results suggest that, even with strong bias against exercising the option, the flexibility to delay the start of the project makes it somewhat more appealing from an investment risk/return perspective, holding the land price constant.

It is important to note *how* the start-delay option adds value to the project. Observe that the target curve graphs for the delay option exhibit a rightward shift relative to those for the inflexible plan. Importantly, this rightward shift occurs over the left-hand tails of the distributions—that is, over the more downside project outcomes. This is the classical signature of a defensive or "put" option that reduces downside risks.

We can also note that, even with the Aggressive Developer Rule, flexibility to delay not only increases value on average, but also is better than the inflexible plan significantly often. The scatterplot in Figure 18.5 illustrates this. It shows, for each of the 2000 trials in the simulation, the difference in the realized IRR achieved by the flexible minus the inflexible model, as a function of the IRR outcome without flexibility. In this case:

- Dots above the horizontal axis are scenarios in which the project with start-delay flexibility yielded a higher IRR than it would have (in the same scenario) without flexibility.
- Conversely, dots below the axis are scenarios where the start-delay flexibility resulted in a worse outcome.

This scatterplot vividly illustrates that the aggressive flexible plan performs better than the inflexible plan:

- Most significantly, when the project performs poorly, as indicated by dots to the left of the vertical axis, the flexible plan performs better than the inflexible plan. This reinforces the concept of the delay flexibility as a form of insurance, as a put option.
- Only about 10 dots are below the horizontal line, indicating that the inflexible plan is better less than 1% of the time.

For the record, but not obviously from the scatterplot, the flexible and inflexible plans lead to the same results in 85% of the cases—the dots that are on the horizontal line. As with most forms of insurance, the delay option is valuable, but we do not often invoke it. The "aggressive developer" rarely delays starting the project.

18.5 Conclusion

This chapter demonstrated how we can use simulation to model and value flexibility realistically and quantitatively in a typical development project.

We focused on the most basic and common type of flexibility, to time the start of a project, which in practice is a delay option. We explored how this option adds value, even when the developer is predisposed (or under strong pressure) to not delay the start of the project. We observed graphically how the start-delay option truncates the downside tail of the outcome distributions of investment performance; it simultaneously increases expected returns and reduces risk.

We also introduced the modeling of decision rules for exercising options. This chapter explored a particular decision rule, which we labeled our "Aggressive Developer Rule." With this rule, the project is only rarely delayed, and the flexibility to delay the project accordingly only adds a small amount of value—less than 5% of the land value. But this is $8 M in the case of the Garden City project, and an extra 175 basis points in the investment's expected IRR. Furthermore, the way that the option adds value—by improving the downside, providing a type of "insurance"—can be quite valuable to many investors.

The Aggressive Developer Rule is only one possible decision rule for implementing the option to delay the project start. And this option is so basic and widely available that we will explore it further in the next chapter.

19

Decision Rules and Value Implications

We Further Explore the Option to Delay the Project Start

LEARNING OBJECTIVES

- Consider different option implementation rules;
- Learn about trigger values;
- Gain deeper understanding of the value of the project start-delay option;
- Review the meaning of value gains from flexibility.

OUTLINE OF THE CHAPTER

19.1 Simple Myopic Delay Rule
19.2 Trigger Values
19.3 Value Implications of the Decision Rules
19.4 Effect of Trigger Values (Start or Delay Bias)
19.5 Review the Meaning of Flexibility Value
19.6 Conclusion

We noted in the previous chapter that there are various ways to model the decision of whether and when to implement the option to delay the project start. Our simulation model is a simplified analog of the real world. Developers may have different philosophies, dispositions, objectives, and constraints. Our initial exploration of the start-delay option was based on what we call our "Aggressive Developer Rule." This rule leads to very limited triggering of the delay option, although, even so, we saw that it adds significant value to our example Garden City project.

In the present chapter, we explore a different, but arguably equally plausible, delay decision rule. In so doing, we take you deeper into the considerations surrounding the modeling of such decisions, and we see the effects that different decision rules can have. This is not just a technical modeling point—it raises basic management policy considerations. In the real world, managers and developers can adopt different decision rules.

Finally, this chapter is also an appropriate time to step back and review the meaning of the discoveries we are making about the value of flexibility in real estate development investments.

Flexibility and Real Estate Valuation under Uncertainty: A Practical Guide for Developers, First Edition.
David Geltner and Richard de Neufville.
© 2018 John Wiley & Sons Ltd. Published 2018 by John Wiley & Sons Ltd.
Companion website: www.wiley.com/go/geltner-deneufville/flexibility-and-real-estate-valuation

19.1 Simple Myopic Delay Rule

An alternative to the Aggressive Developer Rule that we explored in the last chapter is what we will call the "Simple Myopic Delay Rule." The Aggressive Developer Rule was biased toward not implementing the delay option—that is, toward starting the project without delay. The Simple Myopic Delay Rule is more neutral. With this rule, the decision-maker simply looks at the prices in the current year and proceeds with the project unless those prices indicate that the project would be unprofitable (relative to the base case). This rule is myopic because it depends only on the current period's pricing factor realizations. Compared to the Aggressive Developer Rule, the Simple Myopic Delay Rule increases the probability that the developer would delay the start of the project, other things being equal. It doesn't demand so much evidence of unprofitability before triggering the delay. (It also doesn't require as much information.)

As always, if the decision in the current period is to delay, that decision is revisited anew in the next year, and once the project does start, it must continue without further delay, according to the base plan production schedule thereafter.

19.2 Trigger Values

We can further nuance and calibrate profitability based decision rules by setting a "trigger value" that specifies the level of profitability that determines the decision. For example, if we set a trigger value of zero, then the option exercise criterion would be benchmarked simply on positive or negative profitability relative to the base case. For example, in the case of the Simple Myopic Delay Rule, whenever the current profitability is greater than the base case (for the current period in the scenario), the developer would start the project, and otherwise would delay it for the current period.

Alternatively, if we set the trigger value to +10%, then the decision-maker delays the start of the project unless and until the current year's pricing factor realizations are such that the profitability of the project would be at least 10% above that in the base case pro forma for the current year. Similarly, a trigger value of negative 10% would be more aggressive, allowing the project to proceed unless the current profitability was at least 10% *below* the expectation in the base case for the current year.

This type of calibration of the implementation trigger can be applied to any profitability-based decision rule (particularly where we measure profitability relative to a benchmark base case, as noted in Chapter 18). It is more interesting in the present situation to explore this type of decision posture calibration using the Simple Myopic Delay Rule. The Aggressive Developer Rule is inherently "aggressive," by virtue of its "multiple red flags" requirement to delay the project.

In the case of the Simple Myopic Delay Rule, the sign and magnitude of the trigger value level determines the bias in the decision rule. Higher positive triggers produce a bias to delay—that is, to be a bit patient for better conditions. Lower, more negative triggers produce a bias to start—that is, to be less patient and start the project sooner.

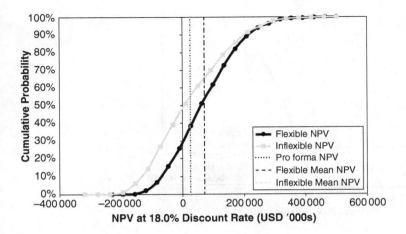

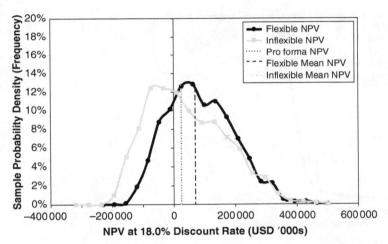

Figures 19.1–19.2

In all cases, decision rules should not be interpreted too literally or narrowly in terms of real-world implications. They are designed to model the general effects of flexibility, and to build the intuition of the real decision-makers.

19.3 Value Implications of the Decision Rules

In Chapter 18, we explored the investment performance implications of the project start-delay option based on the Aggressive Developer Rule. We saw significant, but small, positive effects, as compared to the case where the developer would have no flexibility in implementing the project. With that type of strong disposition to not delay the start of the project, the project was delayed less than 15% of the time; the

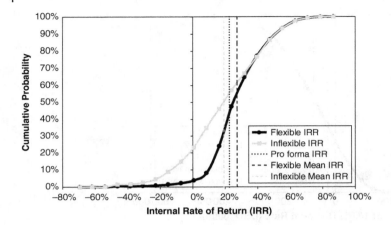

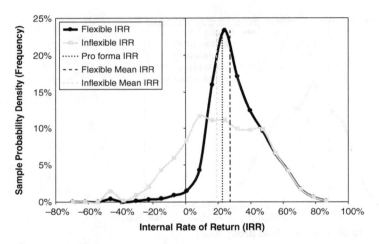

Figures 19.3–19.4

option only added less than 5% to the land value, and less than 200 basis points to the expected IRR.

Now consider the implications of our Simple Myopic Delay Rule with a trigger level of zero. As noted, this rule is "neutral" in terms of any bias either to start or delay the project. Interestingly, this decision rule adds considerably more value than the Aggressive Developer Rule. Comparing Figures 19.1–19.4 with the counterpart Figures 18.1–18.4 in the previous chapter, we see qualitatively similar results, but much stronger in favor of the flexible case. Specifically, Figures 19.1–19.4 show that the project start-delay option increases the:

- Mean ex-post NPV to around $70 M, more than twice that with the Aggressive Developer Rule, and almost three times that of the inflexible project (which is about $25 M). This increase in expected value of about $45 M is over 5% of the gross present value of the project assets.
- Land value by some 20%.

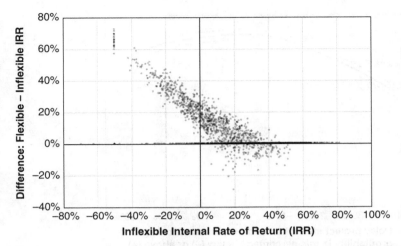

Figure 19.5 Scatterplot of IRR outcomes for start-delay flexibility (Simple Myopic Delay Rule).

- Mean IRR impressively from under 20% to over 27% (over 700 basis points), while the standard deviation in the simulated IRR declines from 24% to 17%.

The figures also demonstrate that this version of the delay option greatly shifts the target curves to the right, compared to the inflexible plan, particularly reducing downside risk (on the far left side). This is a strong indication of the value of this option as insurance, as a put option.

The scatterplot in Figure 19.5 shows that developers are much more likely to exercise the delay option with the Simple Myopic Delay Rule than with the Aggressive Developer Rule. (Compare Figure 19.5 with Figure 18.5 in the last chapter.) This greater caution generally has favorable results. Comparing the project with start-delay flexibility now based on the Simple Myopic Delay Rule to the benchmark inflexible case under the same uncertainty, we see that the flexible project:

- Delivers higher IRR than the inflexible project in about 45% of all scenarios (compared to 15% for the Aggressive Developer Rule);
- Is virtually never beaten by the inflexible project when project IRR outcomes are negative;
- Provides greater extreme downside protection (indicated by the high upward tilt of the scatterplot over the left-hand side of the horizontal axis, more so than in Figure 18.5).

19.4 Effect of Trigger Values (Start or Delay Bias)

The simulation model of start-delay flexibility does more than simply allow us to quantify the value of such flexibility from an investment perspective. We can also use it to explore the implications of different decision postures on the part of the decision-maker. Is it better to be a little aggressive, with a decision bias against delaying the start of the project? Or is it better to be a little conservative and patient, with the decision bias in favor of delaying the project until better circumstances? Or should the decision-maker

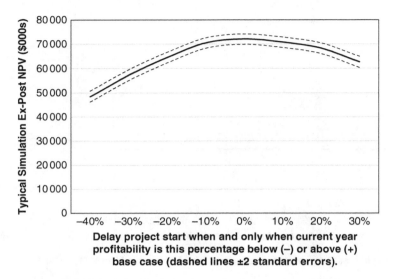

Figure 19.6 Effect of changing level of trigger value for start-delay flexibility.

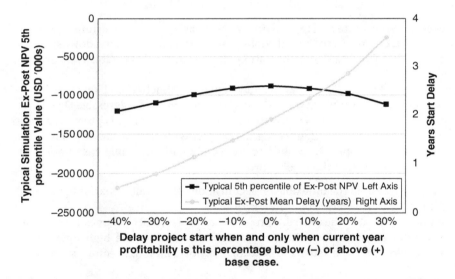

Figure 19.7 Effect of changing level of trigger value on downside results for start-delay flexibility.

aim to be "neutral," in the sense of being unbiased in either direction? This can also have implications for policymakers. When public agencies provide land or zoning incentives to developers, should they require immediate construction of the project, or allow the developers some flexibility to wait?

The simulation model allows us to easily explore this question. Using the Simple Myopic Delay Rule, Figure 19.6 shows the results of varying the level of the profitability trigger value that determines when developers exercise the delay option. As noted, this trigger value level indicates any type and degree of bias for or against delaying the project. In this case, it appears that the best trigger value (the one that maximizes the land value) is at or near zero—neutral bias—that is, neither aggressive nor cautious. However, there seems to be a bit more danger from erring on the side of too much aggression (negative trigger values) as compared to erring on the side of too much caution (positive trigger values). This is seen in the steeper down-slope to the left of the zero trigger value on the horizontal axis, than to the right.

Figure 19.7 shows the effect of trigger values on the downside results. It plots the 5th percentile tail of the outcome distribution (the 5% value at risk) against the trigger value. This reinforces the idea that a neutral disposition is best for the option to the delay project start, even for a decision-maker who is most concerned about downside risk. Figure 19.7 also plots the average time length of delay as a function of the trigger value. At the neutral trigger level, the average delay in the project is slightly less than 2 years. This amount of delay is typical in real estate development, especially for large projects such as Garden City.

19.5   Review the Meaning of Flexibility Value

As you can see by now, incorporating uncertainty and flexibility into the rigorous valuation of a real estate development project can have significant implications for the investment value of the project. This is therefore an appropriate point to step back and review the meaning of these findings.

First, we should review something we said back in Section 10.3, where we discussed the meaning of the added value we apparently found by modeling uncertainty and resale timing flexibility in the stabilized property investment. The type of valuation we are dealing with here is not necessarily market value (exchange value). At least in the first instance, we are exploring private value (or investment value), viewed from the perspective of the developer. Recall that this type of valuation is contingent on the following qualities of the investors or developers:

- Ability and willingness to exercise the flexibility that we are modeling in the simulation; and
- Self-discipline to follow the decision rule to trigger the option.

In Section 10.3, we pointed out a number of considerations that could lead such private investment valuations to differ from estimates of the market value of the asset.

This does not denigrate the significance and importance of the flexibility values that we are quantifying in this book. For one thing, development projects tend to be unique and rare as compared to stabilized property investments. This makes it more difficult to estimate their market value precisely. Our valuation is made consistent with basic economic principles of opportunity cost and the market values of the components of the project. The application of this type of valuation is not just to peg a value, but also to aid in the design and planning and programming of the project. Furthermore, at a deeper level, private valuations underlie, and determine, market values. Buyers will not pay more than their private valuations for an asset, and sellers will not take less than their private valuations for assets they own. The equilibrium prices that we define as market values evidenced by consummated transaction prices can therefore reflect private valuations.

19.6   Conclusion

This chapter continued our quantitative exploration into the value of the start-delay option in real estate development projects, using our archetypical Garden City project as the continuing example. Here, we explored the effects of different decision rules to trigger options, and the different levels of trigger values, reflecting different developer postures toward delaying the start of the project. We found that a simple, myopic decision rule with a neutral bias (predisposed neither for nor against delaying the start of the project) adds most value—more value than we saw in the previous chapter for the "aggressive developer" posture. We found that, with such a decision rule, start-delay flexibility can add considerable value, on the order of 20% of the land value, increasing the going-in expected IRR for the project by over 700 basis points. The option works strongly as a defensive (put option type) mechanism, similar to the way insurance works. The project is delayed slightly more than half the time, with an average delay just under 2 years.

The project start-delay option is just one of the several major types of options available in many development projects, as we enumerated in Chapters 14 and 15. In the following chapters, we will explore several other options, one at a time—beginning in Chapter 20 with modular production timing flexibility.

20

Modular Production Timing Flexibility

We Explore the Timing Option to Pause and Restart the Project Any Time After its Commencement

---

LEARNING OBJECTIVES

- Understand the nature of modular production timing flexibility in real estate development projects;
- Learn how to model and value such flexibility using spreadsheet simulation analysis of DCF;
- Understand how the value of this flexibility depends on the trigger levels for the implementation of the delay option;
- Exploration of synergy or redundancy among timing options: combining modular production with the start-delay option.

OUTLINE OF THE CHAPTER

20.1 Modular Production Timing Flexibility
20.2 Modeling the Modular Production Option
20.3 Value of Modular Production Timing Flexibility
20.4 Effect of Trigger Values (Bias toward Pause or Continue)
20.5 Effect of Combining Start-Delay and Modular Production Delay Flexibility
20.6 Conclusion

The flexibility to delay the start of a project, which we explored in the previous chapter, is common. However, it is only one type of option for the timing of production in development projects. Indeed, Chapter 15 described three different types of timing options: overall project start timing, modular production timing, and phasing. We now look at the second of these.

Modular production timing flexibility is the option to pause the production process of a multi-asset development project after the project has started. To enable developers to implement this flexibility, the project design has to consist of modules that can exist independently. This flexibility is thus an option "in" the project, in the meaning of Section 13.3. It is, in this sense, distinct and separate from the start-delay option of Chapters 18 and 19, which is an option "on" the project.

Flexibility and Real Estate Valuation under Uncertainty: A Practical Guide for Developers, First Edition.
David Geltner and Richard de Neufville.
© 2018 John Wiley & Sons Ltd. Published 2018 by John Wiley & Sons Ltd.
Companion website: www.wiley.com/go/geltner-deneufville/flexibility-and-real-estate-valuation

20.1   Modular Production Timing Flexibility

We introduced the concept of modular production timing flexibility at a general level in Section 15.3. Here, we describe it in a little more depth, and relate it specifically to our Garden City project.

The essential idea of modular production is to give the developer the flexibility to vary the rate of production—for example, of housing units. In some cases, developers can accelerate their production schedule if the market becomes more favorable than anticipated. More commonly, the base plan specifies a normative rate of production. The flexibility that actually exists once the project has begun is effectively the ability to delay or pause the project. For practical purposes, the flexibility to time modular production is thus a defensive option.

We illustrate such an option using our Garden City project, producing housing units. The planning for such a development typically culminates in a base plan that envisions a certain schedule of production. The base plan for the Garden City project is a typical example (see Table 16.1). It specifies a temporal profile of the rate of housing unit production, calling for 144 units to be sold in the first year, 392 in the second year, and so on (850 units altogether).

We model the option to time production using a decision rule that triggers a pause in the sale of housing units in Garden City. This rule acts in years when the market price for housing is sufficiently unfavorable to cause the profitability of sales to dip below a specified threshold level. The simulation model thus reflects the decision rule as follows:

- If demand is stronger than expected, sales prices for the housing units will be higher than in the pro forma;
- If demand is lower than expected, sales prices will either be lower, or there will be a pause in the sales of any housing units if the delay option is triggered.

We model modular production timing as an all-or-nothing option within any given year of a future scenario. The amount of housing in the base plan for that year of the project will either sell out entirely or not be offered for sale at all, according to whether the decision rule triggers the pause option or not for that calendar year. The practical reality may be subtler than this (for example, partial sales are possible), but, for demonstration purposes, the all-or-nothing option well represents the essence of the type of flexibility that could exist. As previously mentioned (Section 17.1), it is important in any simulation analysis to balance the desire to make the model as complete and realistic as possible with the need to keep it sufficiently simple to be practical, and to present the big picture that matters to decision-makers. We should always strive to "see the forest through the trees"!

20.2   Modeling the Modular Production Option

How can we conveniently represent in a computer spreadsheet the essence of the type of modular production timing flexibility described in the previous section? The guiding principle is to retain the general temporal pattern or "shape" (or "profile") of the base plan production timing, only allowing for possible pauses that shift production to later. Put another way, we can open up gaps in the base plan production schedule, but otherwise

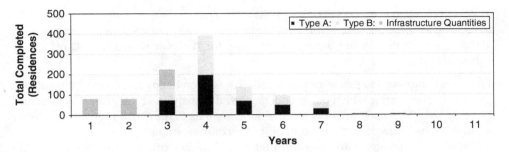

Figure 20.1a Production schedule for the Garden City project's base plan.

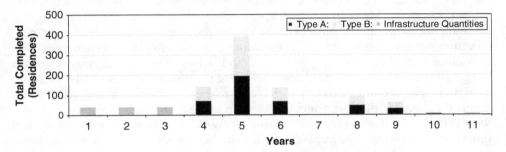

Figure 20.1b Production schedule for one future scenario with the option to delay (modular production timing flexibility).

preserving the temporal profile of that schedule. Figure 20.1a shows the production schedule in the base plan for the Garden City project, a repeat of Figure 16.2a. Figure 20.1b shows an actually realized production schedule in one randomly realized future scenario for the first 11 years. The relative and absolute temporal pattern of production is the same in both panels, except that the exercise of the option to delay production has introduced two gaps in the sequence in the lower panel. (We implement the introduction of this type of otherwise-profile-preserving gap using the "LOOKUP()" function referring to the base plan schedule—see details in the documentation of the Microsoft Excel® templates for this chapter available on the book's companion website.)

In the DCF investment valuation, we implement the analysis of modular production flexibility in the same way as for the overall project start-delay flexibility described in the previous chapter. We represent the flexibility to time modular production using delay decision rules entered as formulas into appropriate cells in the DCF spreadsheet. These rules implement the criteria for exercising the option to stop the project. We base these criteria on the combination of pricing factor realizations within each scenario and threshold trigger values that we specify. For example, in the present chapter, we assume the Simple Myopic Delay Rule, as in Chapter 19.

In detail, the decision rule governs the DCF analysis as follows. In any given year, in a given future scenario:

- If the average profitability of the housing sales based on the current year's pricing factor realizations is below the input trigger value, then we pause the sale of units for that year.

- We check again the next year, and so on.
- As soon as there is a year that passes the criterion, we resume selling housing units at the rate indicated in the base plan schedule for the year where we left off selling houses.

Our model allows us to pause, or resume, in this fashion in any given year, up through a 24-year horizon, after which our model cuts off the analysis. If the project is not complete by Year 24, we assume it will remain incomplete. (This cutoff is arbitrary, but far enough in the future that it has no significant economic impact.)

If we set the trigger value to zero, then this decision rule effectively sells houses only in years when the marginal profit is positive, relative to the base case. However, the exact, actual effect on cash flow is a bit more complicated in our Garden City project. Recall that buyers pay for sales in any year in three equal, consecutive annual installments, based on the price as of the year of the sales contract. Meanwhile, construction occurs equally during the following 2 years, reflecting construction costs prevailing as of those 2 subsequent years, and not in the preceding year when the trigger profit criterion prevailed and the house price was fixed. Nevertheless, construction costs are not nearly as variable as real estate market prices and are not highly correlated with those prices (see Section 11.2.) Thus, the Simple Myopic Delay Rule criterion typically plays out reasonably well in practice. Furthermore, and importantly, it seems to be a reasonably realistic decision rule. That is, it is probably not too different from the way production decisions are actually made in many development projects.

There is a guiding principle for the way we should formulate decisions about flexibility in the simulation model. Decision rules should be realistic, yet sufficiently simple and transparent so that users can easily understand them. It's important for the actual managers, the decision-makers, to be able to relate to the decision model and help to guide its realism.

20.3   Value of Modular Production Timing Flexibility

What is the value of the flexibility to time production in the modular manner described here? In Chapter 19, we saw that flexibility to delay the project overall tends to add about 5% to the apparent gross value of our typical Garden City project, effectively increasing the implied value of the land by about 20%. How does modular production timing flexibility compare to that?

Figures 20.2–20.5 compare the simulated distributions of investment outcomes for the Garden City project with modular production timing flexibility versus with no flexibility at all. No other type of flexibility is considered; the overall project must start immediately at Year 1. These target curves for NPV and IRR assume the base case values for the discount rate and land price (18%, $200 M), with the delay trigger set at zero. Thus, the differences in simulated outcomes in Figures 20.2–20.5 purely represent the value of the modular delay option by itself.

Modular production delay flexibility acts as a defensive option, as in the case of the overall start-delay option analyzed in Chapters 18 and 19. It primarily shifts the

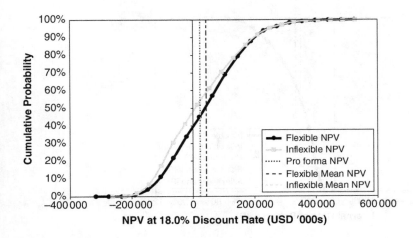

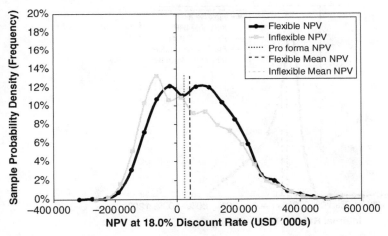

Figures 20.2–20.3

downside (left-hand) tail of the target curves to the right. As it hardly has any impact on the upside tail of the distribution, it also shifts the ex-post mean outcome in a positive direction. However, this positive shift for the modular timing option is not as large as that from the overall start-delay option. Its ex-post mean NPV increases only to around $45 M (instead of $70 M with the start-delay option). Still, this adds almost $20 M to the value of the project from the approximately $25 M NPV without considering any flexibility. The $20 M increase in expected NPV of the project is almost 3% of the gross present value of the project assets to be built.

Importantly from an investment perspective, the expected IRR (at the $200 M land price) increases to 26% with the production timing flexibility, from less than 20% without flexibility. And the standard deviation in the realized IRR reduces to around 15%, from 24%. The increase in mean IRR is only slightly less than what we observed in Chapter 19 with the overall project delay option.

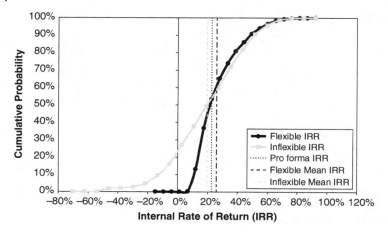

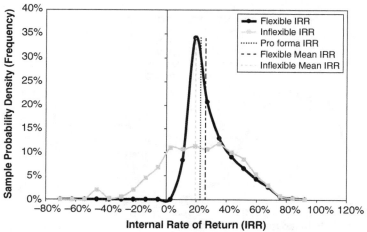

Figures 20.4–20.5

The scatterplot of the joint IRR outcomes in Figure 20.6 reveals that modular production timing flexibility produces a higher IRR only slightly more often than the converse. But there is a strong downward slope in the scatterplot dot cloud. The dots below the zero-difference horizontal axis are only in the lower-right quadrant, and they are not as far below the axis as the dots in the upper-left quadrant are above it. This means that the modular timing flexibility does a good job of providing downside protection, without sacrificing too much upside potential. There is, however, a tendency in moderately upside outcomes for the modular flexibility to modestly reduce the realized IRR, as compared to if there were no timing flexibility. This in part reflects a tendency of the zero trigger level to act too cautiously in the case of modular delay.

20.4   Effect of Trigger Values (Bias toward Pause or Continue)

Analogous to the project start-delay option, negative or positive levels of the Simple Myopic Delay Rule trigger value suggest a decision posture that is biased, respectively, either for, or against, continuing the project. In other words, negative triggers

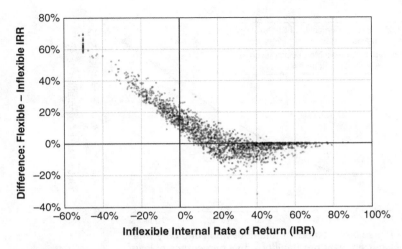

Figure 20.6 Scatterplot of IRR outcomes for modular production timing flexibility (Simple Myopic Delay Rule, trigger=0).

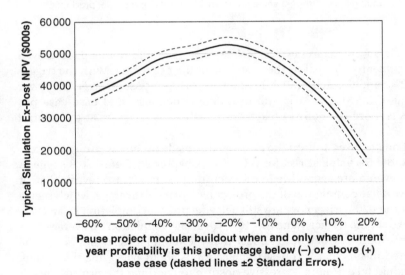

Figure 20.7 Effect of changing level of trigger value for modular production timing flexibility (Simple Myopic Delay Rule).

discourage pausing the production. Conversely, positive triggers encourage pausing the production, as they require more than just zero relative profit in order to continue the sales of housing units.

In contrast to what we saw in Chapters 18 and 19 with overall project start-delay flexibility, in the case of modular start delay, it is better to be a bit aggressive, a bit biased against triggering the pause option, after the project has begun. In part, this may reflect the fact that infrastructure cost is likely to have already been sunk by the time the pause option might be triggered. With infrastructure cost sunk, there is a stronger NPV-based argument to continue the project to completion.

Figure 20.7 reveals that the optimal trigger value for the modular delay option (by itself, without any other options) is approximately negative 20% (or even a little

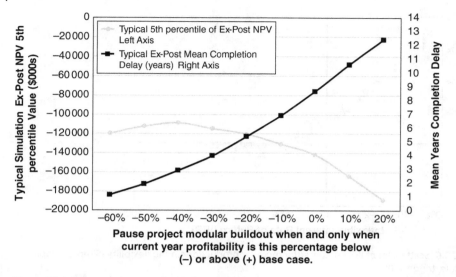

Figure 20.8 Effect of changing level of trigger value on downside results for modular production timing flexibility.

lower)—that is, it is on the "aggressive" side. The project should not be paused even if profitability is currently 20% below the base case of the pro forma. With the trigger set at negative 20%, modular delay flexibility increases the ex-post mean NPV to over $50 M, more than a $25 M gain over the inflexible benchmark and base case pro forma NPV. This is more than $5 M greater than with the trigger set at the neutral value of zero.

Interestingly, if one focuses only on the extreme downside of the investment performance outcomes, the 5% value at risk for NPV (see Chapter 8), Figure 20.8 suggests that we should be even more aggressive in the decision posture. It also reveals that, at the zero trigger, we delay completion of the project by 7 years on average, which seems excessive. Even at the −20% trigger, we are still delaying project completion by an average of 5 years. If we set the trigger value to −40%, we delay completion on average by 3 years, which seems more reasonable. The fact that the modular delay option can be repeatedly triggered means that it is best to be cautious about triggering the option. The developer should take a more aggressive posture to continue the project once it has begun. This contrasts with what works best with the option to delay the overall start of the project, which we examined in Chapter 19. In that case, the "neutral" trigger value of zero gave the best results. These differences make sense intuitively.

20.5 Effect of Combining Start-Delay and Modular Production Delay Flexibility

As we noted previously, an important advantage of simulation modeling of flexibility over the formal option models popular among academic economists is that simulation can represent multiple options simultaneously. We have also seen that two different

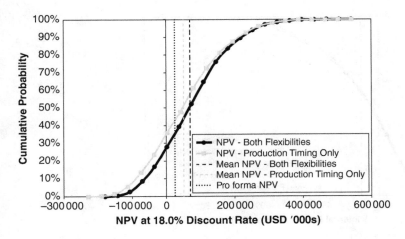

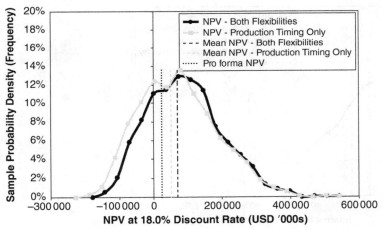

Figures 20.9–20.10

types of defensive timing options, to delay either the start of the project (Chapters 18 and 19) or the production of modules, each enhance project value significantly, but slightly differently. For example, in the Garden City project, the start-delay option added some $45 M to the expected NPV of an otherwise identical project that does not have flexibility, while modular production timing flexibility added only about $25 M (in each case, based on setting the delay decision trigger at its optimal level for mean NPV enhancement). These two options for production timing are not necessarily mutually exclusive. A project might well have both types of flexibilities. How much additional value would we get with both options together?

Figures 20.9–20.12 show the joint value of both options together, compared to that of only the modular production flexibility that we focus on in this chapter. As you can see, adding start-delay flexibility to modular production timing flexibility improves the overall investment performance of the project. For example, it increases the expected IRR from under 27% to over 28%, a gain of over 100 basis points. It also slightly reduces the IRR standard deviation from about 15% to barely over 14%. The dual option project

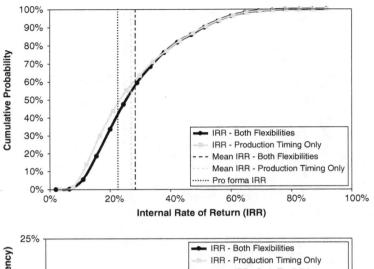

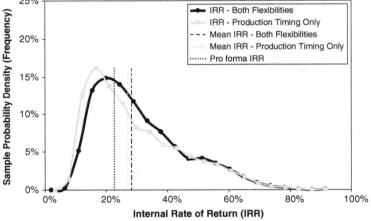

Figures 20.11–20.12

beats the single-option project in almost half of the scenarios, while only losing to the single-option project a little over 5% of the time.

However, the dual option adds very little performance to the start-delay option by itself. The mean NPV outcome is effectively no higher with both options than with just the start-delay option. The two options together do reduce the downside of the IRR distribution in the extreme left-hand tail, where the 5th percentile value at risk IRR is over 600 basis points higher than with just the start-delay option (11% versus 5%), even though the mean IRR is just barely higher.

At least in terms of expectations (mean outcome values), it seems that, once full flexibility exists to delay the start of the project, subsequent modular production flexibility does not add much value to the project (although it may improve the extreme downside performance). In essence, once the developer has the opportunity to delay the start of the overall project, there is, apparently, rarely additional value to further delay in the subsequent production. This also helps explain why the optimal decision posture for the modular delay option is more aggressive (negative trigger level) to avoid pausing the project.

Yet, flexibility in production timing after the start of the project can be valuable. For example, the developer may face constraints on the ability to delay the start of the project. Financial, managerial, or political pressures may force the developer to be aggressive about starting the project. We saw in Chapter 18 how the Aggressive Developer Rule that we modeled resulted in a much smaller gain in value—only about $8 M increment in the expected NPV, and the expected IRR went up to only 21% (with almost 23% standard deviation). But the developer might well be less constrained once the project starts. There might be greater latitude to apply a more advantageous decision posture toward subsequent delays in the buildout of the project. In that case, our simulation model indicates that modular production timing flexibility clearly adds significant value to the project.

The general finding regarding multiple timing options seems to be that the individual options tend to duplicate each other to a considerable degree. Combining options certainly does no harm from an investment performance perspective (and may help the downside exposure), but the effects are far from additive. The value of multiple timing options is only slightly greater than the value of the best individual timing option by itself.

20.6 Conclusion

This chapter presented an in-depth and quantitative study of the investment performance implications of modular production timing flexibility in real estate development projects, using our Garden City project as the illustrative example. We found that such flexibility adds importantly to the investment performance appeal of the project, although not as much as the basic option to delay the start of a project, which was the focus of Chapters 18 and 19.

We also explored the effect of combining the two types of timing options—start delay and production timing. We found that the combination of the two timing options is largely redundant in terms of investment performance. It produces an investment performance only slightly better than that of the better of the two options individually. In the following chapter, we will consider a different type of option, a product option instead of a timing option, as we explore product mix flexibility.

21

Product Mix Flexibility

This Chapter Presents the Option to Change Product Mix, and Examines
the Effect of Volatility on Option Value

LEARNING OBJECTIVES

- Understand product mix flexibility in real estate development projects;
- See how to model and value this flexibility in the simulation analysis of DCF;
- Understand this flexibility as both a defensive and an offensive option;
- Discover how the value of such flexibility depends on the correlation between the pricing of product types;
- Discover the synergy between product mix and timing options;
- See the effect of volatility on the value of development options.

OUTLINE OF THE CHAPTER

21.1 Product Mix Flexibility
21.2 Modeling the Product Mix Option
21.3 Value of Product Mix Flexibility
21.4 Effect of Combining Product Mix Flexibility and Timing Options
21.5 Effect of Correlation in the Product Markets on the Value of Product Mix Flexibility
21.6 Effect of Volatility on the Value of Flexibility
21.7 Conclusion

This chapter focuses on a different type of flexibility—a product option as distinct from a timing option. We look at the flexibility to change the mix of products—specifically, to switch production between different types of buildings.

We see that product mix flexibility is essentially different from the timing options. It is not merely defensive in nature, but also offensive. Product mix flexibility is thus not redundant to the timing options, as the timing options are among themselves, as we saw in Section 20.5. Product mix flexibility adds distinct value to the timing options.

After we include the product switching option in our Garden City model, it is a good time to explore the general effect of market volatility on the value of development flexibility. We can explore this effect on a model that combines all three types of flexibilities: start delay, production timing, and product switching. We consider both the effect of volatility and of correlation between the product types on the investment performance characteristics of the Garden City project.

Flexibility and Real Estate Valuation under Uncertainty: A Practical Guide for Developers, First Edition.
David Geltner and Richard de Neufville.
© 2018 John Wiley & Sons Ltd. Published 2018 by John Wiley & Sons Ltd.
Companion website: www.wiley.com/go/geltner-deneufville/flexibility-and-real-estate-valuation

21.1   Product Mix Flexibility

Product options reflect flexibility in the quantity or type of real estate product(s) being constructed (see Section 13.4). In themselves, they do not affect the timing of the construction. They are "what" options, not "when" options. Product mix flexibility in its pure form would hold constant the total quantity of the product. It is thus different conceptually from expansion options (which we discuss in Chapter 23).

In the case of a project producing a large number of small, relatively homogeneous individual building units, such as the Garden City housing project, "product mix flexibility" refers to the developer's ability to change the proportion of the total quantity of building production in each type of real estate product. For example, some housing units might be of different sizes, configurations, or fit-outs, aimed at different submarkets of housing. Or, units might be aimed at different tenure markets, such as rental versus condominium.

In the case of projects producing one or more large buildings in more discrete quantities, product mix flexibility reflects the developer's ability to change the type of structure on relatively short notice with little expense or operational difficulty. For example, the idea is to be able, perhaps just prior to (or even after) the start of construction, to switch the plans for a building from apartment to hotel, or warehouse to lab space, and so forth.

Product mix flexibility does not exist to a great degree in some, perhaps most, development projects. Developers may have to invest in substantial planning, specialized design, and other preparation to enable this type of flexibility. Is such extra planning and management worth it? The analysis in this chapter shows how to answer that question, and provides some suggestive results based on our Garden City example project.

21.2   Modeling the Product Mix Option

How can we introduce product mix flexibility into the spreadsheet-based DCF valuation model? In essence, we model product mix flexibility in the same way as the production timing flexibility that we considered in the preceding three chapters. We formulate a decision rule in the spreadsheet DCF model. We base this rule on a decision criterion that is observable at the time when the option to switch products can be exercised.

The decision criterion typically compares the relative profitability between or among the types of products. In any given future scenario, in any given year, such profitability will result from the realization of the pricing factors based on our probability and market dynamics inputs.

Recall that, in the Garden City project, we identified two different types of housing units, which we labeled "Type A" and "Type B." For simplicity of illustration, and to explore an archetypical result, we assume that the two types are completely interchangeable. That is, the developer can decide what type to sell each year, and then build this type during the following 2 years. Indeed, to consider an extreme case, analogous to our model of modular production timing in the previous chapter, we here assume that the product mix is all or nothing. We sell either only Type A or only Type B in any given year, and we can switch back and forth from one year to the next.

We use a simple decision criterion. In each year of the scenario, the spreadsheet compares the current price of Type A and Type B houses. Since, for simplicity, we assume that both types of houses have the same construction cost, this criterion effectively compares the current relative profitability of each type of housing product based solely on the relative demand for the two products, which underlies their respective pricing factor realizations. This is a logical basis for the product mix decision in any given year. (This decision rule is also admittedly myopic. It only considers a single year, rather than several. In that respect, it is analogous to the Simple Myopic Delay Rule for the delay option we used in the two previous chapters.)

In general, the analyst can also input a trigger value into the decision rule. For example, this might switch construction from Type A to Type B only if their difference in profitability exceeds the trigger percentage. That is, if the trigger is input is 10%, then:

- The switch to sell only Type A that year will occur only if Type A's current price realization exceeds Type B's current price realization by more than 10% of the base case average projected housing sales profit per unit for that year.
- Conversely, the switch will occur in the other direction, selling only Type B, if the Type A minus Type B profit realization falls below negative 10% of the base case profit projection for that year.

In fact, a trigger value of zero is optimal under the conditions set up for our stylized, archetypical analysis. Any other value would allow the sale of some less profitable houses. Our analysis thus sets the decision rule such that, each year, the developer sells only and entirely whichever type of housing is more profitable, which effectively equates to whichever type has the highest current pricing factor realization.

Our market dynamics assumptions create a high degree of contemporaneous cross-correlation in the pricing factor realizations for Type A and Type B housing (see Section 17.1). In effect, we assume that these two products are very similar, and that their markets are highly correlated. But they are not perfectly correlated. To some extent, each type exhibits its own individual random walk and idiosyncratic noise elements. Specifically, our standard inputs for the Garden City project assume that each type of housing displays annual price volatility just under 20%, with a correlation between the two of around 80%. We vary these assumptions later, in Section 21.5.

Because the Type A and Type B housing pricing factors are not perfectly correlated, one type or the other will randomly turn out to be more profitable in any given year. Our option to switch the product mix responds to the random realization of this relative pricing history across the future scenario. While this model is clearly a simplified version of reality, it captures the essence of how product mix flexibility can work in a real estate development project that produces a large number of relatively small, homogeneous building units, especially if the design of the project allows it.

21.3 Value of Product Mix Flexibility

Figures 21.1–21.4 show typical target curves resulting from the Monte Carlo simulation of product mix flexibility in our example Garden City project. Two features are noteworthy.

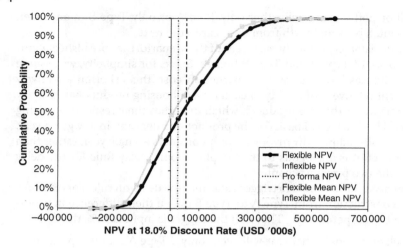

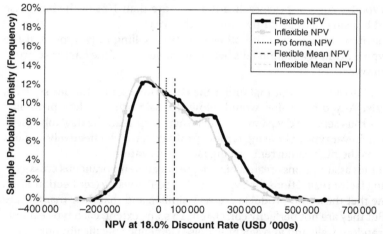

Figures 21.1–21.2

First, it is clear that the product mix flexibility adds value for investors:

- The expected NPV with flexibility is about $30 M greater than that of the inflexible project, equal to 13% of the pro forma valuation of the land, and over 3% of the gross PV of the assets to be built.
- The expected IRR increases over 500 basis points, to approximately 25% from 20%.

Second, the entire outcome distributions shift in the positive direction (to the right on the horizontal axis). The:

- Downside tail, 5% value at risk, of the IRR distribution rises approximately 700 basis points, from negative 19% to negative 12%.
- Upside tail, 95th percentile, rises a similar amount, from approximately 57% to 63%.

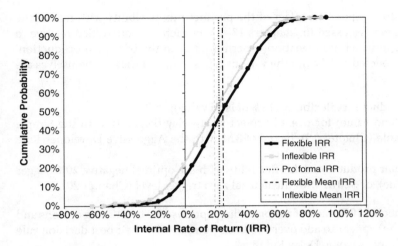

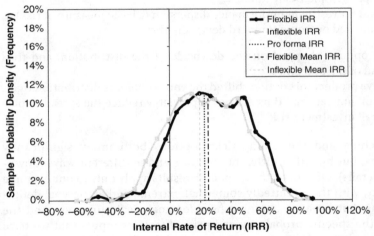

Figures 21.3–21.4

This shift of the entire outcome distribution is different from what we saw with the timing options in the previous three chapters. The timing options primarily only affected the downside outcomes. They were defensive delay options.

In contrast, the product mix option is both defensive and offensive. In effect, it is both a:

- Call on the product type being chosen, while simultaneously being a
- Put on the type being avoided.

The switching option lets developers both take advantage of upside opportunities and avoid downside outcomes.

It is instructive to compare the effect of the product mix flexibility with that of the timing flexibilities we discussed in Chapters 18–20, in each case quantified relative to the inflexible case in which no deviation is permitted from the base plan production. The increases in expected NPV from the various types of flexibilities by themselves are approximately:

- $30 M for the product mix flexibility (13% of land value);
- $45 M (20% of land value) for overall project start-delay flexibility with the Simple Myopic Delay Rule (Chapter 19), or only $8 M with the Aggressive Developer Rule (Chapter 18);
- $25 M for modular production delay flexibility with the optimal negative 20% trigger (11% of land value), or $20 M with the neutral zero trigger level (Chapter 20).

As regards the expected IRR, each of the preceding options (the two timing options and the switching option) appear to add over 500 basis points under their best decision rule settings (for the Simple Myopic Delay Rule).

In terms of the future investment performance dispersion (a basic measure of risk) as measured by the simulated outcome standard deviation, the:

- Defensive timing options chopped off the downside of the distribution, and thus reduced the spread of the outcomes.
- Offensive/defensive product mix option shifted the entire outcome distribution right, but did not chop off any tail, and thus did not appreciably reduce the spread of outcomes or the overall investment risk.

The product switching and the timing delay options both imply significantly increased land value, but by rather different amounts and in different ways (downside tail versus both tails). Of course, these specific results apply only to our example Garden City project, with the admittedly somewhat extreme and archetypal definitions of the options that we are examining here for analytical purposes. And the results depend on the specific probability and price dynamics inputs that we have been using in the simulation. However, we constructed the Garden City example as a typical type of multiple-asset development project, and we believe our pricing input assumptions are realistic for typical real estate markets. Most of the investment performance results are generally and qualitatively robust to reasonable variations in the price dynamics input assumptions, and not biased to be favorable for flexibility value.

The scatterplot in Figure 21.5 provides another perspective on the difference between the product mix switching and the delay options. For the timing options (see Figures 18.5, 19.5, and 20.6), the cloud of outcome dots showing how the IRR of the flexible case outperformed the IRR of the inflexible case, generally:

- Sloped downward from left to right;
- Was higher above the zero-difference horizontal axis over the downside outcomes toward the left of the graph;
- Indicated some scenarios in which the inflexible project outperformed the flexible project, even if these scenarios were few and clustered in the upside of favorable project outcomes.

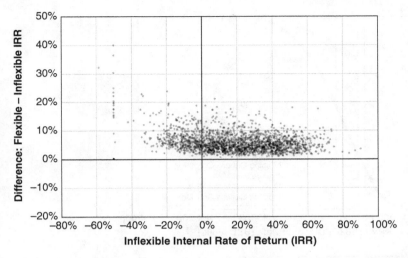

Figure 21.5 Scatterplot of IRR outcomes for product mix flexibility versus no flexibility at all.

By contrast, Figure 21.5 shows that the similar cloud of outcome dots for the product switching option is:

- Not sloped over the horizontal axis;
- Quite evenly above the horizontal axis, except for some (very few) extreme high outliers on the downside;
- Always entirely above the horizontal axis.

The dominance of the flexible case for the product mix option is a result of the zero trigger level. In effect, this steers the project toward always selling a greater proportion of the more profitable type of housing. Chance guarantees that it would be rare indeed for there to be an outcome in which the pricing factors were always identical between the two product types.

21.4 Effect of Combining Product Mix Flexibility and Timing Options

Our product switching option provides a fundamentally different improvement in investment performance than that provided by the delay options. It thus seems likely that the product mix option might combine more complementarily with the timing options. Recall that the two timing options, the start-delay option (Chapters 18 and 19) and the modular production flexibility (Chapter 20), combined together largely redundantly (see Section 20.5). The overall investment performance with the two options together was hardly superior to that of the best of either type of timing option by itself, at least in terms of the central tendency of the result.

Now look at Figures 21.6–21.9. They compare the target curve outcomes for all three options together with the outcomes of just the two timing options together (using the Simple Myopic Delay Rule and optimum trigger values). Notice that the incremental effect of adding the product mix option looks very similar to the effect of

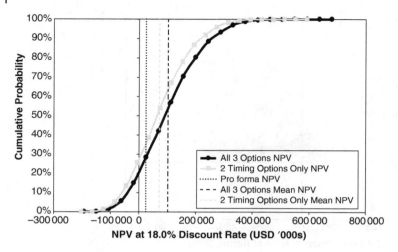

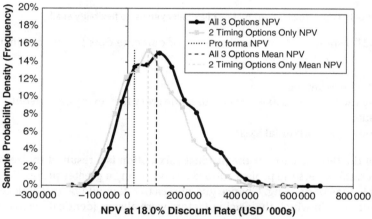

Figures 21.6–21.7

that option by itself (compare Figures 21.6–21.9 with Figures 21.1–21.4). In other words, the product switching option has a largely additive effect on top of the timing options. It improves the:

- Expected NPV by about $30 M to approximately $102 M for the three options combined (over 30% increment in the pro forma land value of $225 M from Chapter 16);
- Expected IRR by slightly less than the effect of the option by itself, but is still significant, adding over 350 basis points, to around 32% for the three options combined;
- IRR 5% value at risk by about 150 basis points, to near 12.5% for the three options combined;
- IRR 95th percentile (upside tail) by some 500 basis points, and, in so doing, slightly increases the spread and standard deviation of the IRR distribution—however, without any negative shift in its downside tail.

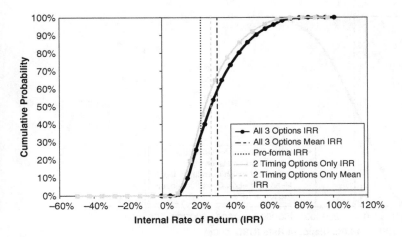

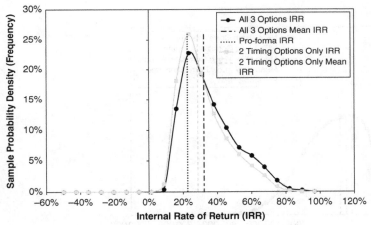

Figures 21.8–21.9

21.5 Effect of Correlation in the Product Markets on the Value of Product Mix Flexibility

The value of product mix flexibility depends heavily on the covariance between the markets for the two types of real estate products. The greater the correlation between the two markets, the less valuable is the switching option, other things being equal (see Section 14.3). In our pricing dynamics inputs for the Garden City example, we have assumed a very high correlation between the two markets, with an annual price-change correlation coefficient of approximately 80% (across time within a given randomly generated future scenario).

Figures 21.10–21.13 show the effect of varying this assumption, specifically of reducing the correlation from 80% to 30%, holding other things constant. The charts

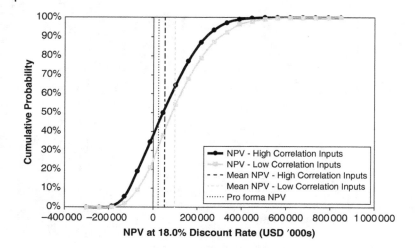

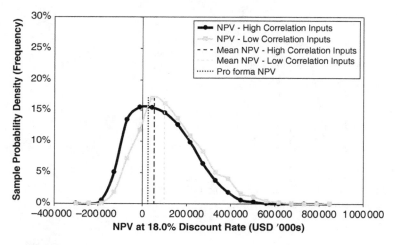

Figures 21.10–21.11

model the product switching option only, without the timing options included in the previous charts. The lower correlation provides the product switching option with more opportunity to improve the project value over the inflexible half-and-half base plan. This improvement occurs broadly over the range of project outcomes. (Notice how the target curves are almost uniformly right-shifted over the project NPV and IRR results.)

These comparisons make an important analytical point about how switching options add value. As noted, they provide simultaneous "puts" and "calls." However, in reality, it may be unlikely that two types of real estate products that could be easily substituted for one another within the same project would have a price correlation as low as 30%.

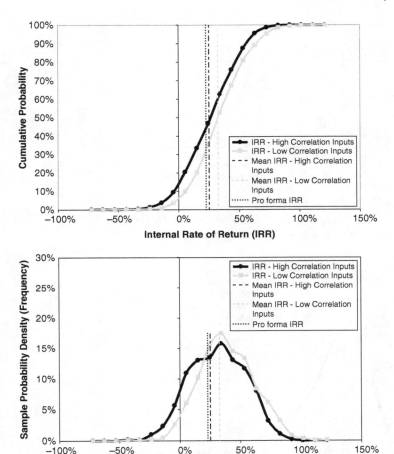

Figures 21.12–21.13

21.6   Effect of Volatility on the Value of Flexibility

Now that we have covered the two timing options and one product option in some depth, this is a good time to step back and explore an important principle of option valuation. The greater the future uncertainty, the more valuable the options become. This is due to the "all gain and no pain" feature of options' right without obligation. Regarding real estate developments, the magnitude of the real estate market price volatility reflects the amount of uncertainty. Options enable the developer to take advantage of upside opportunities and/or to avoid downside outcomes. When we discussed this general principle in Section 12.3, we did so qualitatively, and not quantitatively. So now we ask: How valuable is this favorably asymmetric payoff ability that options have in a typical real-world development project? Our Garden City model allows us to explore this question.

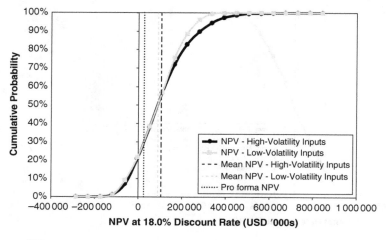

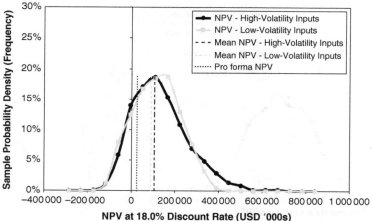

Figures 21.14–21.15

Figures 21.14–21.17 show the effect of two different assumptions about product price volatility on the outcomes resulting from combining our three options together: start-delay flexibility, modular production timing flexibility, and product mix flexibility. The black curve assumes real estate market price volatility of approximately 23% per year. The gray curve assumes volatility of about 17% per year. All other assumptions are the same as in our previous analysis. This range is plausible for property assets in the United States, and we used the same volatility assumptions in Figures 17.6–17.9, which showed the effect on project outcomes without flexibility. (In general, our assumption has been relevant volatility of around 20%. Keep in mind that the relevant volatility is not that of an index or market aggregate, but for the individual Garden City built property, including its idiosyncratic risk.)

The ex-post mean NPV is around $89 M for the low-volatility assumption, and $105 M for the high-volatility assumption. The central tendency of the outcome distributions suggests that the high-volatility case increased the value of the combined options, adding around $15 M to the expected NPV, an increment of almost 7% of the land value,

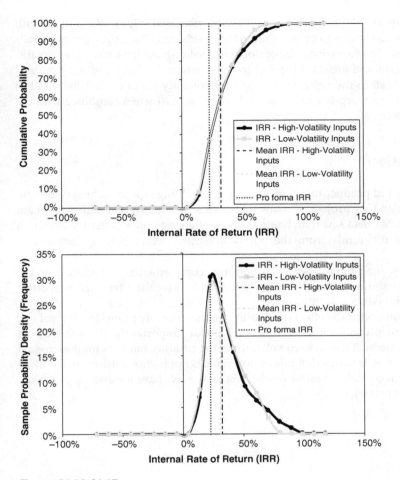

Figures 21.16–21.17

compared to the low-volatility case. This contrasts with the situation without flexibility. In that case, the expected NPV and IRR of the Garden City project is not significantly different in the two volatility scenarios, although the standard deviations of the possible outcomes is, of course, greater in the high-volatility environment (see Section 17.4).

It is important to note that we are assuming the same present value of the built project, across the two volatility assumptions, to see the pure effect of volatility, holding all else constant.

As you can see from the target curves, the increase in land value accompanies a slight increase in the outcome range, or risk, in the project value. The standard deviation of the project's future realized IRR increases from about 15%, with 17% volatility in the built property, to about 17%, with 23% volatility in the built property.

While greater market volatility in real estate clearly tends to increase option value (holding other things equal), it is interesting that the magnitude of this effect is not very large over the likely typical range of volatility in real estate markets.

The curves in Figures 21.14–21.17 suggest that the increased value of the options with greater volatility is due largely to a right-shift in the upside outcomes, the right-hand tails of the distributions. The defensive delay options cut the left-hand tails, but higher volatility spreads these tails and offsets this effect to some extent. In short, the delay options shift the left-hand tail to the right, but the greater volatility shifts the left-hand tail to the left. The two effects largely cancel each other out, at least when combined with the product mix option.

21.7 Conclusion

This chapter explored product mix flexibility, or the building type switching option, in our example Garden City project. We saw that such a product option adds significant value to a project. We also saw that, being both an offensive and a defensive option, it adds value rather differently from the purely defensive delay options discussed in Chapters 18–20.

We also saw how the product switching option is complementary or additive to the timing options. We showed how correlation in the markets for the alternative real estate products affects the switching option value.

Finally, we demonstrated the effect of volatility on the value of options in a typical real estate development project. Other things being equal (importantly, the value of the property assets to be built), increased volatility in the product markets implies greater option value. However, it seems that this option value is not highly sensitive to the likely range of volatility in typical real estate markets, at least as we have modeled these values in our simulation analysis.

22

Project Phasing Flexibility

We Show How to Model and Evaluate the Delay Flexibility Inherent
in Project Phasing

LEARNING OBJECTIVES

- Understand the difference between modular delay and phasing delay flexibility;
- Learn how to model phasing delay flexibility in a spreadsheet;
- Explore quantitatively the value of phasing delay flexibility with a simple two-phase example project.

OUTLINE OF THE CHAPTER

22.1 Modeling the Sequential Phase Delay Option
22.2 Modifying the Garden City Project Plan
22.3 Project Economics
22.4 The Delay Decision Model
22.5 Exploring the Value of Project Phasing Flexibility
22.6 Conclusion

In Chapter 20, we saw that modular production timing flexibility can add substantial value to a multi-asset development project. But, for many real estate development projects, the modular type of production flexibility is not realistic. However, it is widely possible to divide a large, multi-building project into two or more distinct, pre-planned "phases." As described in Chapter 15, phasing flexibility involves a plan to produce parts or sections of the overall project separately, with each phase being able to function independently if necessary. Indeed, the phasing of large projects is quite common. Such phasing generally brings with it considerable timing flexibility—in particular, to delay the start of subsequent phases beyond the base plan schedule represented in the original pro forma. We now explore this subject by considering a modified version of our example Garden City project.

22.1 Modeling the Sequential Phase Delay Option

Phases in a real estate development can be either parallel or sequential (see Section 15.5). Parallel phases do not depend on each other physically or temporally. We can therefore simply model them as separate projects containing start-delay flexibility, as covered in

Flexibility and Real Estate Valuation under Uncertainty: A Practical Guide for Developers, First Edition.
David Geltner and Richard de Neufville.
© 2018 John Wiley & Sons Ltd. Published 2018 by John Wiley & Sons Ltd.
Companion website: www.wiley.com/go/geltner-deneufville/flexibility-and-real-estate-valuation

Chapters 18 and 19. Sequential phases have some sort of temporal dependency, and are the subject of the present chapter.

As we indicated in Chapter 15, a key characteristic of phases is that, once started, they must be completed. Developers cannot (or should not) pause or further delay a phase. Therefore, modeling of sequential phases in a computer spreadsheet has much in common with the modeling of the flexibility to delay the overall project (Chapters 18 and 19). But there are some particular differences. Some phases begin after the first phase in the project.

First, in the present chapter, we will assume that the first phase of the project starts immediately, without flexibility in the project start date. This is simply to distinguish the two types of options: overall project start delay (Chapters 18 and 19) versus subsequent phased production delay (this chapter). One reason to distinguish these options is that overall start delay is much more common. Almost all projects have it. Phasing flexibility is only possible in projects that have phases, which are relatively large projects. Of course, in reality, the existence of overall project start delay does not preclude the existence of phasing in the project. (In Chapter 23, we will discuss the two types of flexibilities together.)

Second, we must explicitly model the temporal or sequential dependence between or among the phases. In the simplest case, the project contains only two phases; so we only have to model delay flexibility for one phase, call it "Phase 2." The modeling of this delay flexibility is similar to the modeling of the modular delay flexibility in Chapter 20, except that, for phasing delay, we do not allow subsequent pausing or further delay of any phase once it has begun. The delay option that we focus on in this chapter exists only between, not within, individual phases.

The mechanism for modeling phase start-delay flexibility is to put a delay decision rule in the appropriate cells of the spreadsheet, as in Chapters 18–20. In each period in the spreadsheet model of the project, the decision rule checks the current (and possibly also recent past) relevant outcomes in the real estate market (as indicated by the realized pricing factors) against user-input delay decision criteria. If user-specified delay trigger values are breached, then the decision rule delays the start of the phase for that period. This process repeats in the subsequent period, through to the end of an analysis time horizon that is sufficiently long to reasonably represent the amount of delay flexibility that exists.

22.2   Modifying the Garden City Project Plan

To explore the implications of phasing delay flexibility for the investment value of a project, we apply our DCF valuation model of the example Garden City housing project. Only now, in order to focus on just the value of the option to delay the start of a phase, we slightly simplify the example.

Table 22.1 presents the base plan for the stylized version of the Garden City project we use for this exercise. The ultimate design and scale of the overall project are very similar to the project introduced in Chapter 16. The main difference is in the temporal profile of the sale and production of the buildout quantities. Instead of the single-peaked temporal profile of Chapter 16, we substitute a uniform sales and production rate over time. Such a temporal profile is more appropriate for a phased project. The plan is to

Table 22.1 Pro forma base plan for two-phase Garden City project.

#	DEVELOPMENT PROJECT PLAN	UNITS	TOTALS	YEAR 0	YEAR 1	YEAR 2	YEAR 3	YEAR 4	YEAR 5	YEAR 6	YEAR 7	YEAR 8	YEAR 9
1	Total Sold	Residences	840		120	120	120	120	120	120	120	0	0
2	Total Infrastructure Quantities	Residence Equivalent	240		80	80				80	0	0	0
3	Land Cost	USD '000s		$170,000									
4	**Phase 1**												
5	Phase 1 Infrastructure Quantities	Residence Equivalent	160		80	80	0	0	0	0	0	0	0
6	Infrastructure Construction Costs	USD '000s	$103,020		$51,000	$52,020	$0	$0	$0	$0	$0	$0	$0
7	Total Sold	Residences	480		120	120	120	120	0	0	0	0	0
8	Total Started	Residences	480		120	120	120	120	0	0	0	0	0
9	Total Completed	Residences	480		0	120	120	120	120	0	0	0	0
10	Phase 1 Revenues	USD '000s	$630,606		$51,000	$103,020	$156,080	$159,202	$107,182	$54,122	$0	$0	$0
11	Phase 1 Construction Costs	USD '000s	$324,825		$0	$39,015	$79,591	$81,182	$82,806	$42,231	$0	$0	$0
12	Phase 1 Profits	USD '000s	$305,781		$51,000	$64,005	$76,490	$78,020	$24,376	$11,891	$0	$0	$0
13	**Phase 2**												
14	Phase 2 Infrastructure Quantities	Residence Equivalent	80		0	0	0	0	0	80	0	0	0
15	Infrastructure Construction Costs	USD '000s	$56,308		$0	$0	$0	$0	$0	$56,308	$0	$0	$0
16	Total Sold	Residences	360		0	0	0	0	120	120	120	0	0
17	Total Started	Residences	360		0	0	0	0	120	120	120	0	0
18	Total Completed	Residences	360		0	0	0	0	0	120	120	120	0
19	Phase 2 Revenues	USD '000s	$506,839		$0	$0	$0	$0	$55,204	$111,512	$168,946	$113,742	$57,434
20	Phase 2 Construction Costs	USD '000s	$261,073		$0	$0	$0	$0	$0	$42,231	$86,151	$87,874	$44,816
21	Phase 2 Profits	USD '000s	$245,766		$0	$0	$0	$0	$55,204	$69,281	$82,795	$25,868	$12,618
22	Net Annual Cash Flows	USD '000s	$392,219	-$170,000	$0	$11,985	$76,490	$78,020	$79,580	$24,863	$82,795	$25,868	$12,618
23	NPV @ 18.0% Discount Rate	USD '000s	$5,117										
24	IRR		18.76%										

#	Project Economics	Time 0 PV		YEAR 1	YEAR 2	YEAR 3	YEAR 4	YEAR 5	YEAR 6	YEAR 7	YEAR 8	YEAR 9
25	Project Economics	Time 0 PV										
26	Built Asset Revenues	$815,306	=PV[V]	$51,000	$103,020	$156,080	$159,202	$162,386	$165,634	$168,946	$113,742	$57,434
27	Construction Costs	$643,378	=PV[K]	$51,000	$91,035	$79,591	$81,182	$82,806	$140,770	$86,151	$87,874	$44,816
28	Implied Land Market Value	$171,929	=PV[y]-PV[K]	$0	$11,985	$76,490	$78,020	$79,580	$24,863	$82,795	$25,868	$12,618
29	Implied Mkt OCC (as IRR)	18.47%	-$171,929									

produce 120 housing units per year over 7 years, for a total of 840 units. (This is slightly less than the 850 units in the Chapter 16 example project). In detail:

- The project begins with infrastructure construction during Years 1 and 2.
- Housing sales begin in Year 1 and proceed uniformly from Years 1 through 7.
- Housing construction starts in Year 2 (as the initial infrastructure is completed), and continues uniformly through Year 8.
- Completions are uniform from Years 3 through 9.
- Revenues reflect the same 3-year installment sale procedure as described in Chapter 16 (three equal installment payments in the years of sale, construction start, and construction completion, with the price fixed based on the year of sale).
- Construction costs are incurred contemporaneously and equally across the 2 years of construction, based on contemporary construction pricing as realized each year.
- Another simplification in this phasing example is that we ignore any product differentiation. We assume that all of the housing is the same type in terms of the real estate market governing the relevant pricing dynamics.

Table 22.1 presents the base plan and base case pro forma for our example project with phases. As is typical with multi-phase projects, the pro forma shows the expected future production program and cash flows in separate parts of the table corresponding to each phase. This is the key feature that distinguishes this pro forma from those we have examined in the previous chapters. The pro forma has four sections:

- The top section (rows 1–3) is the schedule for the overall construction quantities and the upfront land cost (which we now assume is $170 M instead of the $200 M price used for the previous examples, for reasons noted in Section 22.3).
- The next two sections (rows 4–12 and 13–21) correspond to Phase 1 and Phase 2, respectively.
- The bottom section (rows 22–29) tabulates the annual net cash flow amounts for the entire project (including both phases) and the summary expected investment performance metrics. Row 23 gives the NPV net of land cost at the given 18% hurdle rate; row 24 shows the IRR at the given $170 M land price; and rows 25–29 present the project economics we describe in Section 22.3.

Figure 22.1a shows the base plan schedule of production in bar-chart form, and Figure 22.1b shows the base case DCF pro forma. (Compare to Figures 16.2a and 16.2b.) The two phases have the same planned production rate of 120 units per year. However:

- Phase 1 includes the two initial years of infrastructure construction, plus the first 4 years of housing construction—480 housing units altogether.
- Phase 2 includes additional infrastructure construction equal to half of the Phase 1 amount, plus another 3 years of housing construction for an additional 360 units of housing. It brings the overall project production to 840 units (marginally less than the 850 units in the Chapter 16 example project).

Phase 2 thus includes three-quarters of the amount of housing as Phase 1, but only requires one-half as much infrastructure. This is typical. Developers often need to front-load more of the project's overall necessary infrastructure in the first phase, for physical or regulatory reasons. In effect, subsequent phases can often, to some extent, "free ride" on the infrastructure of Phase 1. We assume that the investors must pay for the land entirely up front at Time 0 (and this is also when the economic opportunity cost of the land is incurred).

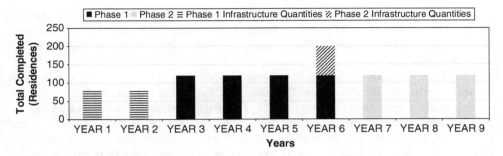

Figure 22.1a Garden City base plan: projected production, two-phase project.

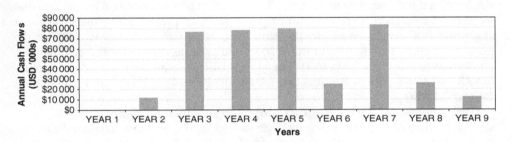

Figure 22.1b Garden City base case: projected net cash flow, two-phase project.

The base plan, Phase 2:

- Begins in Year 5 (4 years behind Phase 1) with pre-sales of its first housing units;
- Must build its infrastructure in the following year; and
- Completes housing construction in Year 9, terminating the entire project.

This plan results in the uniform, continuous housing production seen in Figure 22.1a.

22.3 Project Economics

The NPV of this example two-phase Garden City project differs from that of the previous example. This is because of the way the phased project spreads the rate of production over time. This results in a longer average time until receipt of revenues (or payment of costs), and thus results in lower present values of both benefits and costs. Thus:

- The gross PV of the built assets is now \$815 M instead of the \$883 M of the previous example project, at the same 7% OCC discount rate for these assets (see row 26 in Table 22.1).
- The PV of total construction costs also drops, to \$643 M from \$658 M, at the same 3% OCC discount rate that we discussed in Section 11.2 (see row 27 in Table 22.1).
- Hence, the implied value of the land is reduced to \$815 M – \$643 M = \$172 M in the present version of the project (row 28 in Table 22.1).

If we assume that the project, as designed with the phasing proposed, is indeed providing the highest and best use of the land site, then this implies a lower bid price for the land. For simplicity, we round this to a land price of $170 M, which investors must pay entirely at Time 0.

Apart from the scaling and timing issue discussed in the preceding text, the economics and investment characteristics of the Garden City project remain much as they were in its previous versions in Chapters 16–21. The project's overall pro forma investment risk remains very similar, as its implied market OCC of 18.47% is not very different from the 18.01% rate described in Chapter 16. (Compare the bottom row in Table 22.1 with that of Table 16.1.) This OCC reflects the amount of investment risk in the project as the capital market prices risk in the form of the implied required risk premium in the expected return. (Recall discussion in Section 11.5 and Equation 11.6.) As we noted in Section 16.5, typical practice applies a rounded hurdle rate to the traditional pro forma single-stream net cash flow of the project. We thus retain the same 18% hurdle rate that we applied to the previous version of the Garden City project, since the investment characteristics remain essentially the same. This results in a pro forma NPV for the project of approximately $5 M at the $170 M land price, as seen in row 23 of Table 22.1 (analogous to row 20 in Table 16.1). The $170 M land price provides a pro forma going-in IRR of 18.76% (which is not economically significantly different from the market OCC of 18.47%).

The economics of the Garden City project, as modified for phasing, are thus very similar to that of the original project described in the previous chapters. But the uniform production schedule assumed in this chapter allows us to analyze the effect of phasing delay flexibility with more generality, because the two phases are very similar.

22.4 The Delay Decision Model

As described previously, we assume that Phase 1 does not have delay flexibility; it must commence immediately in Year 1. Phase 2 must follow Phase 1 sequentially. It cannot begin at least until Year 5. But the developer can delay its start indefinitely, as long as conditions in the real estate market are not sufficiently favorable, as governed by the decision rule for delay and its input trigger value level.

The essential measure relevant for the go/no-go decision to delay Phase 2 is the profitability implied by the pricing factors—that is, the current sales prices minus construction costs for the housing units.

The delay decision rule works as follows. In a given scenario (of the many independent random future scenarios, or trials, in the Monte Carlo simulation), in any year in which Phase 2 could otherwise start:

- If the profitability metric is below a trigger value set by the analyst, then the start of Phase 2 will be delayed for that year;
- Otherwise, Phase 2 starts in that year, and then proceeds without further delay or interruption, no matter what happens in the real estate market.

This decision rule is thus essentially the same as the Simple Myopic Delay Rule introduced in Chapter 19. Experimentation reveals that the best trigger value is the "neutral" value of zero (relative to base case profitability). This is the same result we got in Chapter 19 for the option to delay the start of the overall project (see Section 19.4 and Figure 19.6). This is not surprising, since the two options are essentially similar. In both cases, they are the possible initial delay of a production process that cannot be subsequently paused. The second phase is essentially a mini-project by itself. The Phase 2 start delay is like an overall project start delay, except that it cannot commence right away, and it applies only to the Phase 2 part of the project. In this respect, it differs from the modular delay option we were modeling in Chapter 20, where we found that a more aggressive trigger posture was preferable.

22.5 Exploring the Value of Project Phasing Flexibility

The results of the Monte Carlo simulation analysis are shown in Figures 22.2–22.5. As in the previous Monte Carlo results, the target curves represent NPV at the given project hurdle rate (18%) and the IRR at the given land price ($170 M).

First, compare the ex-post investment performance results recognizing uncertainty with the traditional, single-stream pro forma NPV of $5 M (Table 22.1). The mean of the ex-post NPV distribution in the simulation outcomes is not statistically different from the pro forma NPV. As we have seen before, this simply reflects the linearity of the present value function and the fact that our pricing factors come from probability distributions that are essentially symmetric around the pro forma pricing assumptions (that is, we assume the pro forma to be unbiased).

Next, note that the Phase 2 start-delay flexibility provides significant value. Its ex-post mean NPV is around $17 M, some $12 M greater than without the delay flexibility. While this gain is only about 1.5% of the pro forma gross present value of the assets to be built, it is a non-trivial sum, and highly statistically significant. (The 95% confidence range is less than ± $0.9 M in our 10 000-trial Monte Carlo model.) This magnitude of benefit represents 7% of the land value.

As we described in our discussion of defensive (put) options (Chapter 13), the benefit of the Phase 2 start-delay flexibility comes from reducing the downside exposure of the project, shifting the left-hand tail of the ex-post performance probability distribution to the right. We can see this clearly in the sample distributions in Figures 22.2–22.5, where most of the right-shift of the target curves for the case with flexibility occurs in the left half, well below the median performance. This is particularly true in the IRR outcome.

As before, the concavity of the IRR function causes the mean ex-post IRR (the going-in expected IRR) without flexibility to be slightly less than the pro forma going-in IRR—slightly under 17% instead of closer to 19%. Additionally, the:

- Mean IRR of the flexible project averages almost 400 basis points above that of the inflexible project, at over 20% (at the $170 M land price);
- Standard deviation of the IRR outcome is reduced from almost 15% with no flexibility to less than 9% with the phase delay flexibility;
- Downside tail of the IRR distribution, represented by the 5th percentile of the outcome, exceeds that of the inflexible project by some 1300 basis points (+8% instead of –5%).

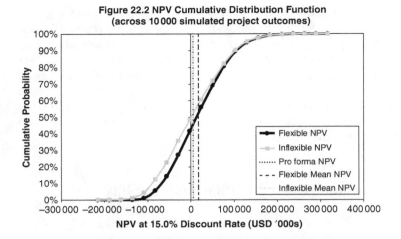

Figure 22.2 NPV Cumulative Distribution Function
(across 10 000 simulated project outcomes)

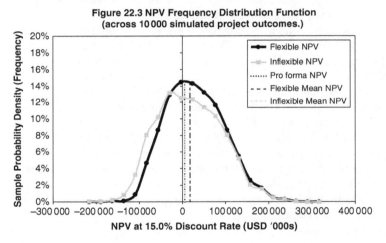

Figure 22.3 NPV Frequency Distribution Function
(across 10 000 simulated project outcomes.)

Figures 22.2–22.3

As the scatter plot in Figure 22.6 displays graphically:

- The flexible project beats the inflexible project in simulated IRR almost four times more often than the reverse happens; and
- In about 45% of the outcomes, the flexibility does not matter, as Phase 2 starts in the base plan Year 5 anyway (dots lying right on the horizontal axis).

Not surprisingly, these results are highly consistent with the quantitative results we found for the option to delay the overall project start in Chapter 19. The difference lies in the fact that the Phase 2 delay option here applies to part of the project, representing less than half its total assets, and cannot start before Year 5. Phasing delay flexibility adds non-trivially to value, clearly improves risk/return investment performance ex-ante, and provides important protection against severe downside

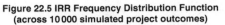

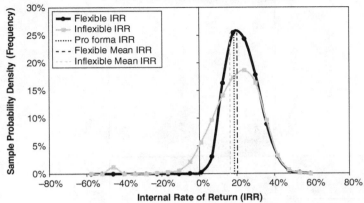

Figure 22.5 IRR Frequency Distribution Function
(across 10 000 simulated project outcomes)

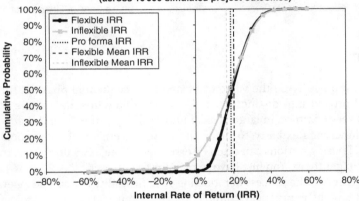

Figure 22.4 IRR Cumulative Distribution Function
(across 10 000 simulated project outcomes)

Figures 22.4–22.5

outcomes that would be of particular concern to conservative investors. Also keep in mind that phasing delay flexibility will often be essentially costless—in the sense that the project owner does not need to incur any additional investment to have this sort of flexibility. It simply requires that the project be designed and planned to allow for the phasing.

Nevertheless, it is important to note that the value of the gain from the Phase 2 start-delay flexibility is small compared to the scale of the project, and much smaller than the gains from production timing flexibility that we saw in Chapter 20 for modular flexibility. This is because delay flexibility limited to only a single subsequent phase is effectively much less flexibility than the type of general stop-and-restart production timing flexibility that we saw with modular production. With effectively less flexibility, we add less value.

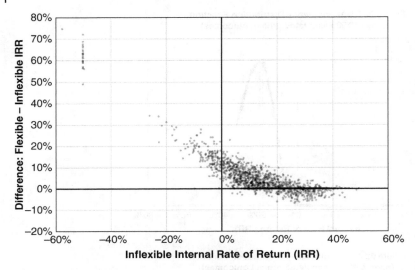

Figure 22.6 Scatterplot of IRR outcomes for flexible versus inflexible two-phase Garden City project.

22.6 Conclusion

This chapter focused on quantifying the value of flexibility in sequential phasing, the breakup of the overall project into distinct parts that must follow in some degree of order. Such phasing is very common in large-scale, multi-building projects, and it generally brings with it inherent flexibility to delay the commencement of subsequent phases (after the first). Phasing options can often be essentially "free"; you don't have to pay anything up front to get them. You just have to plan for the phases.

This chapter walked through the process of modeling such flexibility in a spreadsheet, and then we looked at a realistic practical example, reprising our Garden City project from previous chapters (with modification). We saw that phase start-delay flexibility adds significant value, though not nearly as much as the modular flexibility modeled in Chapter 20.

23

Optimal Phasing

We Now look at Adding Phases, Delineating Phases, and Distinguishing them from Expansion Options

---

LEARNING OBJECTIVES

- Explore the effect of having more phases, holding overall scale constant;
- Explore the best delineation or sizing of phases;
- Understand principles for optimal phasing;
- Distinguish expansion options from additional phases.

OUTLINE OF THE CHAPTER

23.1 Effect of Increasing the Number of Phases
23.2 Principles for Optimal Phasing
23.3 What Is the Difference between a Phase and an Expansion Option?
23.4 Conclusion

In this last chapter of our exploration of the value of flexibility in real estate development projects, we tie up a few loose ends having to do with project phasing. The overall question is: What is the best way to design and program the phases in a project?

- We begin with a natural follow-up to Chapter 22. Since it is good to divide the project into two sequential phases, would it be even better to have three phases (holding the overall scale of the project constant)?
- Second, how should we delineate between phases? That is, how much of the project should we put in one phase versus another, especially in the first phase versus later phases?
- Finally, our analysis of phasing begs a broader question—one that relates back to our typology of development flexibility, introduced in Chapters 13–15. What is the difference between a later "phase" versus what we described as an "expansion option"? We shall see that the key is in the designation of the project's "base plan"—that is, how committed the developer is to carrying out which potential components of the project.

Flexibility and Real Estate Valuation under Uncertainty: A Practical Guide for Developers, First Edition.
David Geltner and Richard de Neufville.
© 2018 John Wiley & Sons Ltd. Published 2018 by John Wiley & Sons Ltd.
Companion website: www.wiley.com/go/geltner-deneufville/flexibility-and-real-estate-valuation

23.1　Effect of Increasing the Number of Phases

We begin by taking a logical next step from Chapter 22, where we examined a two-phase version of the Garden City project. What if we re-cast the Garden City project to be essentially the same, except now we divide it into three phases instead of two?

Let's examine this issue on the same basis as before. We'll continue to examine phase start-timing flexibility only in the subsequent phases, after the first phase, requiring the first phase to start immediately as we did in Chapter 22. The latter two phases must follow sequentially, but the start of either Phase 2 or Phase 3 may be delayed. We apply the same start-delay decision rule and trigger value as with the two-phase project in Chapter 22.

We find that the additional phase clearly adds value. The increase in ex-post mean NPV is strongly statistically significant in our simulations. The rationale is intuitively clear: three phases (with two able to be delayed) has more flexibility to time production than two phases (with only one phase able to be delayed). Our simulations substantiate this point. With the first phase committed to start without delay, the:

- Three-phase project has an average overall completion delay of less than 4 years (reflecting delay in either Phase 2 or Phase 3, or both);
- Two-phase project faces an average completion delay of about 2.5 years.

Importantly, however, the additional value of adding a third phase is not great; it is of minor economic significance, at least in the case of our archetypical Garden City project. It is much smaller than the value of introducing the second phase compared to no flexibility at all. (And recall that adding a flexible second phase added much less value than allowing the entire project to be flexible, as in Chapter 19.) Comparison of the three-phase versus two-phase version of Garden City reveals the following:

- The mean NPV increment due to the third phase is only about $2 M (over the two-phase plan) in a project of $815 M gross present value and $170 M land value. The expected IRR increases by less than 50 basis points as compared to the two-phase project.
- By comparison, the mean NPV increment due to the second phase was $12 M (in the absence of start-delay flexibility for the whole project), and the expected IRR increment was almost 400 basis points (see Chapter 22). And start-delay flexibility for the whole project as a single phase added $45 M (20% of land value) to the inflexible mean NPV, and 700 basis points to the expected IRR (see Chapter 19).

Intuitively, these results would seem to reflect a general rule. Adding more phases (hence, more production timing flexibility), holding overall project scale constant, should increase value, but at a diminishing marginal rate as one adds more phases. The fact that breaking a fixed project into an additional phase adds only a little to the value of flexibility in the project is not surprising after what we discovered in Chapter 20 about the redundancy of production timing options. We noted in Section 20.5 that, if the project has overall start-delay flexibility, adding subsequent production timing delay flexibility does not add as much value as the subsequent production timing flexibility would add by itself if there were no overall start-delay flexibility. Our finding here is similar, again reflecting some redundancy in the options that allow delay of production.

The scatterplots in Figures 23.1 and 23.2 compare the three-phase and two-phase results to each other. Because these projects have slightly different pro formas with different NPVs and IRRs, we cannot directly compare their results—it would be an "apples versus oranges" comparison. The appropriate comparison is each project's difference from its inflexible case. Thus, whether by the NPV or IRR performance metric,

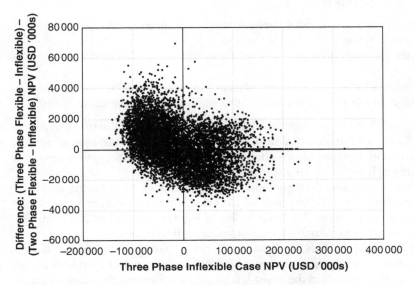

Figure 23.1 Scatterplot comparing NPV for three versus two phases.

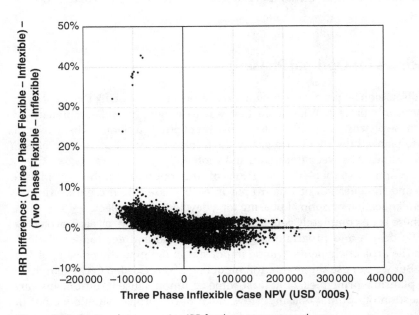

Figure 23.2 Scatterplot comparing IRR for three versus two phases.

the comparison of interest is a "difference of differences." This is the comparison metric shown in the Figures 23.1 and 23.2:

(Three - Phase Flexible – Three - Phase Inflexible) – (Two - Phase Flexible – Two - Phase Inflexible)

In Figures 23.1 and 23.2, the dots:

- Above the horizontal axis (zero-difference line) are scenarios (trials) in which the three-phase project beat the two-phase project;
- Below the axis are outcomes in which the two-phase project beat the three-phase project;
- Exactly on the axis (no difference) are outcomes in which no delay option was triggered, so neither phasing scheme gained more than the other from such flexibility.

Whether by the NPV or IRR metric, the three-phase project beats the two-phase project in over 40% of the outcomes, almost twice as frequently as the reverse occurs. However, there is evidence that adding phases, holding overall project scale constant, is a declining marginal benefit in terms of investment performance.

The third phase adds value defensively, as we would expect, by reducing downside exposure. It provides more flexibility to delay the project in bad market conditions, and thereby avoid or mitigate losses. The scatterplots in Figures 23.1 and 23.2 indicate this through their generally downward sloping shape from left to right.

But this downward slope is only slight, and is almost swamped by the random dispersion in the outcomes. Unlike some of our previous results in earlier chapters, we do see a non-trivial proportion of dots in the lower-left quadrant, indicating that sometimes the two-phase project did better when the project overall was doing poorly. The "insurance" function of the additional flexibility is more limited with the marginal contribution of the third phase.

23.2 Principles for Optimal Phasing

The previous discussion begs a complementary question. Suppose we fix the number of sequential phases in a project: What is the best way to assign physical components of the project to those phases? In other words, given a set of physical elements in an overall project (a "base plan"), how should we group them into sequential phases? In effect, how should we delineate between one phase and another?

The two questions together—the question of the optimal number of phases (Section 23.1) and the question of what to put in each phase (the present section)—define the overall question of optimal phasing for a development project.

Of course, there is no completely general answer to this question, as each project is unique. Specific design and programming issues, physical and economic relationships between the project elements, will be important in defining the phasing of any given project. But we can use the simulation modeling of our Garden City example to identify some plausible principles, or at least some common-sense intuition, answering a basic question of optimal phasing: How much of the project should we put in each phase?

We derive the principles from a study of the range of possibilities in terms of:

- Types of projects (in terms of temporal profiles of production);
- Possible divisions into phases;
- Timing with respect to the real estate cycle.

Our study considers the entire range of possible combinations, but it does not go into excessive detail. The idea is not to be comprehensive; it is to gain insight. As always, we want to "see the forest through the trees."

First, concerning the type of projects, we model the essence of the physical production of the project by defining four archetypical project base plan profiles (Figure 23.3). These cover possible differences in:

- *Duration of project*: 5 and 10 years. These would seem to represent a good range of project duration for major real estate development projects.
- *Temporal distribution of production*: front-loaded, with a peak of work near the beginning of the project (like Garden City of Chapter 16), or uniform over duration (like Garden City of Chapter 22). Again, these would seem to span the main typical patterns.

These base plans, of course, do not depict any production delays caused by the ex-post exercise of timing flexibility.

Second, to explore the optimal delineation of product to phases, we consider the simplest case, in which the project can have at most two phases. Limiting the analysis to two phases provides a parsimonious way to develop the basic intuition that likely applies more broadly. We compare all possible ways of assigning the project's production to the two phases. The comparison in all cases is against the benchmark performance of a project with no phasing and no delay flexibility.

Against this benchmark, we consider all possible schemes for dividing any of the four profiles of Figure 23.3 into two phases. In each scheme, the first phase has no timing flexibility; it must start immediately and proceed to completion without delay. Within this framework, "Scheme 1" places the first year's base plan production in Phase 1 and the rest of the project in Phase 2 (the phase that does have start-delay flexibility). "Scheme 2" places the first 2 years' production in Phase 1 and the rest in Phase 2. And so on. The 5-year projects (whether front-loaded or uniform profile) have four such two-phase schemes (up through "Scheme 4," which places only the fifth-year production of the base plan into the second phase). Similarly, the 10-year projects have nine such possible two-phase schemes, up through "Scheme 9." In addition, we define a "Scheme 0" for each of the four base plan profiles, in which all of the project is put into a single phase that *does* have start-delay flexibility, like the option examined in Chapters 18 and 19 for Garden City. Relative to the benchmark, we therefore have five phasing schemes for each of the two 5-year project base plans (front-loaded and uniform), and 10 phasing schemes for each of the two 10-year project base plans. This framework provides a comprehensive typology for project phasing, given a maximum of two phases.

Third, we need to see how the phasing schemes and base plan profiles interact with the real estate market cycle. Logically, the key driver of the relative success of the alternative phasing schemes would be how the phasing interacts with the real estate market swings in the different base plan profiles—the ups and downs in the market pricing

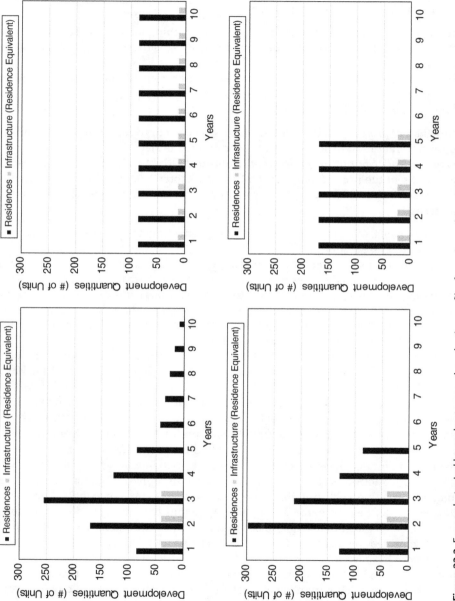

Figure 23.3 Four archetypical base plan temporal production profiles for major real estate development projects.

factors in our simulation scenarios relative to the pro forma projections. This can be most parsimoniously represented by a deterministic cycle. We implement this aspect of the analysis by considering:

- Market cycles of different lengths; and
- Projects starting in different phases of the cycle.

We consider four deterministic cycles of different period lengths: 5, 10, 15, and 20 years. These periods range from being equal to the short (5-year) base plans or half the duration of the 10-year base plans, up to four times the duration of the 5-year plans and twice the duration of the 10-year plans. For each of these cycle periods, we test four different phases of the market cycle as of the beginning of the project ("Time 0"): mid-cycle headed up, peak heading down, mid-cycle heading down, and bottom headed up.

In short, we look comprehensively across all the possible ways in which different phasing schemes could perform, interacting with the market cycles, for the four different base plan production profiles. We replicate the Garden City analyses that we have reported in Chapter 22 and Section 23.1, using the same assumptions concerning the amplitude of the cycles, the discount rate, and the delay decision rule.

We can distill the results of our analysis into a general rule: *Make as much of the project as flexible as possible, as early as possible, but think about the implications of the market cycle.* In more detail, we propose a set of principles:

- As a rule, it's best to make as much of the project subject to start-delay flexibility as possible. Thus, the scheme that has only one phase with full start-delay flexibility often looks best.
- The major exceptions to the preceding general rule are:
  - If the project base plan profile is front-loaded and lasts longer than the market cycle, it's best to put some of the project into a flexible second phase (unless you are at the market cycle peak, in which case you need to do it all in one phase, starting immediately). The idea is to avoid doing the project during down markets and to concentrate it as much as possible into the up-market part of the cycle.
  - If the initial phase cannot have start-delay flexibility, then it's best to minimize the amount of the project in the inflexible first phase. This is because, as we have seen throughout the book, flexibility has value, and more flexibility has more value.
- The preceding rules do not apply to a uniform base plan production profile for projects spread out over a very long time. Their long duration and uniform production "diversify" profitability across the cycle. What they lose in one part of the cycle, they gain in another. Such projects gain relatively little from production timing flexibility, and could, in fact, lose from such flexibility if they start during a recessionary period.

These principles for optimal phasing are neither complete nor comprehensive—nor are they definitive. They derive from a simple, stylized study. But they seem to be consistent with common sense and basic intuition. Combined with our prior findings in Sections 20.4, 21.4, 22.5 and 23.1, we offer these principles as a basis for thinking generally and systematically about the value of timing flexibility and the optimal phasing of real estate development projects.

23.3 What Is the Difference between a Phase and an Expansion Option?

This brings us to the last question that we will take on in this book regarding flexibility in real estate development projects. In Chapters 13–15, we introduced a typology of real estate development project flexibility, and generally distinguished between expansion options and phasing flexibility. We described:

- Phasing flexibility as a type of production timing option, essentially defensive in nature, reflecting the ability to delay the start of a phase of the project if market circumstances are unfavorable;
- Expansion options, whether horizontal or vertical, as product options akin to a call option, an "offensive" type of flexibility aimed at enabling the developer to build additional products in response to upside opportunities.

In some sense, we presented phasing flexibility and expansion options as opposites. In our specific simulation modeling of the example Garden City project in the past chapters, we have provided examples and analysis of phasing options. And we provided an example of one product option: building type mix flexibility. But we have not provided an example analysis of an expansion option. Have we left something out?

We think not. When you get right down to it, in terms of formal, analytical modeling, *an expansion option is not essentially different from another (later) phase of the project.* We can apply the same type of model and simulation analysis to an expansion option as for the phasing options that we illustrated in this and the previous chapter. This is because the distinction between phases and expansions is conceptual rather than formal or mathematical. The distinction reflects the developer's perspective and the corresponding planning decisions. For example, we noted in Chapter 12 that the Bentall 5 vertical expansion in the Vancouver building could be viewed as a defensive ("put" type) option to delay (or abandon) the top floors of the planned building—or, equally, it could be viewed as an offensive ("call" type) option to add five more floors to the base plan. Either way, it is the same option from the perspective of formal modeling and simulation.

Therefore, we may define the essential difference between a later sequential "phase" and an "expansion option" as being that a:

- "Phase" lies within the original commitment for the project, what we have been calling the "base plan"; and an
- "Expansion option" lies outside or beyond that base plan.

Thus, the distinction between an expansion option and a later phase lies in the planning decision of what to put in, and what to leave out of, the "base plan." This decision will reflect basic and specific physical, legal/regulatory, political, economic, and marketing considerations about the project. It will also reflect the production capacity of the developer, and the limits of the financing sources for the project. Crucially important may simply be the amount of demand foreseen for the project within a reasonable period. It may also be valuable to wait and see how the base plan turns out, to see what we learn about the market as a result of the performance of the base plan, before going very far in the planning or design of an opportunity for additional product on the site.

The difference between "base plan" and "expansion option" would be that the developer is committed to the base plan but not necessarily to the expansion. Operationally, the developer (and financial backers) are "very committed" to producing the *entire* base plan quantity, by some point in time, though not necessarily in the originally planned base plan time frame (as we have seen how valuable delay flexibility is). Perhaps we could even quantify this notionally as reflecting, say, "greater than 90% probability" that the developer will fully complete the base plan. The developer would probably have largely lined up financing for the base plan, and has relatively complete and detailed designs and drawings for it.

In contrast, while developers may hope, and perhaps even expect, to realize an available expansion option someday, they have markedly less commitment and planning for it as of the time they start the project. Again, at a notional level, perhaps we could say something like there is "a 40–60% probability" that an expansion option will ever happen, at least within the foreseeable future. It would not make sense to spend too much time and effort yet on lining up financing or completing detailed plans for such a future option.

In terms of the formal modeling and simulation analysis, there should therefore be only a single but important difference between the analysis and valuation of an expansion option and that of the base plan. To reflect that the expansion option is significantly less likely to happen, we should apply different real estate market pricing dynamics to the real estate products included in the expansion option. We would need to have separate inputs of the dynamics and uncertainty governing the pricing factors for the expansion option simulation, compared to the base plan simulation. For example, in our simulation of delay flexibility and phasing schemes in Garden City, we find that we virtually never abandon the project and almost never fail to complete it. In contrast, a realistic simulation including an expansion option should reflect a non-trivial probability that the expansion option will be abandoned. The input pricing dynamics should reflect such a substantial probability of demand not sufficiently materializing for the expansion. Compared to the dynamics governing the base plan pricing factors, expansion option modeling might involve pricing factors applying to the expansion option that have a lower initial value or grow at a lower trend rate, also likely with greater volatility (to reflect less certainty about the ultimate demand).

23.4 Conclusion

This brings us to the end of our journey! In the overall summary to follow, we will say a few words of overall reflection on the exploration we carried out in this book. In this last substantive chapter, we merely tried to tie up a few loose ends about the nature and value of project phasing. We:

- Further confirmed and elaborated the principle that we first noticed in Section 20.5— that production timing options exhibit a fair degree of redundancy.
- Went deeper conceptually into the question of optimal phasing of large-scale real estate development projects. Perhaps the "biggest picture" aspect of this question regards what to put in a base plan that is (nearly) fully committed to, versus what to leave for subsequent expansion options.

What is clear throughout this chapter, confirming our findings from the previous chapters, is that flexibility adds value in development projects.

24

Overall Summary

We summarize the Main Takeaway Points from this Book

LEARNING OBJECTIVES

- Recognize the importance of explicit modeling of uncertainty and flexibility in real estate investment analysis and project evaluation;
- Grasp the basic, practical tools, methods, and techniques for such modeling, using common computer spreadsheet software;
- Gain some insight and intuition regarding the nature and magnitude of the value of flexibility in real estate development projects, including downside outcome protection, upside outcome opportunities, and the value of common-sense and parsimonious, direct, behavior analog modeling.

As they say when your plane touches down, "we hope you have had a pleasant journey," in this case, through this book. You probably had to "fasten your seatbelts" in a few places. But if you have gotten to this point, and we have helped you to think hard about some important questions, then we would like to think we have piloted you through a worthwhile journey. Let's very briefly review and summarize here our (and, we hope, your) journey.

First, most basically, and importantly, we have tried to show how important it is to *explicitly* consider not only uncertainty but also flexibility in the analysis and evaluation of real estate investments, particularly development projects. At the basic level, this point was a big part of the first part of this book. There, we first reviewed the classical DCF valuation model. We showed its fundamental economic basis and characteristics. As good, well-founded, and widely accepted as this classical model is, we hope we convinced you that it leaves out vitally important considerations, unless you enhance it with the type of explicit consideration of uncertainty and flexibility that we have presented in this book.

We pointed out in Chapters 9 and 10 how the explicit consideration of uncertainty and flexibility can be important when analyzing investments in existing, stabilized income-producing property (investment real estate). The particular example we used was the value of the ability to flexibly time the resale disposition of the property asset. But there are, no doubt, other applications relevant for investments in stabilized properties, perhaps in considering decisions about long-term leases or capital improvements, or certainly the right (without obligation) to renovate or redevelop the property (the redevelopment call option). Existing properties may also have expansion possibilities, if they have unused land or density rights.

Flexibility and Real Estate Valuation under Uncertainty: A Practical Guide for Developers, First Edition. David Geltner and Richard de Neufville.
Companion website: www.wiley.com/go/geltner-deneufville/flexibility-and-real-estate-valuation

But the bulk of this book has been devoted to considering uncertainty and flexibility in real estate development projects. This makes sense because such projects present much more scope and opportunity for different types of flexibilities. Indeed, one of the major contributions of this book has been to systematize the study of such flexibility. We offered a structured typology of real estate development flexibility in Chapters 12–15.

As always in this book, we maintain our basic investment perspective as we study real estate development projects, rooted in fundamental economic and financial principles of opportunity cost. But real estate development projects are, in some sense, "more important" than routine real estate investment in existing physical assets. Development projects are "capital formation," the creation of new physical assets. As such, they have a bigger economic, social, and environmental impact than investment in existing structures. This raises the importance of good, complete economic analysis and evaluation. And such good analytical practice requires the explicit consideration of uncertainty and flexibility. Uncertainty is a fact of reality. And flexibility is a fact of reality in development projects. It is impossible to do a complete, rigorous economic analysis and evaluation of development project investments without explicitly considering both uncertainty and flexibility. This book has demonstrated how to do that in a practical and transparent manner.

Throughout this book, we have attempted to present things one step at a time. We hope that, even if you came into this book with relatively little technical background, you have been able to follow it all the way through, at least for its "big picture" decision analysis–relevant implications. We have presented common-sense methods rooted in the spirit of engineering, rather than highly complex models typical of academic literature in the field of economics. We do not claim complete, formal rigor from an academic economic perspective, as this is not our purpose. But we believe that our approach is well rooted in fundamental economic principles, and is consistent with those principles. We gladly sacrifice formal and complete economic rigor in favor of a transparent, common-sense approach that covers the key realistic aspects of uncertainty and flexibility.

We have taken some care to describe the meaning of the quantitative value findings that we present. We have characterized these evaluations as essentially of a private nature of interest to a given decision-maker, not necessarily market or exchange values. But we have applied fundamental economic principles of opportunity cost in deriving our investment value results. Private valuations fundamentally underlie market valuations and the transaction prices that one observes empirically in real estate markets that reflect equilibrium in those markets. Particularly in the case of development projects, which tend to be rare, unique, and therefore difficult to evaluate from a market value perspective, private valuations ("investment values") are of great relevance.

An important part of this book is our presentation of some of the technical "nuts and bolts" of our approach. We have tried to give you enough of a feeling for how we can analyze uncertainty and flexibility in practical ways, using common computer spreadsheet software, so that you can have some sense and confidence about the technical implementation. More details on some of the key technical considerations are presented in the Appendix at the end of the book. Complete technical documentation is provided by the actual computer spreadsheet models (in Microsoft Excel®). These are available in the book's Companion Website. You can use these spreadsheet models, downloadable for purchasers of this book, as starting points or templates to develop your own models, customized for projects you are interested in, and no doubt improved from our humble offerings. (We seek to inspire you, and help you to get started; we don't claim to present a definitive or superior product.)

From the technical perspective, we have made some practical suggestions. We emphasized the importance of keeping the models simple, so as not to lose sight of the forest through the trees. Don't be afraid to abstract from the complete, real-world details of the project. A stylized analysis will usually be more powerful for eliciting the important key insights. Admittedly, there is not a little bit of "art" in this process. Hopefully, the examples we have provided, based on our Garden City project illustration, give some sense and guidance for such craft. And, of course, we need to emphasize the importance of humility. No model, no quantitative analysis, will ever be completely definitive or foolproof. You will never want to let a technical model overrule your common sense and good judgment!

Another principle we have employed throughout the book is to build on existing best practice. We don't want you to reinvent the wheel, or build analyses from scratch, if there is already good practical knowledge out there. This is the principle underlying our practice of using pricing factors combined with existing, best-practice cash flow pro forma projections, for the subject projects or investments. The principal parties in the field already know more than anyone else, probably, about the specific real estate assets that are the subject of analysis and evaluation.

Finally, we have walked you through an extensive study of the value of various types of flexibilities specifically quantified for a concrete example—our illustrative, archetypical Garden City project. We cannot claim that the results that we have obtained and reported in Chapters 17–23 are general or definitive. They apply, strictly speaking, only to the Garden City project under the pricing dynamics assumptions that we have employed. But the project is typical of many medium to large-scale, multi-asset development projects. And the price dynamics that we assume are reflective of current empirical evidence and theoretical knowledge about how real estate asset markets operate, at least in advanced market economies such as the United States and other developed countries.

What do we find? Not surprisingly, we find that there is a lot of risk in real estate development—but also that flexibility can add a lot of value to development projects. Much production timing flexibility in development tends to be, in practice, delay options. These act like "put" options, providing protection against the worst of the possible downside outcomes, much like insurance. This can add value that is a significant fraction of the land value, and that considerably improves the risk/return performance of real estate development investment. Other options provide more upside benefit, such as product type switching options. We often find that individual types of flexibilities by themselves seem to add 10–20% to the net value of the development project (present value of benefit minus construction cost). Therefore, they add that percentage to the value of the land.

But our simulation approach allows the valuation of combinations of several different types of options simultaneously. While there is considerable redundancy among production timing options (the delay options that protect downside outcomes), product options and timing options are more additive and synergistic. Combinations of options may well add up to over one-third of the land value (recall Section 21.4.).

These quantitative results are based on the simple, behavior analog decision rules that we have programed into our simulation analyses in Microsoft Excel®. For example, we use the Simple Myopic Delay Rule, which bases the option exercise decision only on the relative profitability of the project in the current period as compared to the base case projection in the original pro forma for the project. These decision rules are explicitly not optimal or optimized in any formal or rigorous manner. They are practical and transparent, but are simplified representations of how developers might actually make decisions about the exercise of flexibility. It is quite possible that, in reality, developers—at least some developers—could do better than our models in exercising the available options. In that case, our estimates of the value of flexibility may be on the low side.

So, we hope you will now take your newfound knowledge and perspective from this book and go forth and have fun applying it to your own real estate investments and development projects. *"Live long, and prosper!"*

Appendix

Quantifying Real Estate Uncertainty

Let's Think about the Inputs for Real Estate Simulation Models

LEARNING OBJECTIVES
• Understand the big picture of the real estate system; • Think about the sources of future uncertainty for real estate projects; • Learn some practical tips for quantifying uncertainty in simulation; • Understand the nature of real estate price dynamics and uncertainty; • Review some relevant empirical evidence.

OUTLINE OF THE CHAPTER
A.1 The Real Estate System A.2 Sources of Uncertainty and Some Practical Advice for Simulation A.3 The Nature of Real Estate Price Dynamics and Uncertainty A.4 Putting It All Together

In this Appendix, we want to tell you how we arrive at the real estate market price dynamics that we use, and how we simulate future real estate pricing to represent uncertainty, as realistically as we can.

In Chapter 7, we described how we use pricing factors to simulate future scenarios in the real estate market based on dynamics and probability functions that we input into the spreadsheet. We described a very basic and widely used dynamic pricing process known as the *random walk*. We described how private real estate markets include a random walk element but also include some other features: inertia (autoregression), cyclicality, and mean-reversion.

In this Appendix, we want to take you a little deeper into the details, the nuts and bolts of our thinking and method for coming up with these important inputs. We want to give you some feeling for how this aspect of simulation analysis is part science and part art. We use a lot of judgment based on common sense (we think). But we also use some interesting empirical evidence and some relevant economic theory.

The "journey" in this Appendix isn't for everybody. If you don't want to get a little technical, and indeed if you don't want to see "how the sausage is made," then this Appendix may not be for you. We delve into some statistics and economic theory. But, to begin, we want to simply step back and think about the big picture of what we are trying to simulate. Real estate markets are embedded within what we call "the real estate system."

Flexibility and Real Estate Valuation under Uncertainty: A Practical Guide for Developers, First Edition.
David Geltner and Richard de Neufville.
© 2018 John Wiley & Sons Ltd. Published 2018 by John Wiley & Sons Ltd.
Companion website: www.wiley.com/go/geltner-deneufville/flexibility-and-real-estate-valuation

A.1   The Real Estate System

Figure A.1 depicts the real estate system. There are three main elements: the space market, the asset market, and the development industry. The space market trades the rights to occupy and use built space, with landlords on the supply side and tenants on the demand side. Prevailing rental prices and occupancy rates characterize the equilibrium in the space market, and determine the net cash flows that are the fundamental benefit flows accruing to the owners of the property assets (landlords).

The asset market trades the long-term ownership rights of the properties, with investors and owner-occupiers buying and selling the assets. As a shortcut, we can represent the equilibrium price in the property asset market by the prevailing "cap rate," or income yield rate. For example, if a property currently producing $100 per year net income would sell for $1000, then that pricing would be represented by a 10% cap rate. If the prevailing cap rate in the asset market falls to 9%, this would indicate that the price of such a property has risen to $1111 ($100/0.09).

The development industry is where and how financial capital builds physical capital, producing new buildings in the system, replacing older structures, or adding to the overall supply of built space in the space market. The development industry performs a basic calculation. It compares the present value of the expected benefit from a development project to the present value of the expected cost, including the land cost. As described in Chapters 2 and 11, if the computed NPV is positive, development is economical and generally proceeds.

The real estate system is dynamic. It is constantly changing, evolving over time. Exogenous growth and shocks in the economy affect demand for space. Financial capital flows into and out of the asset market and the development industry. When demand for

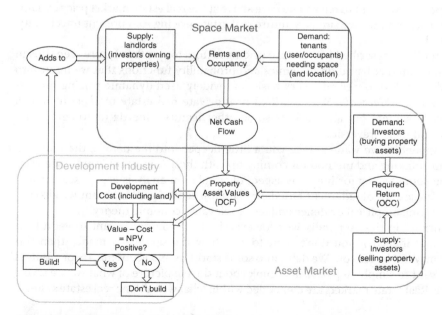

Figure A.1 The real estate system.

space increases, rents and occupancies tend to rise, raising revenues from built properties. Other things being equal, this will raise property values, and this in turn will tend
to stimulate new development—although development can be mitigated by possible
rises in land costs. New development may put downward pressure on rents or result in
increased vacancy in the space market, and this will reverse the preceding trend. Beliefs,
behaviors, and actions in any element of the system will tend to affect the other elements
of the system, at least after some time. The system tends toward a long-run equilibrium,
but often in fits and starts, and with a tendency to cycle around a long-run trend.
Decision-makers in the system—especially investors and developers, and their financiers—
try (or should try) to be forward-looking, to forecast what the future of the relevant
market is going to be. But no one has a crystal ball, and the future is almost never exactly
as was predicted. Uncertainty in real estate markets and the dynamics of real estate
pricing arise through and within all three elements of the system and in the interactions
among them.

A.2 Sources of Uncertainty and Some Practical Advice for Simulation

Uncertainty about the future relevant for a real estate investment or project arises not
only from within the real estate system, as described in the preceding text, but perhaps
even more so, or more fundamentally, from outside the system. The underlying economy and sociopolitical and financial systems in which real estate markets are embedded
provide a constant source of change.

Figure A.2 shows one visualization of this, together with a key point of practical
advice. First, notice how many phenomena and considerations can influence the real
estate system. Many (perhaps most) of these sources of uncertainty are exogenous to
the real estate system itself. Figure A.2 lists 11 such causal factors—effectively, sources

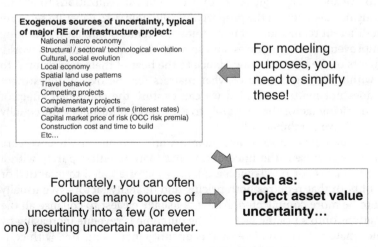

Figure A.2 Simplifying uncertainty for simulation modeling.

of uncertainty about the future. And this list is no doubt only partial. All of these are important phenomena that can substantially change the value of a given location or building for better or worse. We noted in Chapter 5 how difficult it is in practice to forecast accurately even one underlying determinative factor that can be a source of uncertainty (see Figure 5.2 in Box 5.2).

But Figure A.2 suggests a crucial point for simulation modeling. We can often collapse all of the sources of uncertainty into a single factor that captures the combined effect of everything regarding the determination of the value of the investment or project we are analyzing. For example, what ultimately matters from an investment perspective is generally the future value of the asset being built or invested in. Rather than attempting to model all of the possible determinants of this value in a causal structural model, we content ourselves with modeling the kind of dynamics and randomness that appear in historical empirical data about property price evolution. Such data reflects the combined effects of all the determinants of property values, and such values are likely a sufficient metric of investment performance.

This does not mean that analysts should not consider, or indeed study and seek to understand, the underlying causal elements that affect prices and values. Univariate modeling purely reflecting longitudinal time-series behavior is no substitute for a deep understanding of the dynamic causal structure in the system. But an ever-present challenge in effective, practical simulation analysis is to avoid excessive complexity. We must not "get lost in the weeds," and we must not "lose sight of the forest for the trees blocking the view!"

There is no small degree of "art" in this process. An extensive knowledge of historical evidence and economic theory, combined with practical experience in the property markets and a good dose of common sense, are the ingredients behind the art of trimming down the model. The key point is to keep your eye on what will most directly and sensitively affect the output that is most important in the analysis. For real estate investments, this is typically the value of the property asset.

A simple example of this point occurs first in Chapter 9, where we demonstrated the application of simulation analysis to an existing, income-producing property. To generate a future scenario, we applied a single series of pricing factor realizations to all elements of the operating net cash flow of the property. We did not try to generate separate factors to represent different realizations of uncertainty for rents, occupancy, operating expenses, capital improvement expenditures, and so forth. Of course, in the real world, all of these components of the net cash flow "dance to the beat of their own drums" to some extent. But, within the big picture of what matters for the overall investment performance, that does not matter, provided we can capture the combined effect of everything in a single pricing factor that we apply to the overall bottom line (or equally to all elements in an additive combination).

For example, if revenue equals price times quantity, and revenue is what we care about, then we can fully represent the uncertainty that matters either purely with a pricing factor applied to price, or purely with a quantity factor applied to quantity, or some combination of both that requires both pricing and quantity factors. We usually gain little by trying to be more complicated. And it is usually easiest to collapse all the important considerations onto a pricing factor. If the outcome is revenue increasing by 10%, then it does not matter if we simulate that as quantity increasing 10% with constant pricing, or price increasing 10% with constant quantity, or quantity and price each increasing 4.9% ($1.049 \times 1.049 = 1.10$), or price increasing 3% with quantity increasing 6.8% ($1.03 \times 1.068 = 1.10$), or whatever. Generally, the simplest and most elegant approach is to reflect everything in the pricing factor. (Of course, there will be exceptions. Always apply common sense.)

A.3 The Nature of Real Estate Price Dynamics and Uncertainty

Now let us consider the nature of real estate market price dynamics. This also encompasses the question of the magnitude of uncertainty or risk in the future pricing that might be relevant for a given property or project (see Box A.1 for some relevant concepts).

For this purpose, we can identify eight separate sources or components governing real estate price dynamics—that is, how prices change over time. These eight components combine in the real world to govern and characterize real estate price evolution.

Box A.1 The Difference Between Uncertainty and Risk.

In common parlance, when thinking about the future of an investment, the words "risk" and "uncertainty" may seem to refer to the same thing. Whether you call it "risk" or "uncertainty," it reflects the fact that you don't know for sure what the future will bring, and it can cause your investment to perform differently, possibly worse, than you had expected when you went into the investment. But economists often distinguish between the two terms.

In economics terminology, "risk" is quantifiable. Risk can be described by a known probability function. If you know in advance that there is a 20% chance that the bond you are investing in will default and yield a negative 10% return, but otherwise will yield a positive 10% return, then you know your ex-ante expected return is: $(0.2)(-10\%) + (0.8)(10\%) = 6\%$. And you know how much "risk" you face in the investment. This might be referred to as a case of "known unknowns." You don't know if the bond will default, but you know the probability that it will happen and the effect of the default if it does happen.

In contrast, "uncertainty" is when you cannot quantify the probability; you don't know how much risk is there. This might be thought of as a case of "unknown unknowns." Investors are usually much more averse to uncertainty than to risk. But, in reality, most investments do face at least some degree of uncertainty. We may have a lot of historical evidence about the nature of stock market returns, but we don't know for sure what probability functions govern their future returns.

In this book, we often use the terms "uncertainty" and "risk" interchangeably. The phenomenon we are actually dealing with is uncertainty. But we try to convert uncertainty into risk, in effect, in our simulation models, by positing probability functions that we input into the models. It is in this sense that we quantify something that is, in principle, not quantifiable, and we can speak of the "magnitude of uncertainty." We need to do this in order to do quantitative analysis. But we need to be humble. We can never know for sure that our input probabilities are correct. We actually face uncertainty, not mere risk.

This evolution defines the nature and magnitude of risk or uncertainty that investors face. The eight components are:

1) Long-term trend rate;
2) Volatility;
3) Cyclicality;
4) Mean-reversion;
5) Inertia (autoregression);
6) Price dispersion (noise);
7) Idiosyncratic drift;
8) Black swans.

A description of each of these components is given in the following text, together with some discussion about their theoretical basis and quantitative nature or magnitude for the purpose of simulation modeling.

(1) *Long-term trend rate.* The first source of uncertainty is the long-term trend rate. That is, what is the secular rate of change that real estate prices tend to exhibit on average over the long run? (The term "secular" here refers to a long-run trend that persists over time.) This rate is best considered in real terms—that is, net of monetary inflation. This trend component of real estate price dynamics is illustrated in Figure A.3, which shows almost a half-century of history of an aggregate index of commercial property prices in the United States. The property price index is shown in nominal terms, but the consumer price index (CPI), which tracks cumulative inflation, is also shown in Figure A.3. The real change in property prices is the relative difference between the two

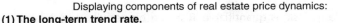

Displaying components of real estate price dynamics:
(1) The long-term trend rate.

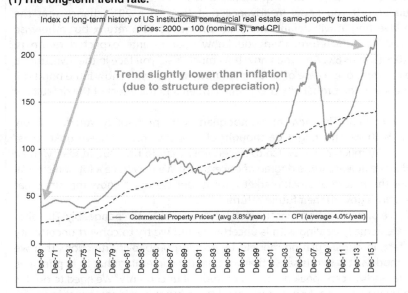

Figure A.3 Commercial property prices, United States, 1969–2016: long-term trend. *Source*: BLS, Moody's/REAL, Moody's/RCA, TBI, Author's estimates.

lines over time. The property price index reflects "same property" price change—that is, the price change experienced by existing built properties, the type of price change that is experienced by investors.

The long-term trend is evidenced by the difference in the value of the index at the end of the history as compared to the beginning, adjusting for temporary or cyclical effects. Over the entire 1969–2016 history, the nominal average rate of property price change was 3.8% per annum (measured by the geometric mean). But, over the same period, inflation averaged 4.0% per annum. If we measure trough-to-trough (1975–2009), the rates are 3.1% for property and 4.1% for inflation. Peak-to-peak (1972–2007), the rates are 4.1% and 4.7%, respectively. Thus, in real terms, property values have tended to decline slightly, growing less than inflation by typically less than 1% per year. This is in spite of the fact that property owners spend money on maintenance and upkeep of the properties. As the buildings on properties age, the property value reflects the depreciation of those built structures. Depreciation generally cannot be fully offset by spending on capital improvements. Thus, it is not surprising that the long-term real price trend rate is slightly negative. However, this depends substantially on the role of land value over time. In places and times where land is very expensive and therefore makes up a large share of property value, the secular trend in property pricing might be more positive in real terms. This would be true if land values tend to grow in real terms, for land does not generally depreciate like built structures do.

Figure A.3 reflects the US national average, where, for properties with average-age buildings, the land value fraction is typically only about half of the total property value. In denser, more land-constrained countries (or in such places within the United States), the secular trend rate might be more positive. But it could be less positive in times and places of low or declining land value. Because we cannot know exactly the future secular trend in property values, this is a source of uncertainty in real estate prices. In most places, it probably ranges between, say, +1% and –2% in real terms (net of inflation).

(2) *Volatility*. This term was defined in Chapter 7 (see Box 7.2). There, we noted that "volatility" refers to the way prices change randomly, unpredictably from one period to the next. Volatility reflects the arrival of news—that is, unpredicted information that is relevant to the value of property. The price movements in each period relative to the prior values (akin to "capital returns," the percentage changes in asset value) are also known as "innovations." Volatility is clearly visible in the long-term aggregate price index shown previously. Figure A.4 repeats that same index, highlighting some clear visual evidence of volatility. It shows up as random movements up and down in the price index.

The key feature of volatility is that it accumulates over time in the price levels. Volatility is the essential feature of the random walk component of asset price dynamics. As noted in Chapter 7, the random walk is "memoryless." If news arrives that is positive, causing prices to rise (positive return in that period), then that holds no implication that prices will either continue rising in the next period or that they would tend to fall back in the next period. Thus, a random bump up in one period is "baked into" the price level as of the end of that period. Any change in the future will start from that new price level which reflects the "bump" from the previous news. In this sense, volatility "accumulates" over time in the price levels. Because the specific price innovations are not predictable in advance, volatility reflects risk, or a source of uncertainty for investors.

Displaying components of real estate price dynamics:
(1) The long-term trend rate; (2) Short-term volatility (that accumulates).

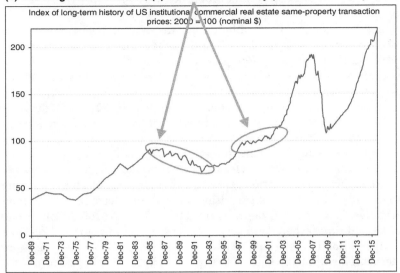

Figure A.4 Commercial property prices, United States, 1969–2016: volatility. *Source*: Moody's/REAL, Moody's/RCA, TBI, Author's estimates.

The historical empirical evidence in the United States, as indicated in Figure A.4 and numerous other similar indices, suggests that market volatility for commercial property may typically be around 10–15% per annum. This compares, for example, with the stock market, which generally exhibits annual volatility closer to 20%. But volatility varies over time and across different property space markets. Real estate price volatility also depends on the frequency at which it is computed, for example, monthly, quarterly, annually, biennially, etc. Because of inertia and cyclicality, real estate volatility measured on an equivalent annual basis is typically greater when measured at lower frequencies (longer "holding periods" in the periodic returns). For example, quarterly volatility might be 5%, while annual volatility is 10% and biennial volatility is 15%, all measured at a per-annum rate.

(3) *Cyclicality.* The next component of real estate price dynamics is rather famous. It is the tendency of property markets to exhibit long-term cycles, upswings followed by downswings or even "crashes." Such cycles are prominent in the long-term index that we have been looking at, which is repeated again in Figure A.5, delineating the long-run historical cycles in the US commercial property market over the past half-century. At least two complete cycles are evident, peak-to-peak, and trough-to-trough. Including the fractional cycles at either end of the depicted history, there are roughly three cycles during the almost half-century covered. The average cycle period is 15–20 years. The index in Figure A.5 suggests that the down-cycles can at least temporarily drop property asset prices by 30–40% on average, more in some markets.

The cycle in the asset market may, or may not, be echoed in the space market. The up-cycle is sometimes characterized by over-building and a rental market "bubble" (such as the late 1980s), but, other times, the cycle is more confined to the asset

Displaying components of real estate price dynamics:
(1) The long-term trend rate; (2) Short-term volatility; (3) Cyclicality; (4) Mean-reversion.

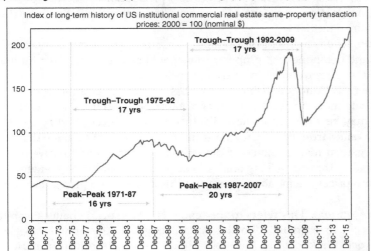

Figure A.5 Commercial property prices, United States, 1969–2016: cyclicality and mean reversion. *Source*: Moody's/REAL, Moody's/RCA, TBI, Author's estimates.

market (such as the mid-2000s). Sometimes the down-cycle is associated with a general economic recession (such as the global financial crisis of 2008–2009). Other times, there is little or no causal connection between the commercial property market and the wider macro-economy (such as the late 1980s). There is some evidence that the property market cycle is related to behavior in the debt market—that is, the relative availability of debt capital for real estate investment. As noted earlier, the flow of financial capital (money) into and out of the real estate market can certainly move asset prices.

Although the tendency of real estate markets to cycle is well known, it is much more difficult to reliably predict the exact nature, timing, and magnitude of the cycles—and, most importantly, the "next downturn." For this reason, cyclicality is an important source of uncertainty and risk for property investors and developers.

(4) *Mean-reversion.* A component of real estate price dynamics that is closely related to cyclicality is the tendency toward mean-reversion. Put simply, mean-reversion is like gravity; it implies that "what goes up, must come down." But, it is symmetrical: "what goes down must come back up too." The idea is that if prices get too far out of line from the long-run trend, they will tend to "correct" or "revert" back toward that long-run trend.

What would cause prices to move far from the long-run trend? It could be a tendency toward herd behavior in capital flows; or, it could be simply an exogenous streak of abnormally good, or bad, news.

What would cause prices to tend to revert toward the long-run trend? It could be powerful economic fundamentals. Real estate assets consist of two components of value: the structure and the land. Structures are produced goods—in some sense, not unlike automobiles or refrigerators. There is substantial price elasticity of supply. The price (value) of structures cannot move very far from marginal production costs, or supply will respond (positively to price increases, negatively to price decreases), putting competitive pressures to keep structure prices near production costs. And, over the long run, structure production costs tend to keep pace with general inflation over time (roughly constant in real terms).

On the other hand, land is neither produced nor consumed, and is much more fixed in its supply. The land component of property value could evolve more like a random walk, without such tendency to revert toward a mean. So, the mean-reversion tendency in real estate is rather weak and unreliable. This makes real estate price evolution more difficult to predict, and more uncertain than that of cars or refrigerators, for example.

Mean-reversion may be stronger at the individual property level (tending to keep individual property values from moving too far from the local market average) than it is at the level of aggregate or market indices. Competitive pressures tend to drive mean-reversion. Astute traders try to buy "bargains" (whose prices are far below average) and sell "winners" (whose prices are far above average). This acts to keep prices somewhat within bounds.

(5) *Inertia (autoregression).* This refers to the tendency of the price changes (capital returns) in one period to partially echo the price changes in the previous period. Technically, this process is known as "autoregression," where the return in period t includes a fraction of the return in period t–1. The result is that, when prices start moving in one direction, they have a tendency to continue moving in that direction, to some extent, for a while.

What could cause such inertia in real estate prices? Inertia reflects the fact that property asset markets are not perfectly informationally efficient. This causes prices to be a bit sluggish or "sticky." When news arrives that is relevant to asset value, it takes a while for that news to get fully reflected in transaction prices. This is because private real estate markets trade unique, whole assets. One cannot simply observe the change in prices at which other assets are trading and apply that change to a private real estate transaction. Each transaction is, essentially, a negotiation between two parties, neither of who knows for sure what the "market value" is of the unique asset they are trading.

Autoregression is similar to, and related to, both cyclicality and mean-reversion. Indeed, autoregression partially overlaps with and reflects those other two phenomena. The difference is that autoregression can act either to push prices toward a long-run mean, or away from it. Autoregression simply carries forward an (attenuated) "echo" of the previous period's price change into the current period's price change. This is depicted visually in Figure A.6.

True transaction price–based real estate index returns are only mildly autoregressive in the United States. Real estate markets aren't too inefficient. Empirical evidence suggests that a typical annual frequency autoregressive parameter might be on the order of +0.1 to +0.3. In other words, the return in period t might include somewhere between one-tenth and one-third of the return in period t–1. (Price indices based on repeated appraisals of the same properties often show much greater autoregression, but this is partly due to the "anchoring" tendency in repeat-appraisals, as the appraisers base their current opinion partly on their previous opinion.)

(6) *Price dispersion (noise).* The preceding phenomena and components of real estate price dynamics are systematic across all or most individual assets. Therefore, they occur at the aggregate level, and are evident in indices of markets or sub-markets. But, now we want to introduce two phenomena that occur explicitly at the disaggregate level of

Displaying components of real estate price dynamics:

(1) The long-term trend rate; (2) Short-term volatility; (3) Cyclicality; (4) Mean-reversion; and (5) Inertia (momentum, autoregression: AR(1)).

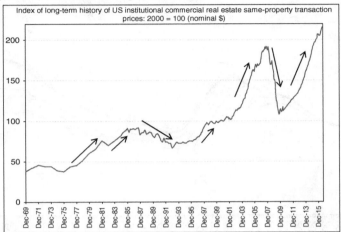

Figure A.6 Commercial property prices, United States, 1969–2016: Inertia (autoregression). *Source:* Moody's/RCA, TBI, Author's estimates.

individual properties, but that are not systematic and therefore do not appear in aggregate indices. The first is random price dispersion, also known as "noise." As we have previously noted, no one knows for sure the exact market value of any property as of any point in time. Transaction prices are negotiated between two parties who both lack such knowledge. The result is that transaction prices are randomly dispersed around the true market values. In fact, the main practical definition of "market value" is that it is the mean of the distribution of possible actual transaction prices. Price dispersion causes an extra source of randomness in realized prices. Prior to any transaction, such noise is a source of uncertainty surrounding the future performance of the property as an investment.

The magnitude of price noise can be quantified in the standard deviation of transaction prices around previously predicted or estimated valuations. It can also be seen in the estimated intercept of regressions of squared residuals onto the time between sales in repeat-sales regressions. Such empirical data in the United States and United Kingdom indicate dispersion standard deviations in the neighborhood of 10–15%, similar in magnitude to price index volatility. But the difference between noise and volatility is that, while volatility accumulates over time, noise does not. Noise happens only when, and if, a property is transacted. In essence, no matter how long the durations between transactions of a property, the magnitude of the noise surrounding its sale price remains approximately the same. In simulations, we model noise as a random "error" around the simulated "true" price level, whereas we model volatility as random deviations in the true returns (price increments).

(7) *Idiosyncratic drift.* The second component of real estate price dynamics that operates at the individual property level and not at the aggregate systematic level is what is called "idiosyncratic drift." This is like volatility—random innovations that accumulate

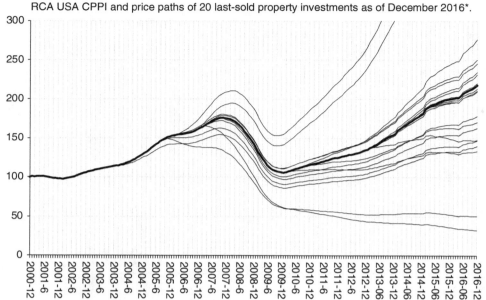

RCA USA CPPI and price paths of 20 last-sold property investments as of December 2016*.

* Pegged to starting value on index (heavy line) at time of prior sale (buy), then tracked at constant rate per month to ultimate sale price deviation at disposition in December 2016.

Figure A.7 Price paths of 20 property investments as of December 2016: idiosyncratic drift.

over time—except that idiosyncratic drift occurs only at the individual property level, uncorrelated with the market volatility. Idiosyncratic drift is depicted in Figure A.7, which shows how individual property price paths evolve separate from and independent of the market value index. For example, the market may be moving up in response to generally strong demand for space, but your particular building may have just lost its major tenant (who decided to move, perhaps, to a newer building). Your property's value just fell, even though the market as a whole went up.

Empirical evidence from US commercial property price indices and the individual property transaction price residuals around such indices suggest that idiosyncratic drift is approximately equal in magnitude to market volatility, typically between 10% and 15% per annum, modeled as a random walk around the market index.

(8) *Black swans*. The last of the eight components of real estate price dynamics and uncertainty that we will identify applies once again at the aggregate level, systematically to all or most individual assets at a time. There are various words for this last type of phenomenon, including "fat tail events," Bernoulli events, Poisson Arrivals, and others. The idea is that, on rare and unpredictable occasions, an event seems to come out of nowhere and have a huge, usually negative, effect on almost all assets. A famous such event was the global financial crisis of 2008–2009. During such an event, it is said that "covariance goes to one"—meaning that there is such contagion or mass panic that almost all assets fall together. A vivid illustration of this is shown in Figure A.8. The figure shows the relative price paths of all publicly traded commercial property investment companies (known as "real estate investment trusts") monthly from 2000

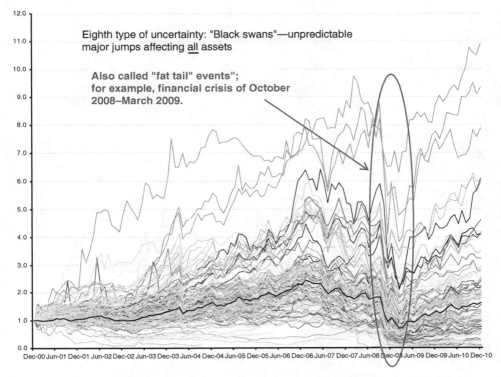

Figure A.8 Effect of the global financial crisis on price paths of all US real estate investment trusts: Black swan event (Financial Crisis, October 2008–March 2009). *Source*: Authors.

through 2010, indexed to a starting value of 1.00. The price paths resemble random walks, with continuously accumulating volatility, until the financial crisis hits in 2008. Then, virtually *all* of the individual stocks collapse together. Black swans differ from normal volatility, in that they strike only rarely and usually bring unexpected losses rather than gains. Their effects also may not be as permanent as normal random walk–type volatility.

A.4 Putting It All Together

The preceding section has introduced you to the eight major components of typical real estate market price dynamics. We have also noted some empirical evidence, as well as theoretical considerations, that help us to quantify and understand the causes and nature of these components.

In our simulation modeling, we program all of these elements into the spreadsheet workbook model, in particular, for the generation of the sequences of pricing factors that govern the simulated future scenarios (Monte Carlo trials). You can see specifically how we do this in the example Microsoft Excel® workbook templates available on this book's Companion Website. The simulation results that we have described in the chapters of this book, including our Garden City example

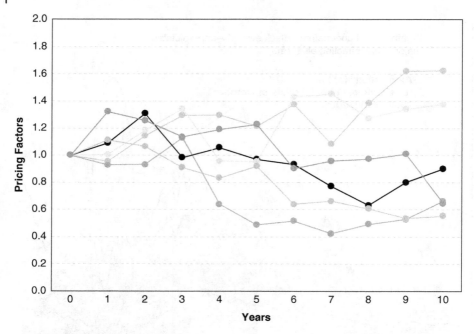

Figure A.9a Pricing factors for six future scenarios based on typical price dynamics: stock market (simulations based purely on the random walk).

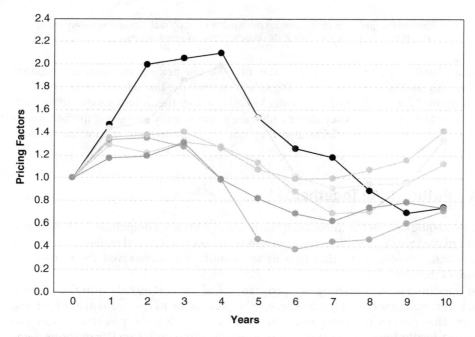

Figure A.9b Pricing factors for six future scenarios based on typical price dynamics: real estate (simulations based on random walk and cyclicality, mean-reversion, and autoregression).

of Chapters 17–23 and the existing rental property example of Chapters 9 and 10, reflect our judgment about a typical and plausible portrayal of the eight price dynamics and uncertainty components described in the preceding section. You can see the specifics in the two input sheets on the tabs labeled "MktDynamicsInputs" and "ProjectDynamicsInputs." The former is for the aggregate market level dynamics, or if there is only one type of real estate product in the project. The latter is for the individual assets or product types, reflecting the price dispersion and idiosyncratic components (items (6) and (7) in the list in Section A.3). The specifics of the formulas and input assumptions are documented within the spreadsheets.

As we noted at the outset of this Appendix, the simulation of real estate price dynamics is as much an art as a science. Ultimately, we are trying to model the uncertainty that exists as we peer into the future from the present, with only the past as a (relatively) solid, observable basis for our modeling. It is important to be humble in any such endeavor. We use our judgment based on our experience, knowledge, and common sense to fashion the generation of future pricing scenarios that "look" realistic and plausible to us. You can see a "picture" of 24 periods of future random pricing factors in the chart at the top of the "MktDynamicsInputs" sheet. Recalculate a few times to see what the generated scenarios look like. Do they look like what you think is plausible and realistic, for the real estate market you are dealing with? You can easily change and play around with the price dynamics and uncertainty parameter inputs in the templates. We do not claim that our inputs are necessarily "correct." Indeed, there is no such thing as *the* correct inputs. (And some of our assumptions are made for pedagogical or illustrative reasons, to demonstrate the possibilities in spreadsheet simulation.)

We would be less than candid if we did not tell you that we give a lot of deference to what we call "the eyeball test." Do the randomly generated future pricing paths "look" realistic and plausible? Do they look like they could happen? Do they have a general appearance similar to the historical, empirically based price indices? If they do, and if the individual component input assumptions seem sensible from a theoretical perspective and consistent with such empirical evidence as is available, then we feel comfortable with proceeding with the simulation analysis. But, even then, we might conduct sensitivity analysis regarding particular results and assumptions that could be critical in a given analysis. Ultimately, the purpose of simulation modeling in this context is to build your intuition and provide insight. It will never by itself provide a definitive and highly specific decision recommendation.

With the these points in mind, take a look again at the randomly generated price paths we showed back in Chapter 7, in Figures 7.1 and 7.2, reproduced here as Figures A.9a and A.9b. Figure A.9a shows pure random walk price dynamics, typical of what is often assumed for the stock market. Figure A.9b simulations also include a non-trivial random walk component, but they also include three other major aggregate market level components described in Section A.3—namely, cyclicality, mean-reversion, and inertia (autoregression). The price paths shown in these charts seem plausible to us (abstracting from any long-term trend), both for the stock market and the real estate market, including the differences between these two types of asset markets. But, we could be wrong. You can make your own judgments and your own assumptions.

Glossary

Autoregression The tendency of changes in one period to partially echo the changes in previous periods. In this text, it generally refers to real estate prices and capital returns.

Basis point One-hundredth of a percent. This is a common unit in the investment industry to refer to returns, and especially to differences between two returns.

Capex Capital expenditures (also called "capital improvement expenditures"); the cost of longer-lived expenditures to improve a real estate property.

Cap rate Capitalization rate; in US real estate terminology, an income or earnings yield, usually based on accounting net income or earnings (rather than a cash yield).

$$\text{Cap rate} = \frac{\text{NOI}}{\text{Property asset value}}.$$

Cash yield rate Current net cash flow divided by the property asset value. Net cash flow = NOI – Capex.

Confidence interval A range of values such that there is a specified probability that the actual value of interest lies between (within) the interval, or bounds.

Covariance A statistical concept referring to how two things vary over time together, or not.

Cumulative distribution function (CDF) The cumulative distribution is the sum of the frequency distribution up to a specified point. It "integrates" the frequency (or "density") of the relative likelihood of each outcome across the range of all possible outcomes. It generally indicates the probability of an outcome being equal or less than a given value.

Current price/income multiple Current price of the asset divided by its current annual income (inverse of yield).

Cyclicality The tendency of the market to have "boom" and "bust" periods.

Data table A Microsoft Excel® function that allows the user to quickly try out the effect on output values caused by different input values for formulas, also used to implement Monte Carlo simulation.

Discount rate, r The rate of reduction per time period of the value of future money amounts in terms of present value; it is how the DCF valuation accounts for time and risk—by converting future cash flow amounts to present values.

Discounted cash flow A fundamental way to value real estate properties based on the opportunity cost of cash flow, time, and risk.

Flexibility and Real Estate Valuation under Uncertainty: A Practical Guide for Developers, First Edition. David Geltner and Richard de Neufville.
© 2018 John Wiley & Sons Ltd. Published 2018 by John Wiley & Sons Ltd.
Companion website: www.wiley.com/go/geltner-deneufville/flexibility-and-real-estate-valuation

Distribution of possibilities The description of the expected frequency of occurrence of outcomes over the range of possibilities.

Effective gross income PGI minus vacancy allowance.

Elasticity See *price elasticity*.

Ex-ante A standard expression meaning "forward-looking," from the Latin meaning "from before."

Ex-post A standard expression meaning "backward-looking," from the Latin meaning "from afterward."

Expected return, expected value "Expected" in such contexts signifies the probabilistic mean, which is a type of "average" across the possible outcomes. When dealing with probability distributions, we calculate the expected value of a variable as the weighted average of the variable over all of its possible outcome values, weighting by the probability of the outcome value.

Fee simple Ownership in "fee simple" refers to absolute ownership in a property, as understood in North America, the United Kingdom, and some other countries, generally without temporal restrictions. It contrasts with other forms of ownership—for example, those limited by time (99 years) or extent (excluding minerals, for instance).

First-order stochastic dominance The situation in which one alternative is never beaten by another alternative over all possible uncertain outcomes driven by uncertain ("stochastic") factors.

Flaw of averages A word play on the "law of averages," which is the (false) notion that future events will balance out toward an average. The flaw of averages says that using average input values to estimate future expected outcome values is a mistake—it gives erroneous or misleadingly incomplete results.

Floor/Area Ratio (FAR) Also called "plot ratio" and "site ratio" in the United Kingdom and elsewhere, as well as several other variants (such as floor space index, FSI); it equals the floor surface area of built space divided by the ground surface area of the land plot on which the building sits.

Forward claim A commitment to buy an asset that will be received and paid for sometime in the future, where the price to be paid is already determined in the present.

Geometric mean A type of mean (average) of a set of quantities, found by multiplying the quantities times each other and then raising that product to the power of the inverse of the number of quantities. In investments, the geometric mean return is the periodic rate of return, which if applied to a given starting value and compounded throughout the holding period will result in a given ending value. In contrast to the arithmetic mean return (the unweighted average of all the returns earned each period), the geometric mean return is unaffected by the volatility of the returns, and depends purely on the beginning and ending values of the investment and the number of periods in the holding of the investment.

Going-in yield rate The ratio of current income (or cash flow) to asset value (or price). Usually applied to the next (first upcoming) year's income.

Going-out yield rate The yield rate at the end of the projected investment, applicable to the resale price at which the investment will be sold. Operationally, it is the ratio of the net cash flow of the next year after the sale, to the reversion value of the investment.

Growth rate, g The projected rate at which the cash flow components of a property will change each year (often also relates to the rate of growth of the asset value).

Hurdle rate A discount rate set by management for its agents to use as the discount rate in DCF and such analyses. Though, in principle, the hurdle rate should equal (or be based on) the economic opportunity cost of capital, the hurdle rate may reflect management procedures for capital budgeting.

IF statements Programmed commands in a computer spreadsheet that are conditional on pre-specified conditions; they automate the process of mimicking investor decisions.

Inertia The tendency of the past to define the future. See *autoregression*.

Internal rate of return (IRR) A mathematical metric to measure investment returns when the investment involves cash flows occurring in more than one future period. Algorithmically, the IRR is the rate that discounts a specified stream of cash flows to a net present value of zero.

Investment value See *value in use*.

Leverage The effect of debt or debt-like obligations on the investment risk and return of the equity.

Mean-reversion The tendency of observations that differ from a long-term mean value to be followed by observations closer to that mean.

Momentum A synonym for inertia. See *autoregression*.

Monte Carlo simulation A repetitive process, based on input probability distributions and a model of the functioning of the project in each period, generating independent, random future scenarios that collectively mimic what could happen in reality, in principle covering the entire range of possible outcomes.

Net cash flow NOI − Capex.

Net operating income EGI − Operating Expenses.

Net present value (NPV) The present value of project or investment asset net of the cost of acquiring the asset.

Normal distribution A particular form of the bell-shaped probability distribution, characterized by its mean value and standard deviation.

Operating expenses Regularly recurring costs for operating a property, such as utilities, insurance, taxes, and maintenance.

Opportunity cost The value of what is lost or foregone or used up because of a given action, based on what otherwise could have been done, in principle based on market values.

Opportunity cost of capital (OCC) The return the investor could expect from investing in a typical asset with similar risk to the subject asset. It represents what the market requires as an expected return on an investment.

Potential gross income (PGI) The amount of revenue a property would generate if fully occupied.

Present value (PV) The value as of the present time of a future money amount, adjusting for time and risk.

Price elasticity Refers to how the quantity of goods or services change because of changes in their prices. *Supply elasticity* refers to the quantity produced. *Demand elasticity* refers to the quantity bought. Generally measured as a dimensionless ratio of changes: percent change in quantity divided by percent change in price.

Pricing factor A ratio that multiplies the original, single-stream pro forma cash flow expectation to arrive at a future cash flow outcome for a given scenario.

Private value See *value in use*.

Probability density function (PDF) The frequency (or "density") of the relative likelihood of each outcome across the range of all possible outcomes. This frequency is relative to all the possibilities.

Probability distribution A common way to refer to a PDF or CDF.

Pro forma A table (or matrix) showing the projected cash flows (income and expenses) for an investment (rows) over time (columns).

Put-call parity A way to view the same flexibility in development from either of two equivalent perspectives—that is, the right without obligation to do something implies the right without obligation to not do it.

Random number A number drawn from a probability distribution that is independent (not affected) by a previous number drawn.

Random walk A process of the random evolution of values over time in which the value is the accumulation of a succession of random steps (increments in value), each of which is independent of any others and of the current value of the process. Often used for modeling stock market prices.

Ratio valuation formula A formula to determine the value of an asset by use of a ratio of asset value as a fraction or multiple of some measure of income, without doing a multi-period DCF valuation.

Return Returns are the basic way to measure performance in the investment business—essentially, how much money you are getting in "return" for the money you invested up front. Return "of" your investment gets your investment back without profit. Return "on" your investment gets you profit or income from your investment. Returns are measured in fractions or percentages of the investment—money amounts divided by money amounts.

Reversion The resale value of an investment asset—in real estate, usually a major source of return "of" the original investment.

Risk-free rate The return that investors can get by investing without any risk, a notional concept but often approximated in practice by the yield on short-term obligations of solid governments with impeccable credit ratings. Also referred to as the "Time Value of Money".

Risk premium The extra expected return that the asset market "offers" to investors to compensate investors for taking on the risk associated with the given investment, reflecting an equilibrium between supply of and demand for investment assets, and the way that the market views risk.

Salvage or terminal value The expected resale price for the property (also see *reversion*).

Standard deviation Denotes the "spread" of a probability distribution. It is a way to indicate how far possible outcomes may differ from the expected value or average of a distribution.

Stochastic A technical term indicating that outcomes are determined over time by the realization of random, unpredictable factors.

Super-normal profit A profit above the opportunity cost of capital; a positive net present value evaluated at a price equal to market value.

Target curve A simple line graph depicting either the cumulative or frequency distribution of the simulated results, typically referring to values of some metric of interest. For an investment, the target metric might be the present value or investment return.

Vacancy allowance The fraction of potential revenue that could be generated by a property that will not occur due to vacancy.

Value at risk (VaR) A measure of the downside exposure faced by an investment, the value at and below which outcomes will occur with a specified probability. An X% VaR of $Y means that there is X percent chance that an outcome of $Y or less will occur.

Value in use The value of an asset for particular owners or users apart from its exchange value—that is, ignoring how much the asset might sell for if it could be traded.

Volatility The variation over time in the returns from (or price changes in) an investment asset.

Yield rate, y The ratio of current net cash flow to price.

Acronyms and Symbols

Capex	Capital expenditures
CDF	Cumulative distribution function
CF	Cash flow
CPPI	Commercial Property Price Index
DCF	Discounted cash flow
EGI	Effective gross income
ENPV	Expected net present value
$E(X)$	Expected value of variable X
FAR	Floor/Area Ratio
FOSD	First-order stochastic dominance
g	Growth rate
HBU	Highest and best use
IRR	Internal rate of return
$IV(B), IV(S)$	Investment value for buyer, seller
MPH	Miles per hour
NCF	Net cash flow
NCREIF	National Council of Real Estate Investment Fiduciaries
NOI	Net operating income
NormProb	Normal probability distribution
NPV	Net present value
OCC	Opportunity cost of capital
$P(*)$	Probability that the outcome (*) will occur
PDF	Probability density function
$PF(t)$	Pricing factor at time t
PGI	Potential gross income
PREA	Pension Real Estate Association
PV	Present value
r	Discount rate
rf	Risk-free rate of interest
RP	Risk premium in ex ante total return
RW	Random walk
VaR	Value at risk
y	Yield rate or cash income yield

Flexibility and Real Estate Valuation under Uncertainty: A Practical Guide for Developers, First Edition.
David Geltner and Richard de Neufville.
© 2018 John Wiley & Sons Ltd. Published 2018 by John Wiley & Sons Ltd.
Companion website: www.wiley.com/go/geltner-deneufville/flexibility-and-real-estate-valuation

Index

Flexibility and Real Estate Valuation under Uncertainty: A Practical Guide for Developers, First Edition.
David Geltner and Richard de Neufville.
© 2018 John Wiley & Sons Ltd. Published 2018 by John Wiley & Sons Ltd.
Companion website: www.wiley.com/go/geltner-deneufville/flexibility-and-real-estate-valuation

CPSIA information can be obtained
at www.ICGtesting.com
Printed in the USA
BVHW010547180520
579786BV00008B/111

9 781119 106494